God Stories

VOLUME SEVEN

"I . . . pray . . . for those who will believe in me through their word, that they all may be one as you, Father, are in me and I in you. I pray that they may be one in us, so that the world may believe that you sent me."

John 17:20–21

The Regional Church of Lancaster County
www.theregionalchurch.com

Dedication

This book is dedicated to the people of South Central Pennsylvania.

Acknowledgments

Thank you to the many contributing authors who made this book possible.

Edited by Karen Boyd, Jessi Clemmer, Jan Dorward, Diana Sheehan, Susan Shiner, Ruth Ann Stauffer, Kim Wittel and Keith Yoder.

Proof readers: Karen Kurtz, Nancy Leatherman and Sharon Neal.

House To House Publications Team: Lou Ann Good and Sarah Sauder

Cover photos: Terry Pfautz, Ann Rodriquez, Mark Van Scyoc

Contact an author

If a particular devotional has encouraged you and you want to tell the author, please email Lou Ann Good (LouAnnG@dcfi.org) who will endeavor to pass on your message.

God Stories 7

© 2011 by The Regional Church of Lancaster County
Lancaster, Pennsylvania, USA
www.theregionalchurch.com
All rights reserved.

ISBN: 978-0-9831560-1-7

Partnership Publications
www.h2hp.com

Unless otherwise noted, scriptural quotations in this publication are taken from the *Holy Bible, New International Version* (NIV). © 1973, 1978, 1984 by International Bible Society. Used by permission of Zondervan Publishing House. All rights reserved.

Printed in the United States of America

Introduction

Set Apart is the theme for this edition of God Stories—stories of being set apart by God and for God. To be set apart is to be dedicated to God's purposes above other loves and loyalties. To be set apart awakens our hearts to what God is doing to transform our world.

This devotional book includes many entries on prayer evangelism to encourage Christ followers to prepare the way for others to be set apart for God. Concepts on lifestyle evangelism are presented through meditations by Lauren Charles (pages 18 and 27) and Bonita Keener (page 203), coordinators for Lancaster Transformed—Street by Street. Also, throughout the year, David Eshleman's practical exhortations will challenge us to share the Good News of Jesus Christ. These meditations are marked by the emblem, "Connecting with our Community."

Each daily entry is linked to scriptural truth. Each one gives us reason to praise God and to pray for similar transformation to come to ourselves and to our region. You may search for a particular author in the index near the end of the book and respond to a particular author by contacting LouAnnG@dcfi.org.

The purpose of God Stories continues to be to cultivate and celebrate oneness in the body of Christ—for which Jesus prayed. As we daily participate in worship in these pages, let us continue to anticipate that we shall become one in the Father and Son even as they are one "that the world may believe" that the Father sent the Son (John 17:21).

In south central Pennsylvania several organizations, whose purpose is to encourage personal and community transformation for the sake of the Kingdom of God, have cooperated to bring this volume of inspirational stories to you. To partner with others for the sake of transformation, use the contact information inside the back cover.

—Keith Yoder, executive team, Regional Church of Lancaster County, on behalf of the participating regional partners

January

JANUARY 1

Never Enough Time?

"My times are in Your hands…." Psalm 31:15

At a missions conference a few years ago, a British instructor made a comment that puzzled me. He said, "American Christians have much to offer people in other nations. However, I would never want an American Christian teaching others about time management." I thought, "What does he mean? We North Americans are productive, hardworking, achievers! If anyone knows how to manage time, we certainly do!"

At break, I went to the man and asked him for further explanation.

"As I see it," he said, "you people always have a huge daily 'to-do' list. You rush through your day, without the least hope of completing every item on your list. Consequently each night you flop into bed, a failure. Day after day you repeat this fruitless cycle. Your behavior demonstrates a belief that there are never enough hours in any day to do everything you need to do. How demoralizing!"

"I would rather believe," he continued, "that God has a different time-management perspective. He knows that there are always enough hours in every day to do everything that He really wants His children to do."

Ah… that was freeing. It made so much sense … certainly God in His love wouldn't frustrate me by giving me more daily assignments than I could possibly complete. Reminding myself of His "timeless" love has helped me to relax more and slow my hurried pace. I've even allowed myself to savor interludes on the porch rocker on a summer evening, or to enjoy a delightful game of chess with my grandchild. Now I can crawl into bed at night, at peace, knowing that what got done that day was sufficient. What God enabled me to finish that day was … enough!

Lord, today is Your day… every hour, every minute, every second. Help me to accomplish Your will, no more and no less… and to be content with that.

John Charles is director of Abundant Living, a family counseling ministry in Lititz.

Photo by Mark Van Scyoc

JANUARY 2

From Generation to Generation

"One generation shall praise Your works to another, And shall declare Your mighty works." Psalm 145:4 (New King James Version)

When I recall my childhood, I can still feel the warmth of hands on my shoulder from two different pastors at separate times. With that gentle touch, each pastor spoke the same words, "Keith, have you ever considered the ministry?"

This question helped to shape the direction of my life. I have been active in congregational service since age sixteen and served as a Christian minister for three decades. Repeatedly I have experienced the Lord setting me apart for new responsibilities. Each came with a hunger for new measures of His grace—God's ability to do God's work in God's way.

Now I focus upon identifying and encouraging a new generation of leaders to be responsible to carry God's message of life-changing truth to the next generation. I am pleased to see so many devoted persons whom God is calling to, preparing for and entrusting with His Kingdom work.

Transformation—bringing about a permanent change in attitude and manner of life—of a region is accomplished from generation to generation. It is a multi-generational task.

As we begin a new calendar year, I believe the Lord gave me these questions to consider: What have I been set apart for in this generation? What is the contribution the Lord has for me to make in this generation? How shall I partner with and encourage members of the next generation in what God has called them to become?

Father, You have entrusted all authority to Your Son. He led the way for us to join in serving You. Show us the place in Your Kingdom where we are to serve, encourage others, and prepare the way for them to serve you. As You transform our lives and theirs, transform our region to reflect Your Kingdom. Through the faithfulness of Your Son, Amen.

Keith Yoder, founder and president of Teaching the Word Ministries, serves on the executive team of the Regional Church of Lancaster County and worships at the Worship Center.

JANUARY 3

Meet Jesus

"These righteous ones will reply, 'Lord, when did we ever see you hungry and feed you? Or thirsty and give you something to drink? Or a stranger and show you hospitality? Or naked and give you clothing? When did we ever see you sick or in prison, and visit you?' And the King will tell them, 'I assure you, when you did it to one of the least of these my brothers and sisters, you were doing it to me.'" Matthew 25:37-40 (New Living Translation)

Can Jesus make it any clearer? When we serve the needy we are serving Him. When we welcome a little child on behalf of Jesus we welcome Him. Jesus said, "Anyone who accepts your message is also accepting me. And anyone who rejects you is rejecting me" (Luke 10:16).

Ask Jesus to open your eyes to someone today who is sick—go visit them, call them, send them a card or an encouraging email. Do you know someone who lost their job or who is discouraged? Maybe someone comes to mind who is hungry—physically or spiritually. Jesus said when you minister to them you serve Him. You may remember He said a cup of cold water given because you love Him will be rewarded.

"God is love." "If anyone has enough money to live well and sees a brother or sister in need and refuses to help—how can God's love be in that person?" (1 John 3:17). When you serve these people by meeting their needs you are serving Jesus. Remember you can meet Jesus today! What a privilege. Jesus reminds us when we obey His commands we will be blessed and rewarded.

Father, I want to meet You today. Help me to be a servant. Open my eyes and give me courage to serve You today.

Dave Eshleman served as pastor and church planter for fifty years.

JANUARY 4

Learning from the Bumps

"He will have no fear of bad news; his heart is steadfast, trusting in the Lord." Psalm 112:7

One snowy Friday evening my husband and I prepared for a grandchildren weekend. Anticipation was high as we looked forward to spending time together.

After a lasagna dinner and a snowman craft, we polished off a huge can of popcorn while watching a video. Soon it was time to bed down for the night.

The next morning as we were cleaning up the kitchen after breakfast, my husband wished aloud for nicer weather. I laughed as I told him it was exactly what we were hoping for … snow. In short order everyone was bundled up and enjoying the beautiful outdoors.

The children headed for the nice smooth driveway in front of the house. Often there were several children on the same sled as they laughed and squealed their way down the hill. It was a merry bunch that trudged back up again.

Interestingly enough, they soon tired of the smooth surface and headed to the back of the house and a slope with a sizable bump mid-way down. The squealing began in earnest as they anticipated and feared the bump and then triumphed in the accomplishment.

Inevitably someone would sled off course and crash into a tree. Occasionally another cousin would stop to help disentangle them, but mostly everyone was concentrating on their own bumps.

I thought about the bumps in my life and the many times I had hung on for dear life. What had I learned from those bumps? How many times had other people helped me? And how many times had I been going too fast to stop and help someone else?

Thank You, Lord, for helping me over the bumps in my life and thank You for providing other people to help me withstand those bumps. Show me when I need to stop and help someone else. Help us to understand the value of the bumps you allow us to experience.

Marie Mumma attends Erisman Mennonite Church and rejoices over grandchildren who teach her real life lessons.

JANUARY 5

Need Superhero Power?

"'For I know the plans I have for you,' declares the Lord, 'plans to prosper you and not to harm you, plans to give you hope and a future.'" Jeremiah 29:11

It was my last public speaking class of the semester, and the assignment was a graded impromptu. Students had three potential topics to choose from and ten minutes to prepare.

One of my students used a wheelchair. As it turned out, only one of the potential topics suited—what power would you choose if you were a superhero? His first thought, of course, was that he would be able to walk. But as he began to construct his speech he realized the enormity of the task. He had so trained his mind to accept the fact that he would never walk, that he struggled to come up with the benefits. In the end, he told the class that he really didn't need to have a superhero power at all. He had God. And that was all the power he would ever need.

It was one of those gut-wrenching moments that occurs when you come face-to-face with true courage. Here was a young man who had learned to accept his limitations and work within them. In the course of the semester, I never saw a trace of self-pity. In fact, he occasionally made jokes about his chair. He knew—really knew—that it could not keep the purposes of God from being fulfilled in his life.

And so it is with each of us. We all have limitations in one form or another. Sometimes God removes them. We experience a miraculous healing, either physical or emotional. Money to pay those outstanding bills appears "out of the blue." But when our constraints are not taken away, I pray we would have a mind set like my friend, Kyle.

Father, may we be set apart to believe You are completing Your plan in us and through us.

Becky Toews serves at New Covenant Christian Church and Lancaster Bible College. This is an excerpt from "Fresh Tracks" at www.beckytoews.com.

JANUARY 6

Green Palmolive Liquid

"But my God shall supply all your needs according to His riches in glory by Christ Jesus." Philippians 4:19 (King James Version)

I was taught that when you pray, be specific and expect God to answer. I remember a time in my life when our means were very scarce —so scarce that we often went without food. I was not upset, I was not angry, but I wasn't sure where our next meal would come from.

One Sunday our pastor challenged us to pray with a childlike faith for things that we needed. We were a young church, and there were many needs. I went home with the sermon on my mind, so I asked the Lord to provide for our basic needs. I was a young Christian so I prayed with the heart of a child. "Lord, I know You will provide us with our needs, but I have a want. Please give me a bottle of green Palmolive liquid detergent." It was a strange request, but in my mind it was a way to confirm a specific answer from God.

A week went by, but I didn't lose faith. Roxanne showed up that Saturday with a bag of groceries saying God had put it on her heart to give me a bag of food. I was so blessed because she was a woman on welfare and had many needs of her own. I invited her into my home and told her to stay until I went through the bag.

"I prayed last week for provisions, Roxanne, but I asked Him for one specific thing. No one knows I did this."

She was distraught thinking, why didn't Marie tell me about the one thing she really needed.

Then I screamed! "Thank you God for the green Palmolive liquid!"

I explained that it wasn't so much the detergent but the specific answer to prayer. We were both so very blessed God provided in so many ways.

Thank You, Lord, for providing all of our needs according to Your riches in glory.

Marie Remp has a ministry of laughter. She is thankful for the grace of God allowing her to be sensitive to hurting people.

JANUARY 7

Celebration of a Life

"Precious in the sight of the Lord is the death of his saints."
Psalm 116:15

Precious, what a beautiful word.... According to the dictionary, precious means highly valuable, costly, cherished and beloved.

Last year I participated in three "celebration of life" services. Some people call them funerals, but when it's a "saint" going home, I think it's more appropriate to call the gathering a celebration of life.

Two friends and one eighty-seven-year-old aunt, all who knew Jesus as their Lord and Savior, passed from this life into the next. Before she died, my aunt said, "I'm not afraid to die; I know Jesus paid the price for me."

One of my friends had been influential in government, but made his mark by serving many newcomers in the Pennsylvania mountains where he lived. His heart to share Jesus was evident in the many testimonials given at his celebration of life service.

My friend had impacted so many lives that his service was attended by the most people I ever spoke to at one time. His passing made me think about the verse above and that it is not how long you live or what you die from but how you lived your life. Your life and your death is "precious" to God, but, what will your children say about you? Who will you have impacted?

It's not about the number of persons who attend your funeral service; it's about your obedience to serve people while you're still alive. Who has God called you to impact this day? Show someone how highly valued they are while they're still on this earth. Remember, it's more important how you live than how you die.

Heavenly Father, thank You that I am as precious in your sight today as I will be the day I come home to be with You. Help me to see the "precious" ones that You desire me to touch and to minister to today.

Steve Prokopchak is married to Mary for thirty-five years and a member of the Dove Christian Fellowship International Apostolic Council, giving oversight to DOVE churches in various regions of the world.

JANUARY 8

Surrendering All to the Lord

"Sanctify them in the truth; your word is truth." John 17:17

The Holy Spirit began whispering to me about how I have not taken care of my body. I had eaten whatever I wanted, whenever I wanted without exercising. As I sat with the Lord to listen more closely, I recognized that it wasn't just my habits, it was my heart and attitude. I was withholding this part of myself. I thought I was justified in eating as I pleased because I had given up everything else to the lordship of Jesus Christ.

As I surrendered this area to God's lordship, I felt a grace, peace and deep love come upon me. The Lord gently encouraged me to make changes and reminded me that with change comes transformation. Okay, I had God's vision, but I had to come up with a plan. There is no perfect plan. But a good plan with good leadership (yes, we can lead ourselves) will produce great results.

I knew I did not want to go on a diet to lose weight, because eventually I'd go off of a diet. Common sense told me that exercise with healthier eating would bring results. So, I joined a gym and committed to cardio and strength training. And I committed to asking the Holy Spirit to help me to learn to listen to my body and to make healthier food choices—more whole, fresh foods and less fast food, junk food and processed food.

My eating habits are definitely changing, and I have consistently met the mark on going to the gym. My body is transforming. I'm losing fat and gaining muscle. I sleep better, have more energy and handle stress better. But, the greatest benefit is that I have surrendered ALL to the Lord, once and for all.

Lord, thank You for Your whispers that lead to surrender and obedience.

Sharon Blantz serves the Worship Center as pastor of care and support.

JANUARY 9

It's Not Over

"I am Alpha and Omega, the beginning and the end, the first and the last." Revelation 22:13 (King James Version)

In a season of lessened ministry, the deadline was past for submitting entries for *God Stories from Lancaster County*. I'd prayed and listened and listened and prayed. Unlike all previous "God Stories" writing opportunities, I was uninspired, worse I felt unassigned. As I sat down for personal God-time, I wondered, "Have I slipped so far? How can I not have a God story?" I felt reprobate.

Then on a stack of reading material I saw the bold letters, "… God Stories." The actual title gripped my heart: "Seizing Your God Story," one of the last articles written by David Wilkerson before his untimely death in an automobile accident. Tears sprang to my eyes as I felt the sweet, gentle whisper of the Holy Spirit, "No, you haven't failed. You're not finished."

These key points from the article are almost an exact mirror of the criteria I hold for a "God Story":

It's an event that can only be described in terms of God showing up to act on our behalf.

It has positive outcome made possible only by God's clear intervention.

That outcome can only be explained in terms of God's power and love.

There is a complete transformation of circumstances, events and people—all made possible only by God.

Later that same day in a public meeting, as the above scripture was read, I heard, "It's not the end until I say it's the end. You're not finished."

And you're not finished either until the "End" says it's the end.

Father, thank You for providing the Beginning and the End through our Lord Jesus Christ.

Ruth Ann Stauffer resides in Lititz with her husband, Al, with whom she enjoys attending Ephrata Community Church, gardening and loving eight precious grandchildren.

JANUARY 10

Only One Ladle

"Therefore come out from them and be separate, says the Lord. Touch no unclean thing, and I will receive you." 2 Corinthians 6:17

In the early 1900s a couple from the village of Schoeneck had a stand at the Reading Market. One day when this husband and wife arrived at the market, they realized they had only brought one ladle with them. The first customer that day wanted cottage cheese, so the lady used the ladle to fill the order. The next customer wanted apple butter, so the lady, out of necessity, used the same ladle to fill the order. That's how things went all day— cottage cheese and then apple butter— apple butter and then cottage cheese! What a mess! There was cottage cheese in the apple butter and apple butter in the cottage cheese—and you really couldn't tell the difference!

The thrust of today's scripture is that, when we as Christians allow "the world" to infiltrate our lives, the difference between believers and nonbelievers invariably becomes fuzzy. Enjoying God's presence requires personal holiness. Since Christians are redeemed from the bondage of sin, St. Paul issues a challenge for us to "come out" from the influences of the pagan world around us in order that we might be "clean" before God. Certainly there's no way to separate ourselves totally from the sinful influences we face. However, as believers we are asked to resist the sin around us, without either giving up or giving in!

Gracious God, forgive me for the times I've allowed the pagan world around me to squeeze me into its mold. By Your mercy and grace, may my resolve to "come out from the world" be quickened and strengthened so that I may stand "clean" before You. In the name of the One who gives me victory.

Paul Brubaker serves on the ministry team at the Middle Creek Church of the Brethren, Lititz.

JANUARY 11

Hit Send

"And then I heard the voice of the Master: 'Whom shall I send? Who will go for us?' I spoke up, 'I'll go. Send me!'" Isaiah 6:8 (The Message)

One morning I received a vision to text my ex-husband a simple note … "I forgive you." Then the Lord said, "When you do this, the gates of heaven will open and an abundance of blessings will pour forth!"

I shared my vision with good friends, and after praying and talking it out, they encouraged me to send the text. I wrote the words but found myself unable to hit the "send" button. One friend ecstatically kept repeating, "Hit send!" Eventually I pressed the button and received a reply from my ex stating he was not able to forgive himself, but he thanked me for forgiving him. I told my ex that the Lord had changed my heart, and He wanted me to tell him that.

This event was huge for me, and it turned out to be the most transforming action I have ever done. I've often heard that forgiveness is not for the other person, but I didn't understand what that meant until I experienced it. Forgiving released me from all bitterness, unforgiveness and anger toward my ex. He struggles with God and his belief in the Lord, so what a testimony that was for him to hear that God truly transformed my heart.

I shared what happened with my children, and when an event arrived that included my ex, there were no bitter feelings among us. I felt only joy and peace—something I thought could never happen. The transformation spoke of true healing as my children watched me in the presence of my ex and saw no confrontation whatsoever.

If you ever ask the Lord, "send me," you'll never know what will happen; but one thing I can assure you, it will be life transforming.

Thank You Lord for making the impossible possible and "sending" me in the most unusual way.

Eileen Christiansen is the mother of two amazing children who get to watch God do His life-transforming work in her life.

JANUARY 12

Just a Little Piece

"When I was a child, I spoke like a child, I thought like a child, I reasoned like a child. When I became a man, I gave up childish ways."
1 Corinthians13:11 (English Standard Version)

Our extended on-site ministry team meets for dinner weekly for fun, food and fellowship. One week we had three birthdays to celebrate. I bought a large, decorated cake and distributed ample pieces of cake with ice cream to everyone. We were sitting around chatting when four-year-old Jonathan came up beside me and rested his head on my arm, just inches away from the remaining cake.

"Miss Joan, may I have another piece?" he asked, cheeks still decorated with chocolate icing. I said he needed to ask his mother, who was seated nearby and heard his question. She laughed and said, "No, Jonathan. You have had enough." Looking down at his large, pleading eyes, I smiled and asked, "What did she say?" With a questioning tone he replied without hesitation, "She said I could just have a little piece?"

How often do we approach the Lord desiring something we know we really shouldn't have? How many times do we plead for just a little more of something when we have had enough? A four-year-old child wanting more chocolate cake is quite understandable, and his naively hopeful answer was sweetly amusing. Does the Father chuckle when I express my dissatisfaction with what has been allotted to me? God has heaped blessings and favor upon me, yet I am still capable of expressing discontent. I want the sweet things to come without interruption even when God has designed a better plan for my growth.

Lord, help me to put away childish things and to find all I need in You.

Joan Boydell and her husband, Bruce, are directors of the Haft, Inc. in New Albany. When there, they attend Living Hope Fellowship in Estella.They are members of Covenant Fellowship in Chester County.

JANUARY 13

Just Say No

"Lay up for yourselves treasures in heaven.... For where your treasure is, there your heart will be also." Matthew 6:20-21 (English Standard Version)

Saying "no" is something that doesn't come easily to everyone, especially for me. I see potential in almost everything. When someone offers to give me an old item for which they no longer want or have space, I believe it's almost impolite to refuse it.

Although I'm not a bona fide hoarder, being an agreeable "yes-man" in this arena is not good. This is especially true when it applies to mission and nonprofit organizations such as the one I lead. In the three years since my wife and I took leadership of this ministry, we have had to remove literally tons of all kinds of Goodwill-type stuff and leftovers, which I stored up for future projects or needs for people who might show up someday. We have rented dumpsters and hired truckers to take away decades of junk. Almost without exception, the stuff was moldy, rusty, hazardous and useless. It was difficult to store and later to find things that were needed.

Well-intended suggestions, emails, tweets, printed material and even kindly offers of help may seriously obfuscate our primary mission and distract us from important goals. Just because such a "gift" may have potential value to someone, somewhere, at some time, does not mean it has value to me in my here and now. I'm learning to say, "No!" or "No, thank you!" A simple two-letter word can make a big difference.

Father, thank You that You do not say, "Yes," to all my ideas and offerings. Thank You for all your many "no's" that have directed my path, ordered my steps and made space for Your purposes in my life.

Bruce Boydell and his wife, Joan, are leaders of the Haft, Inc., a Christ-centered community, whose mission is the development of emerging ministry and marketplace leaders who are in need of refreshing, retooling and rebuilding.

JANUARY 14

Prayer Evangelism

"Ask of Me and I will give you the nations as your inheritance …" Psalm 2:8

The foundation of prayer evangelism is prayer—talking to God about your neighbor before you talk to your neighbor about God. It comes from a heart for the lost out of a passion to see Jesus receive His inheritance.

For so long we have been intimidated by prayer evangelism, concerned about what to say or the reaction we'd receive. What if they ask a question we can't answer or reject the whole conversation? That focus is wrong because it is on us.

God wants us to refocus to see people as Jesus' inheritance purchased by His sacrifice on the cross—to see the glory He receives when a life is changed and the hope that others receive when He comes into their lives. God wants us to see the transformation that occurs as multitudes of lives and the places where people live and work come under His kingship.

We complicate the simple. Prayer evangelism is simple. Begin by speaking peace to your neighbor. Then look for opportunities to live life together. Learn about their needs, and ask God to meet those needs supernaturally. When God directs, tell them the Good News about Jesus.

If we will do our part in prayer, God will do His part in power. In answer to specific, intentional prayer, we have seen Him bring peace to a street in the city known for turmoil and violence. We've seen Him draw people into the kingdom as a family served those who came through a crisis. We've seen Him bring a man to salvation after someone prayed for his physical healing.

God is inviting us to be part of this amazing adventure to see His kingdom come and His will be done across this region and beyond.

Holy Spirit, give us a heart for the lost, a passion to see Jesus glorified and a willingness to be part of what You're doing.

Lauren Charles serves in leadership with Lancaster Transformed Street by Street.

The Regional Church encourages you to participate in prayer evangelism by adopting a street, business, school or other grouping of people. Visit www.lancastertransformed.org and prayerfully consider how the Lord would have you engage in this simple, practical and powerful approach to transformation. Also, see comments by Bonita Keener on pages 19 and 203.

JANUARY 15

Lancaster Transformed

"You who call on the Lord, give yourselves no rest, and give Him no rest till He establishes [Lancaster]* and makes her the praise of the earth." Isaiah 62:6-7 *inserted for Jerusalem

Wherever God has brought revival and transformation to communities around the world, there has always been a common thread: He was invited. If we desire God to come and bring transformation in Lancaster County (and beyond), we must call on Him in prayer, inviting Him to come to our neighborhoods, businesses and schools.

Acts 17:26 says, "God determined the times set for us and the exact places where we should live. He did this so that men would seek him and perhaps reach out for him and find him, though he is not far from each one of us." It is amazing to think that God has strategically placed each one of us right where we live, so that those around us would find Him!

Would you consider adopting your street in prayer, and inviting Jesus to come do a transforming work in the lives of families all around you? As you adopt your street, the spirit of abandonment (the orphan spirit) will be replaced by the spirit of adoption, and the spirit of bondage and slavery will be replaced by the spirit of Sonship.

Newark, New Jersey, was struggling with violent crime when Pray for Newark was put into place in 2008. Today they are the first city to have every street adopted in prayer. Shortly after reaching this milestone, they also reached their first murder-free calendar month in forty-four years. God is changing neighborhoods because of prayer.

If Newark, why not Lancaster? In March 2011, Lancaster Transformed Street by Street was launched to see every person on every street prayed for by name. Let's join together to see sustained transformation in our region.

Father, we invite You to come touch those who live on our streets, work next to us and go to our schools. Give us Your heart for the people You have placed right around us.

Bonita Keener,is prayer coordinator for the Regional Church of Lancaster County www.theregionalchurch.com and helps lead Lancaster Transformed Street by Street www.lancastertransformed.org

See the call to Prayer Evangelism by Lauren Charles on page 18.

JANUARY 16

Equality and Mankind

"Tell it to your children and let your children tell it to their children, and their children to the next generation." Joel 1:3

My six-year-old grandson, Gavin, was taught a beautiful lesson about mankind and equality on the anniversary of Dr. Martin Luther King's death. Gavin listened intently to a recording of Dr. King's dream and the belief that all men are created equal. This marvelous lesson in equality was explained to Gavin in terms a child could understand. Relating the Dr. King story, Gavin was taught to compare equality to his Lancaster Township baseball team where everyone on the team plays together. The players back each other and support one another during a win or a loss. The team is made up of children from different cultures, with individual names, unique styles, personal strengths and weaknesses. When these children all come together, they make up the team. As a child whose character had not yet been prejudiced or tarnished, Gavin found the comparison easy to understand.

When Gavin said his prayers that night, he closed his eyes and prayed, "God, I hope Dr. King has a beautiful dream tonight and that everyone gets to play on the same team."

Dear Heavenly Father, help us to learn from the innocence and example of the child who has not been taught prejudice. I pray that children will make wise and godly choices with integrity.

Barbara Ann Morgan is a member and volunteer of the Worship Center, Leola, and grandmother to Blake Evan, Gavin James and Kyle Morgan Glass.

JANUARY 17

Billboards of Our Lives

"Write his answer on a billboard, large and clear, so that anyone can read it at a glance and rush to tell others...." Habakkuk 2:2 (The Living Bible)

On a recent road trip, several billboards caught my eye: "Welcome to Bridgeville ... if you lived here, you'd be home now!" Or "The little town too big for one state—Delmar—on the border between Delaware and Maryland."

The billboard messages made me chuckle, but they conveyed one clear message about each town that made me want to tell others about it.

In the book of Habakkuk, the prophet questions God on why God was going to use the ruthless Babylonians to conquer Judah. This doesn't make sense to Habakkuk. God commands Habakkuk to write down clearly what God reveals to him, so that those reading it will want to tell others.

Although Habakkuk is a prophet, we see his humanity in the questions he asks God and in his confusion from God's answers. We learn that it's okay to question God, and that we may not understand His answer. Habakkuk ends his writing with a willingness to wait patiently and trust in God's sovereignty regardless of the circumstances.

We are faced with the kinds of questions that Habakkuk asked. We often cry out, "What are You going to do about this, God?" God's response is, "What are you going to do about it?"

Like Habakkuk, question God, but also be ready to respond to His answer. Every day we have opportunities to write God's answer, large and clear, on the billboards of others' lives, transforming both them and us. As they change, others will read it at a glance and rush to tell others about it.

God, help me to be aware of others around me every day and how I can leave an imprint of God on their lives. Give me the strength to obey whatever You call me to do.

Jackie Confalone lives in Shillington with her husband. She is a member of Mohn's Memorial Evangelical Congregational Church.

JANUARY 18

Silence an Angry Person

"A gentle answer turns away wrath…." Proverbs 15:1a

One pleasant, summer evening I drove to Overly's Grove near New Holland. I was inspired and encouraged by the special speaker for Sunday school teachers from Weaverland Mennonite Church. Fellowship with friends was also a blessing to me.

On my way home I was somewhat unfamiliar with the roads. As darkness began to fall, I slowed to a stop trying to determine which way would take me to Route 23. Suddenly one bright headlight shone directly at me, and an angry voice shouted, "You almost hit me!" The man drove his motorcycle right up beside my car and gave a vicious, hard heel boot kick into the door leaving a dent just below the window where I sat. Moving his cycle in front of my car and blocking a getaway, he continued shouting and cursing.

Shaking and praying, I opened my window and said, "I'm sorry, I didn't see you." His response was a torrent of angry words, yelling he would turn me in to my insurance company like he had done to someone else the day before. He gave a command to a girl riding with him to get my license number.

How I prayed someone who knew me would come by to help. No one did. After the young man quieted down a bit, I tried again speaking gently, "I'm very sorry, I have a son who has a motorcycle, and I wouldn't want to cause an accident. Will you forgive me?" Silence … without another word, he drove away.

Frightened and shaking, I thanked my heavenly Protector all the way home and prayed for the aggressive driver.

Two lessons I learned from this experience: God is with me in danger, and a gentle answer turns away wrath.

Lord God, thank You for always being present with us even when we are afraid and that Your Word is true—a gentle response can silence an angry person.

Kathryn Eby lives at Landis Homes with her husband, Harold, and enjoys being a volunteer chaplain there. They are active at Landis Valley Christian Fellowship.

JANUARY 19

Our Father's Stories

"… I will listen to what God the Lord will say…." Psalm 85:8

I recently lost my father. No matter their age or your age, you're never ready to say good-bye. Although he lived in Kentucky, I was blessed to spend time with him, Mom and other family members right before his death. Just four days before his death we were all on the golf course together.

Immediately following his death, we found pictures, books and heard stories about him that we never knew. Time after time I found myself wanting to ask him a question, wishing he was there to tell me more about a particular event or life experience. I just wanted to sit and listen to him share in his own words. I wondered why I hadn't taken more time to ask him these questions while he was still alive.

As I thought about talking with Dad, it made me think about my relationship with God. Do I spend time with my heavenly Father asking Him questions and listening for His voice? Do I take advantage of all the opportunities I am given? Though I wish I'd taken more time to talk with my earthly father, I do have the opportunity to spend time with my heavenly Father before it's too late. I can hear His stories through His Word. I can hear His voice by quietly listening and spending time in prayer.

I had a godly earthly father, and I will get to ask him questions in heaven. But my prayer is that I take the time to ask the questions, hear the stories and listen to my heavenly Father now—all to prepare me for my eternal home.

Lord, help me hear Your stories and listen to Your voice now, preparing me for the day I meet You.

Mona Engle serves as practice administrator for Drs. May and Grant in Lancaster. She attends Living Word Community in York, serving as a mentor mom to young moms.

JANUARY 20

Keys of the Kingdom

"I will give you the keys of the kingdom of heaven and whatever you bind on earth must be already bound in heaven; and whatever you loose on earth must be what is already loosed in heaven."
Matthew 16:19

I remember when I was sixteen; I had just passed my driver's test and received my license. A feeling of importance and confidence welled up inside!

I had just experienced one of the "rites of passage" into the adult world. The first time my dad handed me the keys, with the blessing of his assurance in my ability to drive and care for his car, was indescribable. By giving me the keys, he was giving me the authority to drive his car, in his name. I had to be in agreement with him about being responsible, caring for his property and protecting his good name.

Isn't that what the Lord says to us in Matthew 16:19? He has given us the "keys of His kingdom" to bind or loose on earth what has already been bound or loosed in heaven, in His name and by His authority.

In Matthew 18:18-19, He adds that if two of us on earth agree about anything and everything, then, whatever we ask of Him will be done by our Father in heaven. Now that's exciting, indescribable confidence and authority.

My earthly dad's confidence and generosity translated to me his unconditional love and care. In the same way, my perfect heavenly Father has bestowed on me the power and authority to use His name and "keys" to be about the "family" business and to come boldly to His throne to ask anything of Him. What a privilege to carry the family name of the King!

Father God, Thank You for setting me apart to be one of your royal family. Thank You for lovingly training me to be a "kingdom carrier of your presence" wherever I go and to walk in your authority to bind and loose your will on earth as it has already been done in heaven.

Sue Ferrari is the executive director of Breath of Life Counseling and Chaplaincy Ministries and is a member of Ephrata Community Church.

JANUARY 21

Not My Will

"Thy kingdom come, Thy will be done in earth, as it is in heaven."
Matthew 6:10 (King James Version)

For decades, my prayers were often peppered with requests to God. Not only did I ask for things, I suggested to God how He should answer my pleadings. So many times, I prayed, "Oh, Lord, I've got a good idea." I chuckle remembering the absurdity of some of those ideas.

Time and time again I presented my ideas to God for resolving this problem or that. Important and seemingly life-or-death issues taxed my creativity. I would devise elaborate solutions. God in His great mercy did not answer my prayers as suggested. When His answers were revealed, they were far superior to what I could have imagined. Ephesians 3:20-21 confirms this: "Now to him who is able to do far more abundantly than all that we ask or think, according to the power at work within us, to him be glory in the church and in Christ Jesus throughout all generations, forever and ever."

The scripture verse for today is from our Lord's teaching on prayer. Jesus cautions that we not use vain repetitions (empty phrases) as Gentiles (the heathen) do (Matthew 6:7) . . . for your Father knows what you need before you ask (Matthew 6:8). Jesus continues to show us how to pray: "Our Father in heaven, hallowed be your name. Your kingdom come, your will be done, on earth as it is in heaven" (Matthew 6:9-10).

Many moons passed before I began to pray for His will, not my own. As I meditated on what we call "The Lord's Prayer," God eventually changed my will to His. Occasionally, I still find myself expressing my suggestions to Him in prayer but always with the caveat that His will be done, not my own.

Lord, may I always pray that Your will be done, not mine. For Your will is perfect and exceeds my greatest expectations.

Sally K. Owens lives with her husband, Don, in Lancaster, where they participate in two home fellowship groups. They share many children and oodles of amazing grandchildren.

JANUARY 22

Living the Kingdom

"Your kingdom come, your will be done, on earth as it is in heaven." Matthew 6:10

Every Sunday a group of people gather for a time of musical worship, fellowship, Bible study, prayer and discussion. After an extended time of grabbing coffee and food and catching up with each other, we get "down to business." We get "down to business" each week by asking and discussing the same question, "How have you been a blessing or missional in your life this week?" Or put another way, "How have you lived this week so that God's kingdom and His will was done here on earth as it is in heaven?"

Each week we hear different stories about how our community called Veritas is seeking to live in such a way that heaven literally comes to earth. We've heard stories of serving neighbors, blessings given at a St. Patty's Day Party, prayer for a sick friend, and other opportunities to build relationships with people who aren't part of a faith community.

When Jesus prayed this prayer over two-thousand years ago, He wanted His followers to pray and live the same prayer. He wanted His followers then, and He wants His followers now, to live a life of blessing and service—a life set apart and lived for the sake of others. The gospel isn't just about going to heaven when we die; it's about living heaven now before we die. It's about joining with God in what He's doing in the world right now.

How are you and I living our lives today? What story would you tell if someone asked you, "How have you been a blessing this week?"

Jesus, may Your kingdom come and Your will be done on earth as it is in heaven, and may I play a part in the ongoing work of your Kingdom.

Ryan Braught is the husband of Kim, father of Kaiden and Trinity, church planter of Veritas and a follower of Jesus.

JANUARY 23

Plea for Protection

"Be persistent in prayer, and keep alert as you pray, giving thanks to God." Colossians 4:2 (Good News Translation)

I was only seventeen at the time and driving for only one year. Since my mother had not yet learned to drive, I was her chauffeur for work and other errands. From the time I can remember, she, my four younger brothers and I had suffered horrifically at the hands of our angry, alcoholic father. She was preparing to separate from him, but needed my help. One day the Lord caught us both by surprise when she told me she was pregnant. I was elated and told her that perhaps now I would finally have a sister.

Imagine my horror when she told me that she couldn't have this baby—that I was to drive her to the abortionist. Although not yet a Christian, I knew this was a moral crisis. I refused, reminding her that I would not participate in the murder of my sibling. She said that if I didn't drive her there, she was going to commit suicide. I submitted, but told her that I would be praying that there would be no abortion. She was upset because that's exactly what happened. She agreed to carry the baby to term, and I assured her that I would help in the rearing process. My baby sister Michelle was born several months later.

Sadly, a little over two years later, my mother died. Our father fled, leaving Michelle and two younger teen brothers with my young husband, myself and our four-month-old daughter. Several years later, I was born again and was able to train her, along with our three daughters, in the nurture and admonition of the Lord.

Hallelujah. What a Savior You are! You are a Father to us all.

Denise Colvin is happily remarried to a wonderful man, Rich, who is a pastor. Together, they serve at The Villa Chapel in West Reading. She is the blessed mother of four lovely daughters (one, her adopted sister, Michelle) and ten grandchildren.

JANUARY 24

Light in a Dark Place

"For I know the plans I have for you, declares the Lord, plans to prosper you and not to harm you, plans to give you hope and a future." Jeremiah 29:11

Sitting in the dark one morning around 2:00 a.m., I found myself questioning God about many things. One question, which was heavy on my heart, was the possibility of having to close down the House of Ruth, which is a transitional house for women being released from prison. The room, now dark and empty, was filled earlier with the joyful noise of activity and life. I stared into a dark and lifeless fireplace as I prayed: "Lord, I know that we are here because You put us here, but right now it seems hopeless as if the life is gone from the vision. Has my vision been reduced to ashes? I don't understand. I do know that You are the God of possibilities, and You can resurrect life from ashes. Lord, if that is what You are doing, I will hang in there and wait on You. Please just let me know."

Suddenly, a fire broke out in the fireplace, the same fireplace that moments before was dark and lifeless. A flame lit up the room and my heart at the same time. It was at that very moment that God reminded me that in the face of seemingly hopelessness or impossible situations, He is mysteriously at work in the midst of it all. God does do the impossible. He will bring light into the dark places.

Lord, today I surrender my plans for Your plans, my will for Your will. Please guide my decisions and thoughts to match Yours so that I can experience hope and not harm. Even though things aren't going so great today, I trust the plans You have for me, and I know it's in Your timing, not mine.

Linda Bird is founder and director of Beginning In the Right Direction, B.I.R.D. Ministries and a member of the Worship Center.

JANUARY 25

Inspiring Messages

"If anyone considers himself religious and yet does not keep tight rein on his tongue, he deceives himself and his religion is worthless." James 1:26

So many times I have to remind myself of this verse. Mean words can hurt the deepest parts of the soul, and we don't even realize it. I'm so quick to open my mouth before thinking whether it might hurt the person I'm talking to, or make them angry or offended in any way. I like to use sarcasm a lot.

Now, I try to think before I speak and remember that it has to be Christlike before spoken. The Lord has helped me completely change my way of thinking when I have conversations with others and the people that I love. Now I use positive and sometimes even inspiring messages instead of mean and negative ones.

I struggled with conversations with my husband when I used drugs before I entered myself into a life-change program. I remember being very mean to him and saying the rudest things when I didn't have drugs. I would push him away even though he was just trying to help me. Now I'm changing my life around—all because of the Lord and His determination to help and love me. I finally surrendered my life to the Lord and now my perspective is much better. Although every day is a battle with the devil on my shoulder, I know I have God to turn to. I am teaching my children to walk with the Lord and showing them there is no other way if we want eternal happiness.

Thank You, Lord, for giving me the strength to walk with You so that I can be more like You every day. Thank You for Your knowledge and wisdom to know the difference to change my ways.

Christina Beachy is a stay-at-home mom with two children and one on the way and assists her husband, Jonathan, raising calves. She is in a life-change program at the Lydia Center. She attends Community Fellowship Church.

JANUARY 26

Running on Empty

"Wherefore be ye not unwise, but understanding what the will of the Lord is. And ... and be filled with the Spirit." Ephesians 5:16-18 (King James Version)

The dash of our vehicle lights up with the image of a gas pump. Our fuel is low; a built-in warning prompts us to take notice. In the busyness of the day, we brush aside the warning and rush ahead to accomplish our to-do list. In our minds we justify our lack of wisdom without facing reality. Just maybe, being lucky we'll make it. We drift over to the shoulder of the road as we complain, "What is wrong now .... I have so much to get done."

Reaching for my cell phone, I contact AAA services to report I've run out of fuel. Waiting for assistance gives me time to think and reflect, to sense God's still small voice. Lovingly and gently, His Holy Spirit speaks softly. "My Spirit calls and reminds you when it's time to fill up. Be sensitive and listen, when you're running on empty ... stop and fill up!"

Many times on our spiritual journey we become busy with everything else in our lives. We neglect to fill up with God's Holy Spirit when He calls us to stop, listen and come to Him and fill up.

When the light comes on in your spiritual journey, when you're running on empty, be disciplined in obedience to come to Christ to fill up every day. You will not be sitting along the road learning anew the lessons of neglecting to fill up. Heed the gentle reminder, live in the Spirit. This is the secret of fullness for the journey. Top off every morning; stay full, one day at a time.

Lord, thank You for Your Holy Spirit reminders when I'm running on empty. Help me, please, to have self-discipline and wisdom every day to not run on empty, but to stay filled up, in Jesus' name.

Glenn E. Wagner is a retired carpenter, provides biblical counsel and spiritual mentoring in his home and is a member of White Oak Church of the Brethren.

JANUARY 27

Imitator of God

“Be imitators of God as dear children. And walk in love, as Christ also has loved us and given Himself for us, an offering and a sacrifice to God.” Ephesians 5:1, 2 (New King James Version)

We loaded the car with everything we’d need for our stay in Florida. The computer, suitcases, camera and spare flat screen display were all carefully packed for protection.

We even washed the beautiful new (to me) car before we put it on the Auto Train. So it gleamed in the sun as it hit the wall on the bridge over Tampa Bay.

This isn’t a story about the car, or even about the accident, though a man was drowned two days later when his car hit the same wall and flipped over the edge.

This is a story about a man named Brooks. I can’t tell you his last name because he’d be furious with me, but on the assumption he’ll never see this, I’ll tell the story.

As Peg and I lay in our hospital beds: me recuperating from the heart attack that caused the accident, she from a smashed right shoulder, we wondered where our car was. It was packed full, our gear easily visible through the windows, sitting vulnerable in some back lot.

Along came Brooks. He was there with us in the emergency room suite as Peg was dispatched to surgery and stayed with me until I went off to the cardiac cath unit. He was there with me a day later, though I still don’t recall his visit. He was there the next day with a paper for me to sign, releasing the contents of the car to him.

Brooks is a Christian, a member of my Florida church. He made me stop telling this story around the church.

We talk a lot about Christianity, about living in the Spirit, and about loving our neighbor. Once in a while we meet a Brooks, and we see all that in action, and know it’s for real.

Lord Jesus, I thank You for being with Peg and me in the person of Brooks, and ask that Your glory be reflected in us also.

Tim Wentworth teaches the Bible to homeless people who gather at Lutheran Church of the Holy Trinity in downtown Lancaster every Sunday morning.

JANUARY 28

Real Happiness

"Rejoice with me; I have found my lost sheep." Luke 15:6

In Luke 15 Jesus makes it clear that all of heaven is joyful when one sinner returns home. The Shepherd leaves the ninety-nine and searches for the one lost sheep. If you pray and ask the Lord to open your eyes to the lost sheep in your sphere of influence, He will reveal to you who that sheep is. Pray for that person. Tell God you will be willing to do anything to bring that person into the fold. If you lack that passion or zeal, ask God to give it to you.

Moses and Paul both illustrate that passion with the prayer: "Please forgive their sin—and if not, then blot me out of the record you are keeping" (Exodus 32:32). Paul writes in Romans 9:2-3, "My heart is filled with bitter sorrow and unending grief for my people, my Jewish brothers and sisters. I would be willing to be forever cursed—cut off from Christ—if that would save them."

What would happen if you and I would have the zeal of Moses and Paul? Pray for God to give you a heart of compassion. For most Saturdays of my forty-eight years of pastoral ministry I visited with one or more unchurched families in the community inviting them to church or to consider the claims of Christ.

Whenever you see a U-Haul coming to your area, welcome the newcomers to the community. Offer to help them unload the truck. Show them around town. There is no end to the possibilities including inviting them to church and introducing the children to their new Sunday school teacher or the adults to a small group that has been praying for a new family moving to that address. You will experience joy as you relate to new people and invite them to church and to the Lord Jesus.

Jesus, give me a passion like Moses and Paul. Give me courage to take the initiative to invite new people to worship and to meet you.

Dave Eshleman served as pastor and church planter for fifty years.

JANUARY 29

Preparing the Way

"He will direct your paths." Proverbs 3:6 (New King James Version)

Traveling to pick up Don at the airport when he returned from a trip to India, I received a phone message from paramedics stating they were rushing him to the hospital in Philadelphia. I had just met with my sister who lives near the city. I quickly called her and asked her to lead me to the hospital, which she gladly did. The doctors were testing him for various exotic diseases he might have contracted overseas. I left home in Lancaster thinking I would return in a few hours, but I didn't return until three days later. Looking back, I could see how God had been preparing the way in advance. Even while I was unaware of the upcoming events like a storm brewing on the horizon, God was at work behind the "seens:"

> Contrary to our normal routine of going together to meet Don at he airport, my teens stayed home, which freed me to stay and be there for Don, and enabled them to be at home for school.
>
> My sister "just happened" to be close by and I was able to stay at her house rather than an expensive hotel.
>
> Don became ill shortly before landing on United States soil. Had it occurred while he was either in India or on his lay-over, he would not have been able (or allowed) to return to the United States.
>
> The hospital in Philadelphia was well-equipped to test for the types of foreign diseases he may have contracted.

Thankfully, after several days and multiple tests, doctors discovered it was food poisoning, and, shortly after administering the correct antibiotic, Don began to feel better and was discharged five days after he was admitted.

Thank You, Lord, that You prepare the way before us and are present with us no matter what the circumstances. There is none like You!

Cindy Riker is involved with Teaching the Word Ministries with her husband, Don, and enjoys being a wife, mother and homeschooler and is a member of Manor Church.

JANUARY 30

God Speaks in Unexpected Places

"Come and listen, all you who fear God; let me tell you what he has done for me. I cried out to him with my mouth; his praise was on my tongue. God has surely listened." Psalm 66:16-17, 19

With a heavy heart I joined the Coffee Klatchers at Fairmount Homes on the morning of April 28, 2009. However, I had no desire to participate in the camaraderie that is the norm at these gatherings. Recent tests revealed that our nine-year-old grandson's cancer had reoccurred and his second surgery was scheduled for that afternoon. I breathed a constant prayer: "Lord, thank You for being with Josiah during his first surgery and giving him good reports. Now, Lord we're asking that You guide the surgeons during this second, more serious operation, and give him a complete healing."

Elizabeth rarely comes to the scheduled Coffee Klatcher gathering, but that morning she filled her mug and sat across from me. Each of us bring our own mugs, some designed with advertisements, some from vacation sites and some etched with pretty flowers. Idly, I noted Elizabeth's mug had words on it. Turning the mug around I read the message: "Good Morning! This is God. I will handle all your problems today!"

I sat there, stunned, digesting this message. God heard my prayers! With tears I explained to Elizabeth my concerns for Josiah. I believed the message on the mug was God's way of telling me He has the situation under control!

This experience also offers proof that we can discover God's messages anywhere—even on a coffee mug!

Elizabeth finished her coffee, then pushed the mug back to me. "Here," she said, "take it with you and keep it as long as you need it."

I assured her the message was engraved on my heart. I didn't need the mug.

Although Josiah's operation lasted six hours and was much more complicated than his first surgery, God comforted my heart, gave me His divine peace and healed Josiah in the bargain! Praise the Lord!

Lord, I love finding You in everyday experiences and thank You for healing Josiah!

Grace Graybill and her husband, Paul, are retired and living at Fairmount Homes.

JANUARY 31

Live with Passion and Compassion

"He felt great pity for the crowds that came, because their problems were so great and they didn't know where to go for help. They were like sheep without a shepherd." Matthew 9:36 (New Living Translation)

When I get up in the morning, I frequently thank God for giving his only Son for me. Then I thank Jesus for his willingness to leave heaven and live among sinful men and die a cruel death on the cross. I thank the Holy Spirit for leaving heaven and being willing to live in my sinful heart now made holy by his transforming power. That morning prayer has made a profound difference in my life.

If we have a fraction of God's passion for sinful humanity, we could turn the world right side up. The primary emotional response of Jesus for our world was compassion. Jesus was perfect. If anyone could be turned off by the sin in our world it was Jesus. Instead of looking or reacting with disdain at problem people, Jesus reacted with compassion. Jesus saw people as sheep that had been bruised, beaten and confused. They needed a Shepherd.

Jesus was perfect yet sinners crowded around Him. The more mature we are spiritually the more sinners should feel comfortable with us. It was true with Jesus. His love showed. He was approachable. Both sinners and children were drawn to him. They could tell He was genuine. They felt loved.

Ask God to give you the heart of Jesus toward those who are lost and have no understanding of God's indescribable love for them. He will answer that prayer.

Lord, You came not to condemn the world but to save it. Help me to see people as you see them—sheep without a shepherd. Fill me with the same love and compassion You have for them.

Dave Eshleman served as pastor/church planter for fifty years.

February

Childlike Faith

"I'm telling you, once and for all, that unless you return to square one and start over like children, you're not even going to get a look at the kingdom, let alone get in!" Matthew 18:3 (The Message)

On a cold winter morning in the late 1940s, my mother bundled up my brother James and me before sending us out to play. We talked excitedly about sledding again that day because we had gotten a brand-new sled for Christmas, and its newness hadn't yet worn off.

As James and I scampered out the front door with mother's parting instructions of "Be good, now," we both raced for the sled which we had inadvertently left in the middle of the front lawn the day before. Our exuberance soon turned to frustration when we discovered the sled had frozen fast to the ground because of a slight thaw and then a refreezing. We tugged, pulled and grunted, but all in vain. The sled was securely anchored.

In our frustration, James and I came upon a conclusion. The evening before, Mother had read us a story about faith and prayer from *Uncle Arthur's Bedtime Stories*. Since the characters in the story had exercised the blessed attributes of faith and prayer, we would too. Hand in hand, James and I knelt on the front porch in solemnity before our childhood God. "Dear Jesus," I prayed, "please make our sled come loose. Amen."

There was no doubt in our minds but that God had answered our prayer. So triumphantly we rose from our "prayer closet" and dashed to the sled. Sure enough, on our first tug, the sled came loose. What a boost that was to our childhood faith.

Lord God, forgive me for the times my faith has wavered. Increase my faith to believe that You not only can but also that You will.

Paul Brubaker serves on the ministry team at the Middle Creek Church of the Brethren, Lititz.

Photo by Don Barley

FEBRUARY 2

Let's Empower Our Youth

"These are the twelve he (Jesus) appointed … James son of Zebedee and his brother John (to them he gave the name Boanerges, which means Sons of Thunder)." Mark 3:16-17

How old were the disciples when Jesus called them? I believe Jesus called John when he was in his teens and the other disciples probably in their twenties. In their culture one was not recognized as a teacher until you were thirty. Jesus broke the cultural traditions by calling these young men.

Jesus referred to James and John as "sons of thunder" or "thunderbolts" as the Contemporary English Version states. That can be frightening but Jesus took the risk. We too must take the risk. Empowering youth and young adults will bring new life to our traditional congregations.

We need their enthusiasm. Ask God to open your eyes to see these potential young men and women who have a passion to see people come to Jesus and who relate well with people. Tap them on the shoulder. Believe in them, listen to their concerns. Bless and affirm them in their gifts. Tell them you believe God has gifted them for ministry in extending His Kingdom. As we mentor, pray and walk with them, they will lead us in our church revitalization.

Most people who become Christians accept Christ when they are in their teens or even before. Pray for eyes to see the potential in each youth and young adult and invite them to hear the call of the Lord upon their lives.

The ball is in our court. Jesus said we are to pray to Him to send workers into the harvest. Are we praying? When we pray, He will open our eyes to see these young people. Don't be surprised that many of our Christian workers will be found among our youth and young adults. It happened in Jesus' day. It can happen in ours.

Lord Jesus, make me an encourager for these youth to step out in evangelistic and church planting ministry for You.

Dave Eshleman served as pastor/church planter for fifty years. Presently he is a church consultant.

FEBRUARY 3

Be Prepared

"Preach the Word, be prepared in season and out of season; correct, rebuke, and encourage—with great patience and careful instruction." 2 Timothy 4:2

As young mothers with small children, my neighbor and I spent much time together while our children played. At twenty-eight years of age, I had not accepted Jesus as my Savior. I went to church my whole life but did not know what a personal relationship with Jesus was. My neighbor was a Christian. She was kindhearted, compassionate and had a gentle spirit. There was a peace about her that radiated whenever we were together, and I knew she had something that I wanted. She would gently ask me, without judgment, about my spiritual life. It made me more curious about this peace that seemed to flow from her. One time she invited me to church and our family accepted her invitation. I desired more and more of what I saw and heard until I finally understood what a personal relationship with Jesus was. I confessed that I was a sinner and I asked Jesus into my heart. I became part of the family of God.

I learned a valuable lesson from this precious neighbor and it stays with me to this day. Christians need to realize that people are watching us. It is important to be on our guard and set an example so others can see God in us. My neighbor's example touched me in a way that made me hunger and thirst for God. I saw something in her that was missing in me. I am grateful for her example. From her example, I learned to allow God's love to shine through me so that others may see God and desire a relationship too.

Dear God, help me to be the person You want me to be. May others see You in me so that they too may desire a relationship with You. God help me to be prepared to share with them the peace and joy You have provided me. Thank You Lord.

Cynthia Zimmerman is married to Rick Zimmerman and attends New Life Fellowship Church in Ephrata.

FEBRUARY 4

Rescued Children

"Many, O Lord my God, are the wonders you have done. The things you planned for us no one can recount to you; were I to speak and tell of them, they would be too many to declare." Psalm 40:5

We learned to know an Indian couple who lived here in the States and who later moved back to India. They told us the following story.

Eighteen years ago a girl was born in India. Her mother could not care for her, so her grandmother looked for someone to rescue her. She was desperate and was about to put the baby under a bush to die because it was so ill and very thin. She came upon this Christian couple, our friends, who had taken in other very poor children. She begged them to take this baby. The couple took the child.

With love, care and much patience the child grew and became a beautiful young woman. With many years of careful love, guidance and teaching, this girl saw her need of a Savior. This past Easter she accepted the Lord and asked for baptism. What a marvelous change came into her life. She was very happy and changed her Muslin name to a Christian name—Claire. God preserved her life as a baby and now she is beautiful and full of life. She will contribute much to the lives of others. We thank the Lord for caring people who take the call to care for others seriously. We are grateful to those who adopt children in need and give them a good home and good training. May God bless the many people who have done this and are continuing to care for others.

Thank You, Lord, for opening hearts among us who rescue children and give them hope for a future life.

Miriam Witmer is a retired church leader's wife and intercessor.

FEBRUARY 5

Seeds of Plenty

"Now may He who supplies seed to the sower, and bread for food, supply and multiply the seed you have sown and increase the fruits of your righteousness." 2 Corinthians 9:10 (New King James Version)

As a teenager, I really did not understand the power of the words I wrote and taped to my bedroom mirror, "Here am I; send me."

Today I can still recall the sincerity of my heart as I wrote the words. I thought the commitment to follow the Lord wherever He would take me meant Africa or some other faraway country! God was thinking post-abortion ministry!

In 1999, I was suddenly launched into the lives of broken women; women held captive to abortion's guilt and shame. Pouring over a box of post-abortion Bible studies, I was desperate for a lesson plan. I would soon be meeting with my first post-abortion client. I felt anxious, ill equipped and inadequate.

During the past years, I have grieved with many wounded post-abortion women and have had the privilege of being a witness to God's work of redemption and restoration in their lives. God has certainly been my teacher and has faithfully provided seed for me to sow into these lives. For many, the secret that was guarded in pain and shame in these precious women's hearts has been brought into a spacious place of freedom to share their stories with others as God opens up opportunities. In turn, more women and men are led to the One who heals their hearts and provides seed for them to sow.

Dear Father, Your supply of seed never ends. Fill our hearts with compassion and our words with healing for those wounded by abortion.

Carol Weaver serves at Susquehanna Valley Pregnancy Services as director of Post-Abortion Ministry.

FEBRUARY 6

A Compassionate Heart

"Treat others as you want them to treat you." Luke 6:31 (The Living Bible)

It is the desire of my heart that I be a blessing to others daily. So, each morning I pray that God will send someone my way. If that has been your heart's desire, yet you haven't acted on it because you don't know how, or think you can't do it, let me assure you that even the smallest gestures are still a blessing to others.

For example, there are a lot of hurting people who only need a listening ear. They don't need a solution, or criticism, or anything else. All they need is someone to listen to them … could you be that someone?

Or, how about greeting someone with a smile and saying, "Good morning," or opening the door, or complimenting them. These are all examples of being a blessing to someone that cost little to nothing in terms of time and money.

Is there a single mom who could benefit by your generous offer to babysit while she goes to the grocery store, or maybe just soaks in a tub of hot water to relax and enjoy a peaceful moment?

What about an elderly neighbor … could you invite that person out to lunch? Who enjoys eating alone day after day? What a treat that would be if you included her during all holidays. If she rarely gets a visit from family, welcome her into your festivities and make someone happy. Those long, lonely holidays that were dreaded, now take on new meaning to the recipient of your kindness.

While the list could go on as to how you could be a blessing to someone, I hope you have been inspired to reach out. For by extending a little of yourself to others, you are reaping the harvest of a life full of joy, as you follow God's command to treat others as you want to be treated.

Lord, grant me a compassionate heart that I might reach out in kindness to others in need.

Janet Young attends DayBreak Church and conducts tea presentations and teaches etiquette classes as owner of Over the Teacup.

FEBRUARY 7

Similar Lives, Different Worlds

"'For I know the plans I have for you,' declares the Lord, 'plans to prosper you and not to harm you, plans to give you hope and a future. Then you will call upon me and come and pray to me, and I will listen to you.'" Jeremiah 29:11-12

I was nine-thousand miles from home and on my first mission trip to Fortelaza, Brazil. The connection to the young adults my age came naturally. Surprisingly, language seemed to be no barrier.

While there, I met Karine who spoke no English. I felt a strong connection with her as she shared her story through an interpreter. I felt Karine's hurts, her anger and her heart for God. Although we lived in very different worlds, we shared similar emotions as we struggled with conflicts in growing up and wanting to live for God.

Karine shared her heart because she wanted prayer. I realized right then and there that prayer was the key for a direct line to God regardless of what country we may be from or what language we speak.

After prayer, our hugs spoke volumes to each other. I'm grateful that we are not limited by language barriers, but that we can pray for each other. My heart goes out to Karine and to others I met. She will have a place in my memory forever, and I know the Lord will love her through her trials.

Dear heavenly Father, thank You for gently breaking my heart for what breaks Yours. You allowed me to hear the cry of Karine and not focus on a language barrier ... all because of Your love.

Laurie Zeager was nineteen when she accompanied a mission team to Brazil. She attends DOVE Westgate and lives in Akron.

FEBRUARY 8

Wasteful Love

"How great is the love the Father has lavished on us, that we should be called children of God!" 1 John 3:1

Raised in Lancaster County, I picked up early on the horrors of wastefulness. Time, money, possessions, electricity must be carefully spent or saved. While God calls us to be good stewards of all that He gives us, for me it became tangled up in my own question of value.

Since I homeschool my children, I wanted to learn oil painting with them. I watched videos on YouTube and bought all the supplies. It looked simple enough, and we were excited to start. Yet I kept putting off the actual application of paint to canvas. It wasn't because I was afraid of messing up. It was because I knew I might mess up and waste the canvas. Finally, my husband said to me, "You're worth more than that canvas. Just do it."

As I realized my reason for hesitation, I brought my fear of waste before the Father. I sensed these thoughts in my heart, "You are more important to me than waste. I waste Myself on you in a thousand different ways every day! Flowers bloom for you that you never see, I paint the sky for you whether you notice or not. My love is showered all around you. I don't do this to make you feel guilty, or to get you to do something for Me—I just can't help Myself! I am so delighted with you, My child, that I am expressing My love all the time!"

Father, help me to receive Your love as the lavish gift that it is. I receive the truth that You loved me enough to pour out Your life for me. Open my eyes and ears and heart to the expressions of Your love all around me.

Doe Kopp is married to Dwight and they have four children. She is a homemaker and homeschool mom. They meet as a church with families in various homes.

FEBRUARY 9

Lifeline

"The Lord is my rock and my fortress and my deliverer, my God, my rock, in whom I take refuge; my shield and the horn of my salvation, my stronghold." Psalm 18:2 (New American Standard Bible)

My life had been flowing along fairly smoothly when I sensed the Holy Spirit nudging me to become more grounded in the Word. Up to this point, I had faithfully read the Bible every day, but I sensed a call to a deeper, more deliberate reading and memorizing of the Scriptures.

Instead of reading novels, solving word puzzles and participating in other trivial pastimes, I studied the Scriptures.

Suddenly, without warning, my world turned upside down. Everything I had trusted in failed me and I was left desperately clinging to the Lord and the promises I found in His Word.

One particular morning I awoke in such despair I didn't see how I could face another day. But I forced myself to go to work as usual. I keep a pocket New Testament with Psalms and Proverbs with me and opened it to the topical index. I looked under the heading "despair" and it directed me to Psalm 38: "My iniquities have gone over my head; like a heavy burden they are too heavy for me. I am troubled, I am bowed down greatly. I am feeble and severely broken. I groan because of the turmoil of my heart. Do not forsake me, O Lord my God. Make haste to help me, O Lord, my salvation!"

I could have written those words. They became a lifeline for me, keeping me from drowning in despair.

Looking back, I realize God was preparing me for the storms that would come to rock my world and my faith. The Scriptures became my rock. My foundation. My comfort. My hope.

Lord, thank You for the comfort that Your word gives us. Thank You for being our rock, our strong tower, our deliverer. Thank You for being everything we need You to be.

Dolores Walker, along with her husband, David, is a member of Dove Westgate Church, Ephrata.

FEBRUARY 10

God's Provision

"For your Father knows the things you have need of before you ask Him." Matthew 6:8 (New King James Version)

I felt God calling me to be part of a medical team heading for Uganda for a week of clinics last February. I have been so blessed to be part of medical teams that traveled to Haiti and Kenya in the past, so I knew that I would need a sizable amount of money to cover flights, room, board, food and travel insurance. I began to set aside some money from each paycheck beginning a year before the scheduled trip. I had long ago learned that God's provision was always there for me if I obeyed His call and was responsible to do my part.

The time for submitting my money for the plane fare was fast arriving and I was so happy to find that I had saved the cash I was in need of. And then I received the call. A sweet couple from another state called me one night to tell me they felt God was asking them to send a gift toward my medical trip to Uganda. I was totally surprised as I had not sent a letter of request and could not remember how they would even know that I was going on the team. I thanked them, thinking they would send, say, $50 or at most $100.

Two weeks later I received a call from the mission's office. The gift had arrived. The check was for $1,500. I was shocked. That amount would cover my entire flight to and from Africa. Why would God give me such a bonus gift? I decided to take my extra money to Uganda with me, figuring that God had other plans for the money I had saved.

He did. Some of our Ugandan translators had not been in the budget designed by the pastor planning the trip. Some of the Ugandan pastors and workers had personal needs that were taking a backseat to helping our team with the medical clinics that week and they were trusting God to meet their needs. God revealed all of this to me at the end of our week and I was absolutely delighted to share the extra cash with them, assuring them that God had supernaturally provided for me and now He was doing the same for them. God's provision is amazing.

Thank-you, El Shaddai, that You are the God of more than enough!

Mary Prokopchak leads a small group for Dove Christian Fellowship in Elizabethtown.

FEBRUARY 11

Repercussion of Good Intentions

"He who calls you is faithful." 1 Thessalonians 5:24 (New King James)

As a one-income family, my husband and I share a car. He called me forty-five minutes ago to say he would pick us up shortly, and still my children and I wait for him. I can feel my blood pressure rising because I know I have a pressing errand to complete before dinnertime. My husband uses the car for work, and I usually do not because his hard work allows me to stay home full-time. However, today the kids are not waiting patiently (which means they are fighting with each other) and I'm not acting graciously toward the man I promised to love and cherish.

When my beloved finally arrives, my children and I pile into the car. During the drive to town, I think about my attitude. How many times do I tell my hubby I will be ready in fifteen minutes; yet thirty minutes later, I still run around the house trying to pack my purse or finish dressing? I know this tardiness frustrates him. I find myself humbly praying, "Thanks a lot, God, for reminding me of my shortcomings when I'd rather point the finger at him!"

I feel convicted when I realize how often I don't keep my word. I have good intentions of sending that recipe or praying for that person, but I forget or allow myself to get busy pursuing other activities. Even more troubling is the recognition that sometimes I say what I think the other person wants to hear just so I can look good to them. Ouch!

When people look at us, do they see our faithful God? I want to emulate Jesus, who keeps His Word, and I want people to know they can trust me.

Praise You, God, for Your faithfulness. Where would I be if You did not keep Your word? Make me into a person who reflects Your truth. Amen.

Jennifer Turner resides in Manheim where she helps her husband homeschool their children and sings at Manheim Grace Brethren Church.

FEBRUARY 12

Samaritans on the Loose

"And who is my neighbor?" Luke 10:29

Oh no! We were ten miles away from the Allentown airport when the battery light on the car started to flash. We literally coasted into a gas station directly across from the airport before it died completely. My husband offered to pay a man at the gas pump to take my mom to the gate where she was to catch her flight. "No problem. My wife is headed there right now to return a rental car," he replied. That was only the beginning.

For the next two hours that family (husband, wife, son and cousin) stuck by our side—in the cold, icy rain—trying to help us. It soon became obvious we would have to get towed seventy miles back to our mechanic's garage. But rather than leaving us, the family insisted on staying until the tow truck arrived. So there, in the warmth of their running car, we waited and exchanged stories. All I could think of was, "How do they have the time to do this? We're strangers, we barely speak the same language (they were Hispanic), yet here they are showing us such kindness."

I've thought a lot about the parable of the Good Samaritan since that night … of the priest and Levite who passed by the man who had been robbed, beaten and left on the road to die. Life was about them. They had places to go and people to see. I'll bet they were busy. I'll bet their lives were full of sentences with no commas, too full to be interrupted. Probably not a lot different from mine.

Not so, though, with the Samaritan. And not so with these dear folks. Because of the time they took for us on that cold wintery night, our lives were touched. Changed. Challenged … to slow down and consider God's undeserved mercy.

Father, may we let you interrupt our busy lives and so be set apart.

Becky Toews serves at New Covenant Christian Church and Lancaster Bible College. This is an excerpt from "Fresh Tracks" at www.beckytoews.com.

FEBRUARY 13

Reflect the Glory of Christ

"So all of us who have had that veil removed can see and reflect the glory of the Lord." 2 Corinthians 3:18 (New Living Translation)

As a science teacher in a Christian school, I desire to have a deeper understanding of who God is by studying His creation. I look for things in nature to use as object lessons for spiritual truths to apply to my own life and present to my students.

One of my favorite creatures is the Morpho menelaus, aka the Blue Morpho butterfly. It gets its name from the beautiful color on the upper surface of its wings. The interesting thing, though, is that the wings have no blue pigment in them. Instead, the color is produced by precisely arranged scales on the Morpho's wings that reflect only blue light. This phenomenon is known as iridescence. In the absence of light, the wings are a dull brown and gray.

The Blue Morpho brings to mind 2 Corinthians 3:18, which tells us as believers we are designed by our Creator to reflect the glory of Christ.

The Blue Morpho does not hatch from its egg already able to reflect blue light. Rather, it hatches as a somewhat unimpressive brown caterpillar that spends its time gorging itself on plants. Only after the process of metamorphosis does the creature emerge in all of its iridescent splendor. Similarly, we are unimpressive and self-indulgent prior to experiencing the "metamorphosis" that comes from belief in Christ's work on the cross. The life-transforming power of the cross makes us new creatures (2 Corinthians 5:17), able to walk in the light of Jesus and reflect His beauty and glory.

Father, thank You for Christ's work on the cross, and the Holy Spirit who empowers us to reflect the beauty of Your Son.

Todd Swisher is married to Kati, teaches at New Covenant Christian School and attends Cornerstone Christian Fellowship.

FEBRUARY 14

Tangible Expressions of Christ's Love

"So now I am giving you a new commandment: Love each other. Just as I have loved you, you should love each other." John 13:34 (New Living Translation)

Valentine's Day is an event that some approach with giddiness and high expectations. There are hopes of flowers, cards and surprises, but often those lofty desires are met with disappointment. Some people have a particular dislike for this holiday. Maybe they don't have a "someone special," and this day only seems to highlight the loneliness. I would propose that as Christians, we can take a different perspective on this day altogether.

As followers of Christ, we can live differently among a world that clamors for romance and a self-serving kind of love. We aren't called to live according to the world's standards, but rather, a higher one that instructs us to consider others better than ourselves. Rather than focusing on our wants and desires, what if we would apply the very practical teachings of 1 Corinthians 13 this Valentine's Day? We are told that love is patient, kind, not envious, boastful or proud. It's not self-seeking or easily angered. It always protects, trusts and hopes.

What if each of us viewed today as an opportunity to demonstrate real, Christlike love to the world—not a commercialized, romanticized version of love—but the kind that will be remembered? Today is a day of love—not to be easily angered by the driver that cut us off in traffic, but the kind of love that will be patient with the person holding up the grocery checkout line. Christ's kind of love will not be self-seeking, looking to receive gifts but rather looking for an opportunity to give and serve.

Jesus we ask, as Your followers, that You would give us the grace to supernaturally love others today in the way that You have loved us. May we see those around us who are in need and be a tangible expression of Your love.

Jessi Clemmer and her husband,Todd, serve as senior elders of Koinonia House, a DOVE Christian Fellowship International church in Pottstown.

FEBRUARY 15

Best Practices

"Love the Lord your God with all your heart, all your soul, all your strength, and all your mind. And love your neighbor as yourself." Luke 10:27 (New Living Translation)

Being employed for over eighteen years in long-term care, I have been taught and expected to embrace best practices in this industry. Having many beneficial consequences, creating resident-centered care is evidence of accomplishing these goals. Regulatory agencies and advocates want to make nursing homes and personal care facilities a great place to live and work. However, the required, annual unannounced surveys by the Department of Health can be quite stressful. This almost weeklong survey is one method of assuring quality initiatives are being followed and our own policies are in place. If not, deficiencies are cited, which may include monetary fines if serious enough, with an expected plan of correction. The surveyors' exit interview to announce the "score" results is a time of great stress and nervousness.

I believe that simply put, the best practices of the Scriptures are to love the Lord with all my might, soul and strength and to love my neighbor as I love myself. Pursuing and embracing this best practice every day of the year to assure my heart is Christ-centered will benefit me beyond anything I dare, think or imagine. Perhaps every January should be assessment time and an honest evaluation of my love acts toward my Lord and neighbor. As I heard Sheila Walsh say on a television program lately, it is the Shepherd's job to lead the sheep home. It is the sheep's job to have a tender heart toward the Shepherd. I love that!

Lord, please continue to guide me on my path that leads straight into Your everlasting arms of love.

Beaty Miller, a registered nurse, attends the Worship Center.

FEBRUARY 16

Border Crossing

"Casting all your care upon him; for he careth for you." 1 Peter 5:7 (King James Version)

During time with a mission in Germany, my husband, Omar, and I crossed many borders always carrying passports. Officers never asked to see them, until seventeen days before our return to the States.

The Berlin wall had crumbled in 1989, and we along with Henry and Rainer from former East Germany visited a church in Prague, Czechoslovakia, and toured the old city. On that gorgeous afternoon, we parked our Passat on a wide street and set out to enjoy the sights. After an hour, we returned, shocked to find our car had been broken into.

Our suitcase and Henry's overnight bag were gone. That was bad enough, but then my husband saw that his passport was missing. The selective thieves left the Bibles in his briefcase but took the folder with his passport and German driver's license.

"This was the work of professionals," said Rainer. "We'll never get those things back."

"Then we might as well go," we decided. With much prayer, we cautiously approached the border. Wouldn't you know, this time we got stopped. I handed over my passport, and the Germans showed their ID's. We waited tensely.

Rainer explained that Omar's passport was stolen in Prague.

"You should have gone to the police."

"We did," Rainer said, "but they wanted us to wait for an official translator and we need to get back home."

"You'll have to go back to Prague."

Then silence, except for my whispered prayers, "Lord, please help him to change his mind," and "Let us go through. Please, Lord."

Suddenly, without a word, the officer handed over our cards and motioned for us to go.

After driving across the border we started shouting. "Hallelujah! Thank You, Lord!"

Gracious God, in spite of our foolishness—letting a passport in the car—in Your mercy You rescued us. Thank You.

Martha Denlinger Stahl lives at Landis Homes with her second husband, Clayton Nissley. She is a member of Lyndon Mennonite Church. She has had four books published.

FEBRUARY 17

Authority and Power

"All authority in heaven and on earth has been given to me. Therefore go and make disciples of all nations, baptizing them in the name of the Father and of the Son and of the Holy Spirit, and teaching them to obey everything I have commanded you. And surely I will be with you always, to the very end of the age." Matthew 28:18-20

"You will receive power when the Holy Spirit comes on you; and you will be my witnesses in Jerusalem, and in all Judea and Samaria, and to the ends of the earth" (Acts 1:8).

Jesus assures us of both authority and power. It's one thing to have authority and another to have power. In years past, I was a substitute school teacher. I had the authority because of the position of a teacher, but I did not always have the power. Being a young substitute school teacher in a correctional institution for boys was quite a challenge. I had the position but I had to earn their respect. I have witnessed situations where the principal had the authority but also lacked the respect of the students.

On the other hand one can have the power but lack authority. As a parent you may be bigger and stronger than your child, but it seems that often the child is in charge of the situation. Parents and policemen have the position, but often do not have the power or dynamic they need to maintain respect. A neighbor may have the power to control your neighborhood but not the authority. Therefore he or she is usually resented by their neighbors.

Jesus has given us both the authority and the power to witness for Him. Let's share Jesus with humbleness and with confident boldness. Follow the leading of the Holy Spirit as you witness with Jesus' authority and power.

Father, thank You for giving me both the authority and the power to be a witness for You today.

Dave Eshleman served as pastor/church planter for fifty years.

FEBRUARY 18

Persevering Vision

"Lift your eyes now and look from the place where you are—northward, southward, eastward, and westward; for all the land which you see I give to you and your descendants forever." Genesis 13:14-15 (New King James Version)

God instructed Abram to lift his eyes, and as far as he could see of the land in every direction, was his forever. God instilled a vision in Abraham. As we observe Abraham's life in the years that followed, he was not without opportunities to doubt God's promise in the absence of an heir. But God kept encouraging him, reminding him of the generations that would follow, and finally, when he and Sara were advanced in age, Isaac was born. In Romans 4 it tells us the faith of Abraham was accounted to him for righteousness. Abraham persevered.

In the life of our congregation at Worship Center, we experienced some perseverance. In 1981, Worship Center built its first building, which was to be a temporary all-purpose building with a vision to build a sanctuary some short years later. Ten years passed, fifteen, twenty-five. It took twenty-nine years for the reality of this vision to come to pass. Was it discouraging at times? Yes. Did we have times of doubting? Yes. But we knew the vision God had placed in our hearts. We continued to thank God for our new church building with our eyes of faith on our property. We are now able to celebrate in our new facility to the praise, glory and provision of our God.

Everyone has a God-given purpose or vision. Learning how to walk in that vision on a daily basis is an important key to living a fulfilled life. The Holy Spirit has been given to us to guide us a step at a time in fulfilling our destiny here on the earth.

Lord, thank You for a life with purpose and fulfillment. I thank You for helping me keep my eyes on the vision You have for me.

Pastor Sam Smucker serves as Senior Pastor of the Worship Center, Lancaster.

FEBRUARY 19

The Comfort of a Comforter

"You who are my Comforter in sorrow, my heart is faint within me." Jeremiah 8:18

Sometimes a word jumps out at me and strikes me as important. I was singing a hymn at church the other day that included the word *comforter*, and I had to sit and ponder it for a bit.

I was brought back to days of my childhood in our drafty old house. I didn't mind winter so much because the house abounded with blankets. And there were some that were soft and just perfect for wrapping up in to sit and watch cartoons while drinking some hot cocoa.

A comforter or blanket is a great example of how we can wrap warmth, peace and comfort around us to please our outer body. Now, can you imagine this same feeling from the inside out? This is what Jesus gave us when he left this world. The Holy Spirit is a Comforter—wrapping us in peace and warmth from the inside out. Now, go ahead and drink that cup (cocoa or communion juice), and let Him wrap Himself around your soul.

Dear Lord, You care about every part of our innermost being. Thank You for leaving us with Your Spirit to see us through until we are in the warmth of Your glorious presence.

Tracy Slonaker, director of Christian Education at Harvest Fellowship of Colebrookdale, is warmed by the Spirit.

FEBRUARY 20

Don't Look Back

"Jesus replied, 'No one who puts a hand to the plow and looks back is fit for service in the kingdom of God.'" Luke 9:62

As a young boy, I remember the excitement I felt when my dad showed me how to mow with the tractor mower. One important part of those lessons was learning how to mow a straight line. Dad instructed that in order to mow a straight line, I would need to aim for a clear landmark. A telephone pole was the obvious choice. He told me that in order to make a straight line my gaze needs to stay focused on that pole ahead and to not look back at the path I was making. I must confess, in my first several attempts I didn't always keep my eye on that pole, and the crooked patterns in the grass were evidence of my error.

A few years later, it was my grandfather who taught me how to operate a larger tractor while planting celery. I wanted to do an excellent job. It was tempting to look back instead of focusing on my landmark. Looking back led to some very clear mistakes. Grandpa, who was on the planter, would call to me on the tractor, "Wes, don't look back; keep looking ahead."

This is also sound advice for the believer. As Christians we face many distractions in our daily walk that keep us from seeking and serving Jesus first. Satan's goal is to keep us looking into the rearview mirror of our lives, focusing on our many regrets and sinful choices. While it's true that our past shapes us, it doesn't need to define us. Thus, when we look to Jesus—when we put our hand to the tasks before us today and fix our eyes on Him—the path of our life will be straight and fit for others to follow.

Lord Jesus, thank You for delivering us from our past. Grant us courage to keep looking ahead to our great and glorious resurrection in Christ. Infuse our hearts with a deep passion to trust in your leading.

Wesley D. Siegrist pastors Erb Mennonite Church, Lititz.

FEBRUARY 21

Broken

"And he took bread, gave thanks and broke it, and gave it to them, saying, 'This is my body given for you; do this in remembrance of me.'" Luke 22:19

Broken: I did not understand that word before I lost my son. I had heard the word, I had read about it. I had seen it in others.

I am broken. Some people would say I just have a broken heart. I do. But with the breaking of my heart, my soul broke as well. I am no longer me. I had never known myself as broken, so I have to acquaint myself to my broken me.

No doubt, that "new me" is not worse than the old me. In fact what I considered "whole" before was more broken than the broken me now.

I recognize that my soul needed to break. It needed to break from independence and self-sufficiency. In some ways, knowing that I am broken is a freeing experience. I am no longer in charge. I am in need of other people's advice. I am craving comfort. I don't mind that people are walking in and out of my heart to inspect and to see what can be done to mend it, to discover for themselves the real me. I am no longer guarded that other people might find out what is going on inside of me. To pretend as if I'm "together" is becoming a strange idea.

God is close to the brokenhearted. Losing my son has broken me. Was there no other way God? Was there no other way to be close to you God?

I am reminded of Your words before You departed from this earth: "This is my body broken for you." Your perfect body, Your perfect heart, Your perfect life … broken. Broken for me so that my life could be whole.

I don't feel whole God, I am broken. Maybe to be whole is to be broken. Forever dependent, forever not in charge of my life, forever transparent for people, who walk in and out of my life, to know my every need, my every tear, my every thought….

If this is what you wanted of me, You got it, God. I am broken, I am surrendered to You. I am forever a stranger to myself and at home with You.

Josef Berthold is pastor of West End Mennonite Fellowship.

FEBRUARY 22

Out of the Pit

"He also brought me up out of a horrible pit, out of the miry clay, and set my feet upon a rock, and established my steps." Psalm 40:2 (New King James)

I was in love with Jesus, but I opened a door and the enemy came in like a flood. I thought I could dabble in sin and then walk away. Instead the enemy drew me in further. But God, who is faithful and long suffering, rescued me from the hand of the enemy and brought me out of the miry clay. I couldn't do it in my own strength, but He wooed me back to Himself.

The road to recovery and restoration was not an easy one, but God continued to be faithful and walk me through the process. Sometimes it was difficult to distinguish His voice from all the lies I had believed. But He broke the power of the lies with His truth.

He called me up higher, to a life I had not known previously. He asked if I was willing to surrender my life to His control. Then He taught me about His Father's heart for me. When I received His unconditional love, it caused me to love Him more and understand just how much He had done for me. His love caused me to desire that I never hurt His heart again.

He calls me higher every day now, to live a lifestyle of thanksgiving and speaking His words of life.

Father, thank You for rescuing me and saving me, for calling me to Yourself and working in me, energizing and creating in me the power and desire, both to will and to work for Your good pleasure, satisfaction and delight.

Alice Brown serves as an intercessor for Teaching the Word Ministries, attends Acts Covenant Fellowship and enjoys treasure hunting.

FEBRUARY 23

His Name Was Peter

"Satan hath desired to have you .... But I have prayed for you."
Luke 22:31-32

Peter was a full-blooded Gypsy residing with his family in mid-Wales. One Sunday morning he returned home to an empty house. A note on the kitchen table read, "The marriage is over. I've taken the children and left. Please don't come looking for us. Your wife."

Peter was devastated. In a state of depression he considered his options. He thought suicide. He had a hand gun, but did he really want to die? Intoxication would give temporary relief, but it wouldn't change the reality of his missing wife and children. What about church? He'd never been inside a church and had little understanding of what it would do for him—he decided to get drunk.

Later, Peter headed for the local pub. Suddenly, a hand without a body took control of his car. In minutes, the startled man found himself in front of a Pentecostal church where I was a guest speaker. Hesitantly, he entered the sanctuary and took a seat near the front. He endured the music and prayer before I was introduced as a friend from the United States.

My message for the evening was taken from Luke 22, the words of Jesus to Peter: "Satan has desired to have you.... But I have prayed for you." Peter immediately wanted out. How could this preacher know about him? In my conclusion I said that perhaps there is a Peter here for whom Jesus has prayed. If so, I invite you to come forward. The Gypsy literally ran to the front giving me a full-body embrace. His tearful words were, "To think you came from America to tell me Satan wanted me." We parted as brothers in Christ.

Thank You, Jesus, that You know the hearts of all people. You are able to do exceedingly abundantly above all that we are able to ask or think. Your name be praised.

Glen Sell, Manheim, has served as evangelist, pastor, Bible teacher, overseer, family counselor and newspaper columnist. He and his wife, Ethel, are members at the East Petersburg Mennonite Church.

FEBRUARY 24

Compassion for a Troubled Teen

"God is our refuge and strength, a very present help in trouble." Psalm 46:1 (King James Version)

Tom had such anger problems that one day he literally smashed a window with his head. I came into work that day and saw the shattered pieces of glass.

"What happened?" I asked. The story came out that this troubled teen was triggered by a negative remark and vented his anger by becoming violent.

Tom had to face me as he went through the cafeteria line, and his head hung low. I excused myself and took him aside. He looked up at me with sad eyes and asked, "Miss Marie, are you disappointed in me?"

I always encouraged this cute, sharply dressed young man. He and the rest of the troubled teens at this facility needed to be encouraged. My answer to Tom was, "No, I'm not disappointed in you. I love you, and I am praying that you will be able to control your anger." I knew it was the grace of God that covered me as to what I should say and when.

Tom was humble. I didn't know if this young man had ever heard an encouraging word or felt the presence of God's love. He'd often say, "Thank you, Miss Marie. I appreciate your encouragement."

To this day, I continue to pray for those teens who were forced to live in a self-contained facility because of their troubled past. I pray the words I said to the boys might have planted seeds and broken the barriers of anger.

Dear heavenly Father, may I continue to be an instrument to those who have never felt God's love.

Marie Remp has a ministry of laughter. She is thankful for the grace of God allowing her to be sensitive to hurting people.

FEBRUARY 25

Firm Ground

"Then the priests who bore the ark of the covenant of the Lord stood firm on dry ground in the midst of the Jordan; and all Israel crossed over on dry ground, until all the people had crossed completely over the Jordan." Joshua 3:17 (New King James Version)

I think we are kings and priests and called to bear the ark. What is the ark? The presence of the Lord.

As we bear the presence of the Lord, we stand firm on dry ground. We stand firm in the midst of the Jordan. We stand firm in the midst of the waters that surround us and can drown us.

A place of crossing, a place of going into the new, a place of danger and of promise ... as long as we stay in the presence of Jesus, we cross over in the midst of the waters, firmly on dry ground.

When we stay and bear the presence of the Ark of God, it causes those around us to also cross on dry ground. Why? Because we carry the presence of the Lord.

The presence always goes before, just as the ark went before.

We are called to carry it, to really hold it, just like the priest held that very heavy, weighty ark and stood on dry ground.

Many times we try to enter the water without the ark, we go before God tells us or we wait too long. We think we can do this alone. Why would we want to enter the Jordan without the One who called us to cross it?

We are called to enter the water, only with the presence of God in us. Don't get in the water without the ark.

God, today we choose to enter the waters only if You are with us. We choose to carry Your presence with us at all times.

Kim Zimmerman and her husband, Brian, are the founders and directors of City Gate Lancaster and the City Gate Prayer Room.

FEBRUARY 26

The Lost Shall Be Found

"Do not be anxious about anything, but in everything, by prayer and petition, with thanksgiving, present your requests to God." Philippians 4:6

I had just purchased new glasses with the newer-style frame. Even my thirteen-year-old granddaughter told me they were "cool."

I was scurrying around to get ready to go to church when my husband called, "Are you coming?" Just before I readied myself to go, I had been reading in my recliner chair. As I put my glasses on, something felt really off. I could see easily out of the left lens, but the right lens was really strange. As I removed my glasses, I noticed that the entire lens was missing.

We were on a time crunch. I asked my husband to help me search for it. We looked at all the usual places but to no avail. I felt the urge to pray, "Please, God, help me find the lens to my glasses. I can't read without them, and I do need them to drive. You are an all-knowing God, and You care for even the smallest details of our lives. I trust You to guide me. Amen."

I had checked around the recliner where I had been sitting. When I reached down each side of the chair I felt the glass. It was intact, not broken! Thank You, God.

He does care. He directs us when we take the time to ask. So often I think I must solve problems myself, and as a last resort I ask God for help. I am determined to change that with HIS help.

God, thank You for caring for us like You do. I trust in You for even the smallest details of my life. You are an awesome God.

Ruth Robenolt lives in Watsontown with her husband, Ronald. She is retired from Bucknell University. They attend the Community Mennonite Church in Milton, where Ruth is the Director of Pastoral Care.

FEBRUARY 27

Let Your Light Shine

"How, then, can they call on the one they have not believed in? And how can they believe in the one of whom they have not heard? And how can they hear without someone preaching to them? And how can they preach unless they are sent." Romans 10:14-15

Helen, my wife, spends time with our neighbor showing love and sharing the difference Jesus makes in her life. However, she felt checked by the Holy Spirit that it was not the time to confront this neighbor concerning her relationship with God.

Later, my wife found out that a person had knocked on the neighbor's door and asked if she was a Christian. When she answered no, she was told she was going to hell.

The neighbor said, "When I heard that a preacher was moving across the street I was angry. But you are different. No matter what I say, you accept me." Within weeks, the neighbor and her family came to our church and became new creations in Christ Jesus.

Francis of Assisi said to the effect, "Witness 24/7. If necessary, use words." There are times when the witness of our actions and good works are most effective. However, there are other times when we do need to use words. Jesus came and lived a perfect life but if He would not have explained salvation to us, we would still be lost. Someone suggested that we take Saint Francis' words and say, "Wash, if necessary use water." We need both deeds and words.

As Apostle Paul wrote: "How can they hear without someone preaching to them? And how can they preach unless they are sent?" People need to know why we live as we do. The Holy Spirit will prompt you to share how Jesus is making a difference in your life.

Father, help me to both live and speak for You today.

Dave Eshleman served as pastor/church planter for fifty years. Presently he is a church consultant.

FEBRUARY 28 & 29

Selfless Love

"And the King will answer and say to them, 'Truly I say to you, to the extent that you did it to one of these brothers of Mine, even the least of them, you did it to Me.'" Matthew 25:40

Each year our ministry holds a festive day for families to come learn about homelessness and poverty. One of the coolest things about that day is that homeless persons, staff, neighbors and the public are all hanging out and interacting with each other.

Last year, our staff recognized a homeless man shuffling around the festivities. He seemed to be enjoying the food and the festive atmosphere, but his clothes were unclean, his socks were dirty and worn and most noticeable—he had no shoes.

Staff and friends began talking among themselves to determine whether or not anyone had an extra pair of size thirteen shoes to give to the homeless man. While folks were busy problem solving by talking, a resident in the Water Street LifeRecovery program, who just a few weeks before had been living on the street, walked slowly up to the homeless man. The resident took off his own black dress shoes, sat them on the ground next to the man's feet and said, "Yea, they look like they will work."

The homeless man stepped into his new shoes, smiled and shuffled on. The resident smiled and walked off in his stocking feet.

It was a sacred moment—a moment of generosity, compassion and selfless love. A moment where the Kingdom of God was present and I am certain our King smiled.

Lord, thank You for inspiring examples of compassion and generosity. Grant me the willingness to love others with selfless love and a generous heart.

Jere Shertzer is president/CEO of Water Street Ministries, serves on the executive team of the Regional Church of Lancaster County and attends Ephrata Community Church.

Photo by Lowell Brown

March

MARCH 1

My Past

"As for you, you meant evil against me, but God meant it for good." Genesis 50:20

Once I understood the sovereignty of God, everything in my life fell into place. Until that moment, anger, from earlier mistreatment, wrapped its tentacles around me tightly.

My spiritual journey had gone hither and yon until I started attending a church that teaches that God is sovereign over every aspect of life, not just salvation, but all events, both happy and sad.

"Can God use my painful past for good?" I questioned. I believed that God kept me through the dark places, but I had not considered that He used those places to shape me. Was I limiting the power of Almighty God?

I had known that God was my Father. Some say that a person with an untrustworthy earthly father may not view God as a loving, dependable Father. But for me, the very opposite is true. With an often-absent Dad, I relied on my heavenly Father since early childhood. Yet the sadness and hurt remained. I began to examine my belief.

At a Bible conference, I nodded in agreement with speakers teaching God's sovereignty over nature, nations and more. But over my past? By conference end, the Holy Spirit opened my eyes. As tears flowed, I sang with others the Charles Wesley hymn "And Can It Be That I Should Gain." The sting of the past vanished as I viewed my life through a different lens. Anger's grip was loosed and vanquished, never to reign over me again.

Like the biblical Joseph, I recognized that each event helped shape me into the daughter God wanted me to become. I now embrace all aspects of my life, seeing them as a beautiful tapestry created by the sovereign Weaver. The work of my heavenly Father continues.

Lord, thank You for all the events of my life. I trust You to use each one for my good.

Sally K. Owens lives with her husband, Don, in Lancaster, where they participate in two home fellowship groups. They share many children and oodles of amazing grandchildren.

MARCH 2

And a Dog Shall Lead Them

"What have I done to you to make you beat me these three times?" Numbers 22:28

Mr. O'Rourke is a rather old, somewhat overweight Golden Retriever who was a former sightless person's dog. How he came to be a part of our family is a story in and of itself.

O'Rourke was adopted from the National Blind Society located in Morristown, New Jersey. He was put up for adoption because his former owner abused him. These types of dogs are trained, at quite a significant expense, to guide a specific sightless person, and they cannot be transferred to another blind person.

It is hard to fathom that an animal of such a fine breed, and with all the training it has gone through, could be treated with such indignity and disregard, especially by the one it was trying to help. So our home and family became not only the benefactor of a wonderful dog, but he in turn enjoys the "green pastures" during his retirement years.

Such a dog story has often reminded me that I, too, have abused and ignored the One who has loved me from the very beginning—the Lord Jesus Christ. I was blind and He made me see. I was bound by the chains of sin, and He set me free by being nailed to a wooden cross. In reality, he was abused for my adoption.

The Lord uses all sorts of people, things and yes, animals. If He could use Balaam's donkey to teach him, then I guess He could use the Outlars' dog.

Dear Lord, in that You have made all creatures great and small, may I never become too big and haughty to think that You can't use the smallest among us so we might know that we are Your children and You are our Father.

Dr. Sandy M. Outlar serves as community relations director at the Lancaster County Christian School. He and his wife, Joye, live in Landisville and attend Wheatland Presbyterian Church.

MARCH 3

Dead Woman Walking

"My old self has been crucified with Christ. It is no longer I who live, but Christ lives in me. So I live in this earthly body by trusting in the Son of God, who loved me and gave himself for me."
Galatians 2:20 (New Living Translation)

During a time of confession in small group, I shared that being vulnerable has led to many physical, emotional, spiritual and relational acts of betrayal. I feared the enemy would one day succeed in destroying me.

Afterward someone accused me of not making a "positive confession," and I felt betrayed again, becoming vulnerable. Through the night, I kept confessing that my fear is nailed to the cross and bound away from me. I claimed that I am forgiven, and then I forgave the person who had criticized me.

God reminded me that when we are raw and exposed, we either hide behind the fig leaf of shame or we stand naked and unashamed before God as He reveals His love, acceptance, mercy and truth. Words began stirring around in my spirit that I felt would expose the truth from the Lord. As I meditated on them, the Lord revealed the trickery of the enemy and the truth that the enemy can't kill me. I'm already dead. I'm dead. Dead woman walking!

It's no longer I that live, but Christ that lives in me. The truth has set me free! God preserved my life before I received Him. When I gave my life to Him, He came to dwell in me. My life is in His hands, not the enemy's. I willingly lay my life down to follow Christ, to love Him, to serve Him, to glorify Him.

God, I am grateful that when Jesus suffered on the Cross, I suffered with Him. When He died, I died with Him. When He was buried, I was buried in death with Him. And when He was raised, I was raised from the dead with Him.

Sharon Blantz serves the Worship Center as pastor of care and support.

MARCH 4

Always Be Ready to Give an Answer!

"Always be prepared to give an answer to everyone who asks you to give the reason for the hope that you have. But do this with gentleness and respect, keeping a clear conscience…." 1 Peter 3:15-16

Some Christians never talk about their faith. They have the philosophy: my life speaks for Christ or my life is my witness. In one sense this is the most egotistical philosophy anyone could have. In essence they are saying: my life is perfect. Just look at what I do, or how I act and you will see Jesus and who He is. This is a half-truth. (Admittedly there is no such thing as a half-truth.) It's true that we are Christians modeling the life of Christ, but the problem is none of us are perfect models. John writing to Christians says: "If we claim to be without sin, we deceive ourselves and the truth is not in us" (1 John 1:8). James writes: "We all stumble in many ways" (James 3:2).

People need more than models. They need a Savior and Lord. Our life, as imperfect as it is, must point people to Jesus but also we need to verbalize our faith. We need to explain that Jesus is our source of life. We must share with the unbeliever that we need daily cleansing because of our sinful nature. This means there are times when we do not model the life of Christ. He was sinless. We are not.

We need to witness both in word and deed. As James writes: "Faith without deeds is dead" (James 3:26). Peter writes, "Be ready to give an answer to those who ask about why you have a hope for the future."

Lord, help me to live faithfully for You and to boldly and confidently share with others the good news of salvation.

Dave Eshleman served as pastor/church planter for fifty years. Presently he is a church consultant.

MARCH 5

The Big Picture

"You have made known to me the path of life; you will fill me with joy in your presence, with eternal pleasures at your right hand." Psalm 16:11

When I graduated from high school, I knew that I didn't want to be a teacher, secretary or a nurse, but I did want to go to college. I liked to read and write, so I majored in English, Liberal Arts. I naively thought I would become a famous writer.

After college, I waitressed until my mom found out that a local printing company was hiring. I applied for a typist's position, but they said to me, "You have an English degree. You're a proofreader!" I wasn't exactly sure what one did, but after six months of training, it fit my skills and personality exactly. Two jobs later I was proofreading books and eventually decided to work freelance at home. I had experience and lined up two customers.

Then it happened. My retina detached. At first, I wasn't aware of it. Scar tissue formed and I needed two operations. My sight in my right eye could not be restored.

My eyesight was very important in my business. Who would hire a one-eyed proofreader? One customer dropped out and the other one waited six months for me. Eventually the people who owned and worked at that publishing business recommended me to the customers I have today.

Looking back over my career path, I see God's fingerprints all over my life: education, good training, discontent that led me to the right job (books, the only way to sustain a freelance business). Even the timing of my eye surgeries was the best. God knew the big picture and provided for me every step of the way. He is so good and so very personal. It's amazing!

Can you pinpoint the ways God has guided your path? Thank Him for every time He helped you along the way, even the rough spots.

Heavenly Father, thank You for guiding me on my life's path. You truly have a plan for me, and I do not want to stray from it.

Sharon Neal serves with Susquehanna Valley Pregnancy Services, Lancaster Evangelical Free Church (shepherding team, kids' and women's ministries) and proofreads for Bible Visuals International and the Regional Church of Lancaster County.

MARCH 6

Good All the Time

"Through the Lord's mercies we are not consumed, because his compassions fail not. They are new every morning; great is your faithfulness." Lamentations 3:22-23 (New King James Version)

As I rounded the corner, the church's street-side sign stood out to me. "When circumstances are bad, God is still good." The sign typically displayed some clever saying, but that night the message had a life of its own. I somehow knew I would need to cling to it in the coming days.

Our eight-year-old son, Scottie, had been sick for the past day and couldn't keep anything in his system. Hoping to keep him hydrated, I had driven to the store to buy Gatorade. By 9:00 a.m. the next morning, he could hardly walk into the doctor's office. The doctor quickly assessed his condition. He called an ambulance and said, "I'm afraid we're dealing with diabetes."

On the way to the emergency room, my adrenaline was pumping, but I had an inner peace. The sign's message came back to me — God was good and He was in control. He was good eight years ago when he graciously gave us our son, despite the miscarriage of his twin, and despite the diagnosis of a chronic illness and the lifestyle changes that loomed ahead of us, He was still good. Circumstances were changing, but God was the same.

The next week was filled with long days at the hospital learning the many requirements of caring for our son. God showed His goodness in the excellent health care at the hospital and the prayers, meals and babysitting provided by our extended church family. That week I no longer needed a sign to remind me that jobs are lost, bank accounts drain, circumstances change, health declines, but God's goodness never fails.

Lord, thank You for being good all the time. Help me to remember during difficult times that You are in control and give good gifts to Your children who trust in You.

Elisabeth Natter plays piano and cello as part of the music ministry of Cornerstone Presbyterian Church in Ambler.

MARCH 7

Don't Be Distracted

"I run straight to the goal with purpose in every step." 1 Corinthians 9:26 (New Living Translation)

"Remember that in a race everyone runs, but only one person gets the prize. You also must run in such a way that you will win. All athletes practice strict self-control. They do it to win a prize that will fade away, but we do it for an eternal prize. So I run straight to the goal with purpose in every step. I am not like a boxer who misses his punches. I discipline my body like an athlete, training it to do what it should. Otherwise, I fear that after preaching to others I myself might be disqualified" (1 Corinthians 9:24-37).

Paul had a goal. That goal was to "become a servant of everyone so that I can bring them to Christ" (I Corinthians 9:19). Jesus had a similar goal: "to seek and save the lost" (Luke 19:10). He says, "I have come to call sinners to turn from their sins, not to spend my time with those who think they are already good enough" (Luke 6:32). Many Christians have lost that focus.

Pray for your neighbors, your work peers, your school peers by name. Ask God to give you eyes to see how you can build a bridge of relationship to them so you can share Christ. Paul says he became a servant of everyone. Do you and I see ourselves as servants to our neighbors?

Ask yourself what you can cut out of your busy schedule so you have time to be a servant to them. It is often the good things that remove us from doing what is best. Do we need to read the newspaper every day? What about TV and Internet time? Are our hobbies re-creating us? Can we use them to build bridges to share Jesus?

Lord, help me to run straight to the goal with purpose in every step. And help me to become a servant to everyone so that I can bring them to Christ. Amen.

Dave Eshleman served as pastor and church planter for fifty years. Presently he is a church consultant.

MARCH 8

Ordered Steps

"A man may make designs for his way, but the Lord is the guide of his steps." Proverbs 16:9 (Bible in Basic English)

This week I knew the Lord was guiding my steps. I began the day by going to Sewing Circle at our church. On my way I stopped at Root's Country Market and the traffic was just the way I like it. At noon I had an appointment in Mt. Joy, while in the area I stopped at the Reusit Shop. As I left the shop, going east on Route 230, I saw a line of traffic waiting to turn left onto Manheim Street so I decided to take an alley to avoid the congestion and came out on Manheim Street farther on.

Little did I know by doing that I would be getting ahead of an ambulance going to an accident at an intersection on the Manheim road. I was able to slip past the accident and get back to quilting at the Sewing Circle. On my way home from the Sewing Circle I needed to go through a one-lane covered bridge. I saw no one coming into the bridge from the opposite direction, so I proceeded through the bridge. Just as I left the bridge a vehicle passed me heading into the bridge. If he would have entered the bridge three seconds earlier while I was still in the bridge, we would have had a head-on collision.

Each time one of these instances happened, I said, "Lord, You are here." That evening I attended an intercessors prayer meeting. The speaker said that morning a group was praying for the prayer intercessors who would be meeting together in the evening. I am convinced that God heard and answered their prayers. It was an encouragement to pray without ceasing.

Thank You, God, for answering prayers and ordering our steps. Thank You for guiding and protecting us.

Miriam Witmer is a mother, grandmother, greatgrandmother and a prayer intercessor. She and her husband, Howard, live at Landis Homes Retirement Community and attend Erisman Mennonite Church.

MARCH 9

God Is in Control

"Find rest, O my soul, in God alone; my hope comes from him."
Psalm 62:5

The news was devastating. In a moment I went from believing I had a condition that would resolve itself after I delivered our third child, to being told by a pulmonologist that I had a very rare, degenerative lung disease, known as LAM (lymphangioleiomyomatosis). There was nothing I did to get the disease, and there was no way to know how fast the cysts growing on my lungs would destroy the healthy lung tissue I still had. I would always have shortness of breath and be prone to spontaneous lung collapses. There is not a known cure. If the disease in my body is aggressive, I will need a lung transplant.

My husband and I left in a state of shock. We looked on the internet for information, but most of it was inaccurate or outdated—and bleak. We finally stumbled upon a foundation dedicated to researching and finding a cure for LAM. Their motto is: A Breath of Hope.

Hope. I needed it badly. I realized, however, that my hope couldn't come from a doctor, other LAM patients' stories or even a foundation. I have access to the one, true source of hope: the Creator of the universe and my body—the God who controls all things. He knew before I was formed that this disease would invade my lungs. He will be with me throughout my journey with this disease and the daily challenges it brings.

In one moment, my life changed forever, but in another moment, I was reminded that really nothing had changed. God was still in control. He could still be counted on to offer comfort. He is the source of all hope. I needed to keep looking to Him each day for my strength, just in greater measure than I had before.

Thank You, Lord, for being in control and therefore, I can put my hope in You!

Rebecca Nissly, Community Bible Church (Marietta), serves as Business Manager at Susquehanna Valley Pregnancy Services.

MARCH 10

God Is Constant

"We gladly suffer, because we know that suffering helps us to endure. And endurance builds character, which gives us a hope that will never disappoint us." Romans 5:3-5 (Contemporary English Version)

I was angry with God. I was in the midst of a very difficult transition and was drowning in resentment. To get some distance from the situation, I went on a mission trip and thought I was making good progress at overcoming the bitterness that had begun to build inside me, but God knew more work was needed.

Toward the end of the trip, I was asked to share with a group of people and defend the very situation I was criticizing. I thought, how dare God ask me to do such a thing! God knows very well how I feel about this situation. As I inwardly ranted, God was already bringing healing. Through Scripture and the encouragement of other people, I was finally able to see the positive aspects of the transition in which I was living. I proceeded to share joyfully with the group as I had been asked. There is a verse in the Apocrypha in Sirach 2:1 that says, "My child, when you come to serve the Lord, prepare yourself for testing." I had forgotten that my first priority was to serve God.

Afterward, I humbly returned to God in awe of the mercy shown to me. My anger was replaced with praise; joy overtook bitterness. Nothing about the circumstance had changed, but I had a new perspective and was ready to step back into the difficult situation trusting that if God could change my heart so radically, then God could bring good out of any trial I encountered.

Heavenly Father, times of transition can arouse feelings of joy or of fear, but, God, You are constant. To be set apart for You does not mean a life of ease, but it does mean that You give hope even in times of uncertainty.

Christa Mylin has served overseas with Mennonite Central Committee and in the United States with Eastern Mennonite Missions. She attends New Danville Mennonite Church.

MARCH 11

The Prayers of the Righteous

"The prayer of a righteous man is powerful and effective."
James 5:16

Mr. Smith (not his real name) was ninety-seven years old, nearly blind and very hard of hearing. I had to shout at him during his visit so that he could hear me. He expressed his appreciation for the work of Water Street Ministries and particularly the work of the medical and dental clinics. He also thanked me for my involvement there.

He explained that he could not read much anymore because of his poor vision, but he always made time for his morning devotions first, before his tired eyes surrendered the ability to read. He lamented that he could not do much anymore because of the toll that age had taken. I told him that I was glad that he still was reading the Word and gently suggested that he could still pray. "Oh, I do a lot of that, doctor," he replied. "I have a list of fifty people that I pray for every day, as well as many organizations like Water Street, and I pray regularly for you and your practice too."

I was immediately humbled as I realized that his contribution to the Kingdom was far greater than mine! He took the battle of prayer seriously and he believes (and so do I!) that his prayers are heard and that it brings to bear the power of an Almighty God on those for whom he intercedes! As he painfully struggled up from the chair and slowly made his way out of the exam room, I realized that despite all of his physical limitations, he was close to the heart of our Lord, and our Father wants time with us more than the many activities that consume my day!

Lord, may we spend more time in your presence, talking to and getting to know You!

Chip Mershon is a family physician, is on the boards of Water Street Ministries and Water Street Health Services and attends Lancaster Evangelical Free Church.

MARCH 12

Nothing Is Too Hard

"The Lord said to Abraham, 'Is anything too hard for the Lord? At the appointed time I will return to you, about this time next year, and Sarah shall have a son.'" Genesis 18:13-14 (English Standard Version)

God promised Abraham that Sarah would bear a son. Do you remember their response? They laughed. Abraham fell on his face and laughed; Sarah laughed to herself. "We're too old."

Their visitors replied, "Is anything too hard for the Lord?"

Last January, my husband and I received an invitation from a ministry in Cuba. "We're having a conference in May, and we want you to come and teach," it read. I laughed. There were so many obstacles between us and travel to Cuba! We needed U.S. government permission. We needed Cuban government permission to enter on a religious visa, because it's illegal for foreigners to do religious work in Cuba without specific permission and sponsorship from a denomination in Cuba. We needed money for plane tickets and lodging and supplies. Yes, I must confess, I shook my head and laughed. There was no way.

But my husband applied for the U.S. travel permission. Friends in Cuba applied for religious visas. Other friends pledged financial support.

One sunny day in April, an official-looking envelope from the U.S. Department of the Treasury arrived: we had a license to travel! Then came the email from our friends in Cuba: "We have your religious visas!" An unexpectedly large tax refund check and a bonus from work sealed the deal. God had made a way!

Abraham and Sarah had a baby, Isaac—and through them, all the families of the earth have been blessed. We were privileged to go to Cuba and teach, to watch God pour out His blessings, on us and through us.

Be encouraged: when we are set apart for God's purposes, the way will open!

Lord, help us to remember that nothing is too difficult for You. Help us to listen for Your direction, to trust that You will make a way, and to rejoice daily to see you at work all over the world.

Laurie Mellinger is dean of academic programs and associate professor of Spiritual Formation at Evangelical Seminary in Myerstown, and a member of Mountville Mennonite Church.

MARCH 13

Sacrifices that Cost

"I will not sacrifice to the Lord my God burnt offerings that cost me nothing." 2 Samuel 24:24

I wept and laid my heart bare to the Lord after each of three miscarriages. I simply would not be comforted, because the cost of my children's lives seemed too great for any justification. Still, I knew God was good, so I sought Him.

Then, God showed me the story of King David and Araunah. When David told Araunah he wanted to purchase his threshing floor and build an altar upon it, Araunah offered him not only the threshing floor but also the oxen and the firewood at no cost. But David insisted upon paying Araunah for it, saying, "I will not sacrifice to the Lord my God burnt offerings that cost me nothing" (2 Samuel 24:24).

It was as if God whispered into my heart, "I know the cost of the sacrifice you have made. I know exactly how precious it is to you. It is precious to Me, too, and if you will only offer it to Me, I will honor it and receive it as a fragrant and holy sacrifice." I came to understand that God did not discount my children. He knew exactly how valuable they were to me, and that made them all the more worthy.

So, just as Jesus committed His own spirit into the hands of His Father when He died on the cross, I chose to commit the spirits of my unborn children into the hands of my Father in Heaven. In exchange for what was most precious to me, I have received that which is of greater value than anything, a deeper relationship with Christ.

Father, You are worthy of even the greatest of all sacrifices, and yet You made that sacrifice for me, that I might live and know You. Thank You for Your Son, Jesus Christ.

Nicole Schwartz is a wife and mother of two boys. She participates in a simple home church in Maytown, and she serves as a volunteer counselor for Susquehanna Valley Pregnancy Services.

MARCH 14

You're Going Blind

"Yea though I walk through the valley [of affliction] I will fear no evil: for you are with me." Psalm 23:4 (New King James Version)

My parents tell me I began talking about becoming a foreign missionary at age three. I have no recollection of this, but I do know it was the only calling I ever considered. I trained to become a Licensed Practical Nurse, thinking it would be helpful when serving the Lord abroad. I accepted a call into ministry at age twenty-one. When I married April 22, 1957, my wife shared my enthusiasm for missions, and we promised a local mission's agency that we would go abroad in a year.

A month after marriage we discovered parenting was also in the offing. Life was bursting with excitement and anticipated change. Then, July 1957, I went to an ophthalmologist for a routine eye checkup. After a very thorough examination the doctor pushed back his chair, looked intently into my face and said, "I have bad news for you Reverend; you're going blind."

"Going blind," how could this be? Surely there must be some mistake. We were only married three months. Within a year I would be a daddy. We would soon be making preparations for going abroad.

Instead of going abroad, I accepted a call to serve as pastor of a newly planted church in Gaithersburg, Maryland. Five years later, I entered full-time evangelism, a ministry that ultimately became interdenominational and international.

What about my eyes? God gifted me with sight from the corneas of two donors who willed their eyes. That's another story. Physically and spiritually I can say, "Once I was blind, but now I can see." To God be the glory.

Thank You, Father, that no matter how dark or deep the valleys we face, Your hand is there to guide and lead into the brighter tomorrows if we are willing to trust. Blessed be Your name.

Glen Sell, Manheim, has served the Lord as evangelist, pastor, Bible teacher, family counselor, overseer and newspaper columnist. God gifted him and his wife with an itinerant ministry in Wales for more than a decade.

MARCH 15

No Matter What

"Who shall separate us from the love of Christ? Shall trouble or hardship?" Romans 8:35

I can still see this picture in my head whenever I hear Kerri Roberts' song: "No matter what, I'm gonna love You, No matter what, I'm gonna need You, I know that You can find a way to keep me from the pain, but if not, if not, I'll trust You."

My stepson, Dustin, and daughter-in-law, Kelsey, were in their room at Ronald McDonald house in Philadelphia. They said to my husband Darrell and I, "Listen to this song This is true for us."

From the beginning of the pregnancy it had been a rocky road. One of the first ultrasounds revealed there were possible problems with their unborn son, and with each subsequent ultrasound (and there were many) they heard things such as "he could have Down syndrome; there is no connection between stomach and esophagus; possible dwarfism...." And the list went on.

Kelsey delivered Colby five weeks early, and several hours after delivery, Colby and Dustin went by ambulance to Children's Hospital of Philadelphia. Two days later the little guy had major surgery to connect his esophagus and stomach, and a few days later the diagnosis of Down's was confirmed through blood work.

So here sat Dustin and Kelsey on their bed, not knowing how long the stay in the Neonatal Intensive Care Unit was going to be, or what the future held for them and their son, but knowing "no matter what, I'm gonna love You, no matter what, I'm gonna need You."

It was a holy moment as Darrell and I observed this scene. No, none of us knew the future, but we knew our God. I think I'd be correct to say hundreds of God's people prayed throughout the pregnancy and the five-week stay in Neonatal Intensive Care at Children's Hospital.

Colby is a cute little red-headed guy who brings such joy to his family and so many others. He continues to amaze his doctors with his development—no matter what ....

Lord, thank You for loving us, no matter what.

Nyla Martin is the director of Columbia Pregnancy Center, Susquehanna Valley Pregnancy Services.

MARCH 16

Death to Life

"Truly, truly, I say to you, unless a grain of wheat falls into the earth and dies, it remains alone; but if it dies, it bears much fruit."
John 12:24 (English Standard Version)

Death is a key principle of transformation—personally and regionally. It's a truth that makes all the sense in the world according to the government of God. From death comes life; it's a core tenet of our Christian faith.

But we are terrified of it, and we often do everything we can to avoid the principle of embracing death in order to experience life. We cling to the things we have come to experience as life ... relationships, careers, worship styles, ministry contexts, small groups, family dysfunctions, neighborhoods and so forth. When God chooses that one of these is to die in order that new life may grow, we often react strongly, pushing against His call to our death in order to stay in a self-imposed and self-controlled construct of safety and security.

It's a clear truth: Jesus asks for everything. Our call is that of a cross. To live is Christ and to die is gain. Without the death of the seed, there is no new growth, and without new growth, there is no harvest.

Dear heavenly Father, help us to embrace the death to which You are calling us and allow us to experience abundant life. As we experience Your call to brokenness and receive Your healing, this path of resurrection and hope comes as we walk with You through the power of the Holy Spirit.

Jay McCumber serves as lead pastor at Cornerstone Christian Fellowship in Lebanon and as president of the Lebanon 222 team.

MARCH 17

Changed Cities, Changed Lives

"And we, who with unveiled faces all reflect the Lord's glory, are being transformed into his likeness with ever-increasing glory, which comes from the Lord, who is the Spirit." 2 Corinthians 3:18

I recently attended my annual family reunion in Weirton, West Virginia. When I was a young child Weirton was a steel town, as were the Pennsylvania towns Pittsburgh and Industry, which are other familiar places of my youth. Each of these towns were very dirty places as the steel mills belched thick black smoke from their stacks. I remember returning home with my white socks almost black.

In the past few years, something has happened to these towns. Steel has been replaced as the major employer by other jobs and slowly but surely the atmosphere in the towns cleaned up. My recent trip revealed that Weirton is a much cleaner town than I remember even though the mill is still in operation. It seems it is almost a totally different place.

This got me thinking of how our lives are a lot like those steel towns of forty and more years ago—all dirty with black soot, so to speak. But, when we receive Christ, we begin to clean up. We need to remove the sooty sin that veils us from the truth of God's Word. Paul describes this changing as a transformation with ever-increasing glory. We are to be in the process of becoming more and more like Jesus. As we continue to transform, people begin to see Jesus in us. That should be our goal: Becoming a living reflection of our Savior.

Lord Jesus, help me clean myself up so that I can become a more accurate reflection of You.

Kevin Kirkpatrick is the pastor of Terre Hill Bible Fellowship Church and serves on the executive team of the Regional Church of Lancaster County.

MARCH 18

Pathways to God

"Jesus said, 'I am the way, the truth and the life. No man can come to the father except through me.'" John 14:6 (New Living Translation)

When I talk of pathways to God, I'm not talking about a pathway to other gods. I am talking about the Creator God whose Son is Jesus Christ. We come through Jesus to our heavenly Father. Also we all come through the blood of Jesus Christ, the new life-giving way. However, since God made us all different, with different spiritual temperaments, we find closeness to God in different ways.

Gary Thomas, in his book *Sacred Pathways*, lists nine common ways that people take to draw near to Jesus. For example, "Abraham had a religious bent, building altars everywhere he went. Moses and Elijah revealed an activist's streak in their various confrontations with forces of evil and in their conversations with God. David celebrated God with an enthusiastic style of worship, while Solomon expressed his love for God by offering generous sacrifices. Ezekiel and John described loud and colorful images of God, stunning in sensuous brilliance."

Which of the nine sacred pathways seem to be more helpful to your approach in walking with Jesus: (1) Naturalists: Loving God in the outdoors, (2) Sensates: Loving God with the senses, (3) Traditionalists: loving God through ritual and symbol, (4) Ascetics: Loving God in solitude and simplicity, (5) Activists: Loving God through confrontation, (6) Caregivers: Loving God by loving others, (7) Enthusiasts: Loving God with mystery and celebration, (8) Contemplatives: Loving God through adoration, and (9) Intellectuals: Loving God with the mind.

When we share Jesus with people we need to allow them to approach Jesus through their spiritual temperament. Let's not force people to come to Jesus through our spiritual pathway. Give them the freedom to follow the refreshing pathway of the Holy Spirit in their lives.

Father, I thank You that You have made us all different. Help me to celebrate the difference and learn from others as they share their close and life-invigorating walk with You.

Dave Eshleman served as pastor/church planter for fifty years.

MARCH 19

Pray Always

"Pray without ceasing." 1 Thessalonians 5:17

I always knew prayer was important. I am learning that prayer is life. We are to be people of prayer. In City Gate Prayer Room, where we watch and pray, we often have people come in and ask for prayer. This story tells us of the power of prayer, and how far the hands of prayer go.

Our neighbor saw us praying, and she came in. She took several steps and leaned against the wall, weeping. "I need you to pray," she managed to say. "The doctors told us my husband is dying of cancer." Immediately we began to pray with her and for her husband, declaring scripture and encouraging her. We hugged and she left to go back to work.

The next night as we were in the Prayer Room again, she came back over. "I have never felt this kind of peace before. I did what you said, and read all the Psalms last night." I really only gave her two to read, but she couldn't stop reading the Word, and as she read, it brought peace to her. She even started to share with her husband about prayer and the Word.

Several weeks later, our landlord came into our Prayer Room. He said to me, "Jane told me how much you have been praying with her and how much prayer has helped and meant to her, and I wanted to thank you for praying for her; that is really amazing." I felt called to ask him if he needed prayer. And sure enough, his wife was suffering from breast cancer.

That is how prayer works. It changes you. You share what prayer has done, and then it moves to the next person. And they begin to pray. This is how we pray without ceasing.

God, teach us to pray even more. Let us be people of prayer, praying always and being watchful.

Kim Zimmerman and her husband, Brian, are the founders and directors of City Gate Lancaster, and the City Gate Prayer Room.

MARCH 20

Yes, Lord

"Oh, taste and see that the Lord is good; Blessed is the man who trusts in Him!" Psalm 34:8 (New King James Version)

As an early teen, I was an immature believer. I let my mind wander to yearning for a boyfriend. I made some poor decisions and went my own way instead of God's way.

So for every grade, it seemed I was crazy about a certain boy. It was all in my mind, the boy never found out, but my focus was all wrong. I didn't consider God at all in my thinking in this direction.

Then I wondered what was wrong with me, that no boy ever looked in my direction.

The one I sat beside as a senior seemed more like a brother and we got along fine. But he had a girlfriend and I was crazy about another boy.

Finally God got my attention and I began to seriously consider His plans for my life.

The first step was to surrender my life and goals to Him. I remember distinctly saying to Him, "Lord I'm yours, and I submit to You the direction of my life and the plans You have for me. If You bring into my life a husband, I'll be grateful and thank You. But if not, I will be satisfied and not look for anyone. You are first in my life and I thank You for being in control and guiding me. I love You. You are all I need."

With my eyes fixed on Jesus, it came as a surprise several years later, when Richard asked for a date. We grew to know and love each other and I realized the Lord had brought him to me. We celebrated sixty years of marriage before the Lord had him graduate to Glory. When I learn enough I'll graduate! Hallelujah!

Lord, You are so good and kind and faithful to those who let the decision with You.Thank You for turning my heart to You. Thank You for blessing me. You are precious.

Mary Ruth Lehman attends ACTS Covenant Fellowship and is involved in various prayer groups in the region.

MARCH 21

Jesus' Clothes

"... my ways higher than your ways and my thoughts than your thoughts." Isaiah 55:8-9

My two-year-old son came home from Sunday school with a coloring page of Jesus on the cross. Over the next days and weeks, we went over the details of the story of how Jesus died, but repeatedly, he returned to one detail: "What happened to Jesus' clothes?" Later, when I explained how Jesus was raised from the dead and went to heaven, his response further revealed his prioritizing of the lack-of-clothing detail: "Well, God probably gave him new clothes in heaven."

While I smiled and fondly laughed at my son for the way his brain was processing information of a story his two-year-old mind cannot begin to comprehend, his fixation convicted me of mine. How often am I focused on one small detail and missing the big story? When I am dwelling on the hardships that our church doesn't have never-ending supplies to make my ministry easier, am I missing important ministry? When I worry about getting work done while my children are growing up (and away from me) before my very eyes? And anytime I focus on material objects or appearances?

Life is overflowing with distractions and details to help me miss the larger story of the growing of God's kingdom. I want to cultivate the nature of being set apart and the eyes to see the larger picture beyond my fixations and distractions.

Lord, help me to remember that Your amazing story of love is so much bigger than the details. Help me not be distracted by surface details and instead be able to pinpoint the heart of matters.

Renee Lannan, a member of New Cumberland Church of the Nazarene, volunteers in children's ministries and writes articles, devotionals and fiction while her small children nap.

MARCH 22

Saying Thanks

"I thank my God every time I remember you." Philippians 1:3

The little church where I grew up celebrated its two-hundredth anniversary this year, and they invited all who had attended and everyone in the community for a weekend of celebration. I thought about all the happy memories I had through the years growing up there. More importantly, I thought of the many people who had influenced my life in a godly way—pastors who preached the Word, Sunday school teachers who taught Bible lessons and missionaries who told stories of their trips and communicated God's love for all people. To this day, people in that congregation have a spirit of service and a willingness to help those in need. Their godly example of service with a generous and cheerful heart has made an impression on me.

Two words overwhelmingly came to mind as I pondered all this: "Thank You." I felt that I had to return to this church to say thanks to as many as possible. Some of those I would have liked to have thanked are in heaven with the Lord now, but others are senior saints in their eighties or nineties. I realized that if I delayed, it may soon be too late to say thank you on this earth.

It's amazing the power of a simple thank-you. Some of those dear people got tears in their eyes as I thanked them for being a godly influence in my life. Saying thank you benefits the one giving thanks as well, and I know it made me feel good to express the gratitude in my heart.

Who needs to hear a word of thanks from you? Think of those who have influenced your life in a positive way. I would encourage you to make a visit, pick up the phone or write a letter to say thank you.

Lord, show me who I can thank and help me to do it soon—before it's too late.

Jane Nicholas lives with her husband, Bill, in Elizabethtown. They are grateful to have celebrated their twenty-fifth wedding anniversary in 2011.

MARCH 23

Reflecting the True Light

"In the same way, let your good deeds shine out for all to see, so that everyone will praise your heavenly Father." Matthew 5:16 (New Living Translation)

Most of us would agree that our world is getting more evil and violent. We are surrounded by much pain, overwhelming needs, hopeless despair and deep darkness. Sometimes we feel compelled to try harder to be salt and light to our needy world. But wait ... recently I was challenged by this verse about light from Jesus' Sermon on the Mount teaching. We really don't create the light. We don't have to try harder. We simply shine or reflect the light of our loving heavenly Father.

Scientists tell us that the moon makes no light of its own, but reflects light from the sun. One writer states, "Think of the sun as a huge light and the moon as a mirror." That is exactly how God wants us as believers to live. Jesus is the true light, the Son. We are like huge mirrors reflecting His love, mercy and glory. Let's all be very conspicuous, to be seen by all.

Will you and I be good reflectors today? Note that the good deeds are done by us, but all praise goes to our Father God in heaven. I don't believe God is as concerned where we go to do that reflecting, whether around the world in mission trips or to spend time with or encourage our next-door neighbor. The key is to let the true light shine through us, being active reflectors of the love and light of Jesus.

Lord Jesus, thank You for Your mercy and grace. Help us be reflectors of Your love to all people we meet today. May they see and glorify our heavenly Father because of our deeds.

Nelson W. Martin is director of Support for Prison Ministries, a Lancaster County based prison ministry and prison chaplain program. He and his wife, Anna Mae, live near Lititz and are active at Millport Mennonite Church.

MARCH 24

Crisis Leads to Freedom

"I will walk about in freedom…." Psalm 119:45

The phone call that came at 7:15 a.m. marked the beginning of spiraling events in my life. The man I had lived with for fifteen years was dead. Three weeks later my father was diagnosed with esophageal cancer. Six months later I attended another funeral of a loved one. Within a few months, my house went into foreclosure and I needed to move.

I considered moving back home where I could help with an aunt who had Alzheimer's and my best friend who was dying of a brain tumor. Instead God opened many doors to show me I needed to come to Lancaster County. Looking back, I can see God's little miracles through all these events and how He led me step-by-step. One of my life's greatest breakthroughs happened nine months after my father's death. That is when I recognized the need to be delivered from things that had been a part of my childhood, which had influenced decisions that I had made as an adult. With the help of mentors, prayer counseling and most of all my Lord, I spent three years moving from the worldly me to become the person God had truly meant for me to be from the beginning.

It's still a day by day walk with God directing each decision, each interaction and each direction in my life. When I meet someone who is going through a crisis of faith, I know it is an opportunity to encourage them that joy and freedom can follow.

Thank You, Lord, for crisies that become a testimony of Your grace, mercy and love. May we all use the blessings, knowledge and changes delivered by You to encourage and give comfort to others as they walk through their times of fire.

Connie Martin provides lay prayer ministry/counseling to women at her home and attends Petra Christian Fellowship.

MARCH 25

Joy and Purpose

"When they said, 'Let's go to the house of God,' my heart leaped for joy." Psalm 122:1 (The Message)

With a spring in her step, she was bursting with enthusiasm and beaming with a bright, contagious smile. She passed me in the corridor, full speed ahead. I called out asking where she was headed with such gusto. She quickly replied, "I am late for class … to learn more of the Lord and His church." I called after her, "So it's true, one is never too old to learn new things?" Without pause and with deep conviction she replied, "Never! Never is one too old to learn new things from the Lord!" I smiled thinking to myself, now that is how I want to grow old. I should mention this woman had celebrated her hundredth birthday several years earlier.

This woman was a matriarch of faith and faithfulness. I thought of all the incredible scope of change she experienced in life, community and the church. Disappointment and loss provided much opportunity for bitterness to take root. Yet her love for the Lord and the church permeated her total being. With lasting joy, lasting faith, lasting faithfulness and a fierce hunger for more of God in this centenarian, her desire to know the Lord was so beautiful and refreshing. What a model and heroine of faith!

Evidence abounds of the fading or absence of such foundational characteristics among many Christians. Whatever defines our framework in understanding, God also establishes the benchmark for living life—thus shaping our joy and purpose. The Apostle Paul declares, "If what was fading away came with glory, how much greater is the glory of that which lasts?" (2 Corinthians 3:11). Does my heart leap for joy to enter into the house of the Lord? Am I energized to press into the inexhaustible depths of the Lord? This alone is greater; this alone is lasting.

Lord, may my heart leap for joy today. Refresh me through Your Presence and Your Word.

Brian E. Martin serves as lead pastor at Weaverland Mennonite Church in East Earl. He and his wife, Shirley, are parents of three married children, one young adult at home and they have three grandchildren.

MARCH 26

Delivered from Fear

"I sought the Lord, and He heard me, and delivered me from all my fears." Psalm 34:4 (King James Version)

When my husband and I were missionaries, we were stationed at a place called Kiwi, in what was then Dutch New Guinea. Kiwi was on a plateau of necessity, allowing room for an airstrip. Airplanes were our only means of transportation except for walking. On one side of the plateau there was about an eighty-foot drop—straight down to the river below. Our house was perhaps one-hundred yards from the edge of the cliff, and we had small children. I became very afraid that one of my children would fall over that precipice.

One day my three-year-old asked if she could throw away a rotten piece of passion fruit. I said, "Sure," thinking she would throw it in the trash can. A minute later, I saw her running toward the edge of the cliff. It was too late to yell for her to stop, so I just watched in terror as she threw the passion fruit over the edge and then turned running back to me with a smile of accomplishment.

That night I couldn't sleep, I was too gripped by fear. Finally I prayed, "Lord, I can't live here with this fear. Please take it away." I started thinking about all the Scriptures I had memorized about fear: Psalm 23:4: "I will fear no evil: for thou art with me …." Isaiah 41:10: "Fear thou not; for I am with thee …." and Psalm 34:4: "I sought the Lord and He heard me and delivered me from all my fears." I pondered these and other scriptures for a long time, until a great peace came over me. I knew I was where God wanted me to be, so I consciously and willingly placed my children in His hands. He took away my fear, and of course, took care of my children.

Our Father, I thank You for Your lovingkindness and Your patience with me in my weakness. Thank You for Your precious Word that gives such peace. Help me to always trust in You for everything.

Lorrie Lockhart, a retired missionary, attends Calvary Church in Lancaster.

MARCH 27

What Greater Cause?

"Each one should use whatever gift he has received to serve others." 1 Peter 4:10

When I was a child, we had a motto in our living room that made a huge impression on me. It read, "Your life will soon be past, only what's done for Christ will last." Although I have come to believe the motto would have been more theologically correct if it read, "Your life will soon be past, only what's done with Christ will last," it still made an impact on my life.

In Luke 15 Jesus tells us three stories: the lost sheep, the lost coin and the lost son. That which is important to Jesus is what is lost. The lost need to be found. Believers need to hear and be challenged to do all they can to help others who are lost find hope in Jesus. Jesus came to seek and to save the lost. Jesus modeled serving (see Philippians 2:5-7). When He left heaven he came to serve and to rescue you and me from our sins and give us His very life. His life was a life of service. "Jesus went around doing good and healing all who were oppressed by the Devil, for God was with him" (Acts 10:38).

The church must be involved in our local communities. What concerns the people of the community concerns us. Sometimes we need to be a voice for the voiceless, whether they are abused children, those without healthcare, orphans, unwed mothers or those caught in human trafficking. Let's help to clean up our schools. We cannot be silent.

Celebrate the joys of serving. When we serve others, our faith is made stronger. When I help those in need, my needs look smaller. Jesus says in serving the "least of these," we are serving Him.

You're never closer to Jesus than when you're serving, loving and engaging the poor and hurting.

Lord Jesus, I dedicate my life to serving You by serving others.

Dave Eshleman served as pastor and church planter for fifty years. Presently he is a church consultant.

MARCH 28

God Always Keeps His Promises

"So shall My word be that goes forth from My mouth; It shall not return to Me void." Isaiah 55:11

There I was, working out on a treadmill and watching the Food Network. That combination is just as bad as going grocery shopping when hungry. I was not helping myself by watching all of the delicious meals they were creating. I was simply increasing my appetite and cravings for food. On the other hand, it gave me new ideas to try to improve my bland cooking.

I was on a mission to keep my New Year's resolution by exercising on that treadmill. I had set some goals and made promises. Five months later, the promises fizzled away until I broke those promises I had made.

Broken promises might be experienced within ourselves and those made to our friends, family members or co-workers, but we will never experience broken promises from God and His Word. His promises to us are more secure than thick concrete.

His Word will not return void. You can be certain that He hears your prayers. He may not answer them right away, but He has His reasons and we need to simply trust Him.

New Year's promises and resolutions to ourselves come and go, but God's Word always stays the same. So, don't make promises to yourself that are too hard to keep and set yourself up for failure. Make obtainable goals and you will start to feel good regarding your accomplishments.

Thank You, Lord, for Your Word to us, filled with Your loving promises to always be with us. I'm grateful that You never go back on your promises.

Lisa M. Garvey is a member of Hosanna! A Fellowship of Christians in Lititz and involved in women's ministry and prayer ministry.

MARCH 29

Sippy Cups and Jesus

"For the word of God is alive and active. Sharper than any double-edged sword, it penetrates even to dividing soul and spirit, joints and marrow; it judges the thoughts and attitudes of the heart. Nothing in all creation is hidden from God's sight. Everything is uncovered and laid bare before the eyes of him to whom we must give account." Hebrews 4:12-13

Our family babysits several children. Recently, a four-year-old asked me what the word *real* meant. He went on to explain that his mom told him that Santa wasn't real, but he could see him, and Jesus was real, but couldn't be seen. Using some verses from the Bible, we had a great and meaningful discussion about faith, Jesus and the salvation message.

That conversation reminded me of a day many years ago when a neighbor called to tell me that my firstborn child, age three and a half years old, who was playing in her home, had just asked Jesus to live in his heart. He was playing with her five-year-old daughter. The five-year-old had been memorizing Bible verses, and she used them to help my son understand the message of salvation. I rushed over to their home to talk to him and was confident that he truly had made a conversion.

Twenty-three years later, he is still serving Jesus. Even very young children can understand the truth of scripture.We know that His Word is alive and powerful and does not return void. In a world filled with wild fantasy, stress and danger, faith in the only true God is a wonderful and stable anchor for a child!

Lord, as with the simple faith of a child, set us apart through faith in Your Word.

Bonni Greiner, a motivational speaker and blogger, offers daily advice for young moms from an older mom in the admonition of Titus 2. Her blog site is http://www.mombyexample.com.

MARCH 30

One Accord

"How good and pleasant it is when brothers live together in unity.... It is as if the dew of Hermon were falling on Mount Zion." Psalm 133:1, 3

Our church evangelism and missions team discerned that we should be involved in the Lancaster Transformed vision of prayer evangelism. As a team, we watched the "Transformation in Newark" video. It became apparent that Tim Hess, the leader of this team, had a passion for prayer evangelism. From that point we began to trust the Lord what that would look like for Byerland. We were in one accord to pray street by street in Pequea Township. The discernment process led us to focus on the southern portion of the township. The plan was then introduced to the congregation. A map of this portion of the township was enlarged. Pins with individuals' names were placed on the street name located on the map so people could focus their praying.

Three United Methodist and two Mennonite churches planned to meet for a community worship service. However, due to rain, Byerland hosted the service. Worshipping together was a beautiful picture of the body of Christ. Mike Sigmann spoke on the unity that comes down from the Father in heaven, Psalm 133. This was a powerful prophetic word for everyone gathered. The Lord directed Mike to address how disunity can be found in the body of Christ and in our township. The service closed with crying out in prayer for His unity to come over this region.

Father in heaven, let the dew of one accord fall over this region today: my home, where I work, and study ... in every relationship to the glory of Jesus.

Joe Garber pastors at Byerland Mennonite Church in Pequea Township.

MARCH 31

Fitted for Gospel Shoes

"Make level paths for your feet...." Hebrews 12:13

One cheery spring morning, I had met a good friend at a coffee shop in Lancaster. We were meeting to discuss a difficult situation that had befallen a ministry that reaches out to children. The organization had asked us to come and help them to resolve their problems.

While in the midst of our coffee and conversation, a man came into the shop, no doubt in pursuit of his morning pick-me-up. Before he ordered, he looked down at my friend's feet and said, "Where did you get those shoes? I would like a pair like those!"

With due respect, I looked at the shoes, which were showing signs of wear, and wondered what about those particular shoes had captured this man's attention. Could it be how comfortable they appeared, or was it the style?

In any case, what came into my mind were the words from Romans 10:15: "How beautiful are the feet of those who bring good news!"

So as we returned to our prior discussion of how to be of service to a hurting ministry, the thought came to me that the answer might be found in the condition of one's "spiritual feet." Could it be that we were to communicate sound, biblical counsel (Good News) in the spirit of a peaceful and blessed approach? Our feet needed to be custom-fitted with the shoes of the Gospel of peace (Ephesians 6:15).

Dear Lord, as we trod the path of sometimes rocky lifestyles, may we wear well the Gospel shoes that can meet the needs of hurting people. May we be custom-fitted with the Gospel of peace by the Shoemaker of our soul.

Dr. Sandy M. Outlar is the liaison to Christian schools based out of Lancaster Bible College. He and his wife, Joye, live in Landisville and attend Wheatland Presbyterian Church.

Photo by Mark Van Scyoc

April

APRIL 1

Friends

"It is better to trust in the Lord than to put confidence in man. It is better to trust in the Lord than to put confidence in princes." Psalm 118:8-9 (King James Version)

I was sitting in court waiting for the hearing of one of "my kids" on an offense he committed prior to moving into our house. Being my first time in court, I found the proceedings fascinating. Then came a case that surprised even the judge. He looked at the charges, looked at the defendant, looked back at the charges, and back at the defendant. "You have been charged with passing a counterfeit twenty-dollar bill at a local drug store?" he asked.

"Yes your honor."

"Where did you get the counterfeit twenty-dollar bill?"

"I made it in my basement, your honor."

"And why did you think you would get away with it?"

"Your honor, my friend was working that night and I thought he would let it pass, but he turned me in."

We often lean on our friends for support, encouragement, advice or just camaraderie. Every human, no matter how strong, has a breaking point. There always comes a time when our friends let us down. Rather than supporting us, we find them needing us to support them. They betray us, their advice is poor and their demeanor drags us down instead of lifts us up.

Jesus experienced all that. The disciples whined, fought, jockeyed for position and fell asleep at key times when they should have been supporting Him. However, through all their failures, He was always faithful. After His resurrection, Jesus did not punish Peter for his denial at the trial. Jesus restored him and gave him new responsibilities. If our trust is solely in the Lord, He will not let us down.

Father I trust in You and no other. My friends may fail me and betray me, but You will be with me always.

Steve Hershey is a teacher and speaker at White Oak Church of the Brethren. Steve and his wife, Brenda, have opened their home to young adults.

APRIL 2

For Whom Do You Consecrate Yourself?

"Jesus said, 'For them I sanctify myself that they too may be truly sanctified.'" John 17:19

Who is the "them" Jesus is referring to? Jesus is referring to his disciples as he sends them into the world. The New Living Translation helps clarify this: "As you sent me into the world, I am sending them into the world. And I give myself entirely to you so they also might be entirely yours" (John 17:18-19).

Let's ask ourselves: For whom do we sanctify (purify or consecrate) ourselves? Just as Jesus lived a pure life for his disciples, we live a pure life for others. They see our lives and as a result are encouraged to move on in their Christian walk.

Jesus was motivated to live a pure life for us. Therefore we are motivated to live a pure life for others. Jesus promised blessings to those who live pure lives: "God blesses those whose hearts are pure" (Matthew 5:8).

To be pure in heart means that we are focused. We are not double-minded. Unfortunately, we are doubled minded in almost everything we do. When John Bunyan was told that he preached a good sermon, he responded saying that the devil told him that when he came down the steps from the pulpit.

Do we work to please Jesus, or work to receive praise from our employer? When we read our Bible, pray or attend worship is it to draw closer to God or because it gives us a pleasant feeling that we have done what is best and fulfilled our duty? There are few things that even the most dedicated Christian does with unmixed motives. This is why Paul writes to the Church: "He made you holy by means of Christ Jesus, just as he did all Christians everywhere—whoever calls upon the name of Jesus Christ, our Lord and theirs" (1 Corinthians 1:2).

We always need grace. Peter reminds us with his final words: "Grow in grace" (2 Peter 3:18). We need his grace continually to live in joyful freedom. The neat thing is that Jesus is there to give us His grace.

Jesus, purify my motives so others can see You and be drawn to You.

Dave Eshleman served as pastor/church planter for fifty years.

APRIL 3

Bracing a Tree

"Nevertheless, God's solid foundation stands firm ... if a man cleanses himself ... he will be an instrument for noble purposes, made holy, useful to the Master and prepared to do any good work." 2 Timothy 2:19-21 (New King James Version)

Aghast, I looked at the structure to which my husband was proudly pointing. After an earlier conversation about the sagging crepe myrtle tree branches, he decided to brace the tree with materials he had on hand from his shed. It was a combination of boards of different lengths and various nails hammered in at odd angles. The result was a lopsided wooden frame surrounding the tree. As my husband waited for my response, I prayed for tact and wisdom. I finally said, "Well, it looks like it will do the job." He knew that I was less than enthusiastic. We decided to leave it in place until it was time to prune the tree in the fall. As different people saw it and raised an eyebrow, I simply grinned and said, "It's my husband's tree house."

During the time I spent on the back patio while the "tree house" was there, the Lord reminded me how necessary this ugly structure was. It was like the process He goes through with us when we need extra strength. He wants to brace us and hold us up. Sometimes it is not a pretty sight. Although He is the Master Carpenter, He is limited by the materials on hand because we hold onto things that keep us from fully allowing Him to raise us up. If I allow Him to hold me up during the hard times, I'm sure I will come out with my "branches" going in the right direction. Even when He is pruning me, I can rest assured that He already knows the end result will be a beautiful testimony to Him.

Lord, thank You for knowing exactly how to reinforce my body, mind and spirit during the times when I need strength. Thank You for bracing me even when it is not a pretty sight.

Angie Plantz is married to a handyman and lives in Harrisburg. She serves in the Celebrate Recovery, Grief Share and women's ministries at Christian Life Assembly in Camp Hill.

APRIL 4

Papa God

"But the Lord still waits for you to come to Him so He can show you His love and compassion. For the Lord is a faithful God. Blessed are those who wait for Him to help them." Isaiah 30:18 (New Living Translation)

Philadelphia International Airport was my destination, the first leg of my journey to Ohio where I would attend an in-depth training day for post-abortion ministry. I was traveling alone, and the evening before, my husband reviewed the directions he had written. Yep, I knew how to get there.

And then it happened. My path onto Route 322 East off of Route 1 was blocked. A taxi in front of me faced the same obstacle. I followed the taxi along the shoulder of the road as he made a U-turn and another attempt onto Route 322, to no avail. Obviously, the taxi wanted this route. Confident he would find the way, I did not panic, but became his shadow. After meandering through a huge business complex, we emerged onto Route 322. I breathed deeply, thankful the crisis was over.

Suddenly the taxi pulled off the road and the driver began motioning for me to pull over. I slowly passed him, reconsidered and pulled in front of him. The driver approached my window and informed me that the road was blocked ahead by an accident. Panic threatened to attack again as I said, "I need to get to the Philadelphia Airport!"

"That is where I am going. Follow me," he replied. He told me what roads to look for, "in case we are separated," and off we went. As I drove I thanked Papa God for providing someone to help me. He knows me, and He certainly knew I needed help.

As we traveled unfamiliar roads, I was able to easily follow. At each merge onto a highway, the driver turned down his window, raised his arm, and pointed to where we were turning. Finally we were on I-95. I knew the rest of the way. The driver gave a final wave and was gone in a flash. I felt like I had just received a huge bear hug from my Papa God.

Father God, You know the way even when all we see is a roadblock. Draw our gaze to You and lead us in the way of truth.

Carol Weaver serves at Susquehanna Valley Pregnancy Services as director of Post-Abortion Ministry.

APRIL 5

Messy Faces

"Purify me from my sins and I will be clean; wash me, and I will be whiter than snow. Oh, give me back my joy again; you have broken me—now let me rejoice." Psalm 51:7-8

I find it amazing that my son, Michael, gets spaghetti sauce not only on his chin but on his forehead. I mean, how do you get it there?

At times we as parents don't notice the stains until we look down at his smiling face. "Whoa, your face is dirty!" Quickly we wash his face.

We aren't much different when it comes to our relationship with God. We get messy and sometimes we don't realize it until God points it out and says to us, "Whoa your heart is dirty; time to wash it."

My love for my son doesn't change when he has a messy face. I love him with spaghetti stains or without. However, I love my son enough not to leave him in that condition; I wash his face. So it is with Jesus, He loved us enough that He refuses to leave us in our messy, sinful state. Jesus shed His blood so we can be clean and washed white as snow. Like a dirty child getting bathed, so are we washed by Christ's sacrifice.

The world can make us dirty, our choices can make us dirty. However, God is always eager to redeem and cleanse us of every speck of dirt. Many of us see ourselves as dirty sinners, but is that truth? Nowhere in the Bible does Paul address the church as sinners; instead, he calls us saints. Our view of ourselves needs to be that we are dearly loved children of God. You were bought with the blood of Jesus Christ, and when you realize that you are a child of God, things start to change. You see your messiness more clearly and quickly run to the Father for cleansing. You start to make better choices and desire a deeper relationship with the Father.

My son, Michael, does not think of himself as a dirty, messy kid who has sauce on his face 24/7. Instead he knows he is my son and is loved by his daddy, and no matter what, his daddy will take care of him. If I, as an imperfect father, can do this for my children, how much more can the greatest Dad in the universe do this for us?

I pray that we will rest in Your forgiveness and truth, that we recognize that we are cleansed and washed white as snow by the blood of Jesus Christ. Thank You for Your love, grace and for cleansing me today. I love You, Daddy.

Mike Wenger is executive director of TNT Youth Ministry.

APRIL 6

New Is Better than Old

"But now He has obtained a more excellent ministry, inasmuch as He is also Mediator of a better covenant, which was established on better promises." Hebrews 8:6-7 (New Living Bible)

What a difference a weekend can make! Passover for the disciples had to be the worst day of their lives. Their Lord, master, friend and miracle worker was the one who had always pulled them through. Whether it was needed food, calming a ferocious wind, freeing a demonized man or raising a dead child, Jesus had always had a solution. Now Jesus was gone, dead, in the tomb. All hope was lost. The disciples' hearts must have weighed a ton. Emotionally they had to be crushed, physically exhausted, spiritually in doubt, full of fear and confused.

Then Sunday came! Jesus was alive! Suddenly all the things that had transpired began to make sense. Prophetic words that were spoken years ago suddenly became clear.

There are many things that we could write concerning this most powerful and the most important day in history, but I want to draw your attention to one: God never takes something from us unless He has something better for us! When Jesus cried out, "It is finished" and rose from the grave, the new and better covenant was put in place. If God of the Old Testament performed all the miracles He did, defended His people, healed, provided for and cared for them under the old covenant, think of what He desires to do under a new and better covenant!

When I consider all that God did under the old, I think my level of expectation sometimes falls way short of all that He desires to do in and through me under the new. Go ahead, raise your level of expectation. You are functioning under a new and better covenant. Expect great things. You will not be disappointed.

You are alive, Jesus. We come boldly to Your throne of grace to ask for help in our time of need.

Ron Myer serves as assistant international director of DOVE Christian Fellowship International.

APRIL 7

Passover: A Mystery Revealed

"For this is my blood of the New Covenant which is being poured out for many for the forgiveness of sins." Matthew 26:28 (The Living Bible)

During my Jewish childhood, I often questioned why my family didn't celebrate Easter. I used to gaze out my window on Easter mornings, watching my Christian friends parade down the street in their best clothes to go to church. I wondered why this day was so important to them.

About the same time as Easter, our family's Passover Seder was held. The story told of God's chosen people, the Israelites, being freed from slavery in Egypt after more than four hundred thirty years in captivity.

I grew up questioning many things about God. Why were there different beliefs honoring the same God? Why was Christianity such a predominant religion when the Jews were God's chosen people? I wasn't aware that Jesus was a devout Jew, the root of the world, and the Gentiles the grafted branches. Later, I discovered that Jesus and the "men" in the Last Supper picture were celebrating the Jewish observance of Passover—but that Passover was different. Thanks to Jesus, now my Messiah, I understand how the Jewish and Christian faiths connect.

The Bible revealed that Y'Shua was indeed my personal Messiah. He didn't come to destroy the law but to fulfill it. My eyes were opened to the beautiful transition between the Old and New Testaments and how Passover revealed the story of Easter. Blood was used to confirm and seal the covenant laws the Lord had given the Israelites. Christ, the spotless Lamb of God, shed the final blood sacrifice during His crucifixion. No longer was the blood of a lamb used as the symbol of our ancestors' freedom from slavery. Jesus' blood, shed for all, is the final sacrifice that brings us freedom from eternal death into eternal life.

Pray for the Jewish people everywhere that they may, too, know our precious Messiah.

Jan Dorward is a Messianic Jew attending DOVE Westgate Church, Ephrata. She's grateful for all the opportunities God has laid before her, including writing, editing and presenting Messianic Passover teachings.

APRIL 8

'Woulda, Coulda'

"A man with leprosy came and knelt before him and said, 'Lord, if you are willing, you can make me clean.' Jesus reached out his hand and touched the man. 'I am willing,' he said. 'Be clean!' Immediately he was cleansed of his leprosy." Matthew 8:2-3

I was driving in my car, singing along with the contemporary music group Third Day, when I mis-sang some lyrics. The words were similar, and it did not seem like a big deal until I thought about the difference in meaning between the two words.

I sang something to the effect of "Jesus 'could' save us," when the lyric actually was "Jesus 'would' save us."

Of course, Jesus could go to the cross and die for us. Every one of us has the ability to die. And there is no doubt that he could save us from our sins. However, if I went to the cross, it would save no one, because I am not the perfect sacrifice that Jesus was.

But what truly shows God's compassion is that He "would" do it. Jesus knew He "could" save the world, but that did not make his suffering any less torturous. It was His decision more than His ability that saved us.

What love! I cling to the above passage in Matthew that shows Jesus enthusiastically telling the leper that He was willing to help him. He is willing, if only we "would" ask him.

And since we are called to be His own, we need to be an example of this. "Could" I give my worries to Him? I think that is possible. But "would" I? We "could" do anything for Him. But the question is, what "would" you do for Him?

Dear Lord, what would you have me do for You today? Please grant me a willing spirit to do it.

Tracy Slonaker, director of Christian education at Harvest Fellowship of Colebrookedale, would like to publish some novels to God's glory, if He is willing.

APRIL 9

Seed Money

"Now he who supplies seed to the sower and bread for food will also supply and increase your store of seed and will enlarge the harvest of your righteousness." 2 Corinthians 9:10

Shortly after we were married, we received an advertisement for sponsoring a needy child. We received a picture of little Mario from Guatemala and agreed to sponsor him for eight dollars a month. Soon we took another child and then another and another. We purposely took them all in Guatemala in case we would have a chance to travel there to see them.

Several years later, a team in our church was forming to travel to Guatemala to do work in a school for ten days. We inquired about the trip and the leader quickly signed us up. Before long my wife, Laurie, and our six-year-old daughter, Becca, were on the way to Guatemala to see our four sponsored children. It was an amazing experience and led to more visits.

During the past twenty years we have made numerous trips to Guatemala building lifelong friendships. But that's not all. That seed money of eight dollars a month eventually inspired us to adopt a child from Guatemala in 1995. The baby we adopted was also Mario, but we renamed him Joshua. The seed also led to our children learning Spanish, living in Guatemala, and serving in other countries with YWAM.

While living in Guatemala, our daughter, Becca, worked in an orphanage and encouraged us to adopt eight-year-old Isaiah. Isaiah has been with us for four years and desires to help his native people someday. It is our hope to live there someday and run an orphanage full-time. Our seed money has definitely gone a long way.

Thank You, Lord, for seeds of love in us. I pray that we will always plant seeds in Your Kingdom, and that You will harvest them at the proper time.

Brian Fulmer is the owner of Crossroads Property Management Inc. and leads the mission program at ACTS Covenant Fellowship in Lancaster.

APRIL 10

For Such a Time as This

"For if you remain completely silent at this time, relief and deliverance will arise from another place … Yet who knows whether you have come to the kingdom for such a time as this?" Esther 4:14

I think God wants us to grab a deeper meaning from this whole story of Esther. As we are reading this year on being set apart for God, we can all agree that the story of Esther is one of the finest examples of being set apart for kingdom work.

We see that Esther has a choice to make. To go in to the king and chance being rejected or killed, or to be offered the scepter to come near. We often find ourselves in this same situation. Do we remain silent and let things pass, or do we risk it all and go in to the King?

I want to submit a thought to you. The King loves you. The King really loves you. He is already holding out the scepter to you. You do not have to remain silent.

Esther was already chosen as the favorite of the king. She already has his favor. She knew that. We are chosen by the King. We have His favor. Esther knew the king loved her. She was convinced that the king loved her. Am I convinced that the King loves me?

We are in this incredible moment in time, when God is calling us to come near. And like Esther, we can come near, because we can have confidence that the King really loves us. We do not have to remain silent, because the King has already offered us the scepter, His favor.

God, most loving Father. Let me feel the depth of Your love and be confident in how much You love me. Let me live in such a time as this, where I know and am convinced of the love of my Father.

Kim Zimmerman and her husband, Brian, are the founders and directors of City Gate Lancaster, and the City Gate Prayer Room.

APRIL 11

Within a Split Second

"The good man does not escape all troubles ... But the Lord helps him in each and every one. God even protects him from accidents." Psalm 34:19-20 (The Living Bible)

At our mountain retreat in Tioga County, our family could have perished. It was a perfect day with my son, his family and some friends. While we were enjoying dinner our four dogs started barking uncontrollably. We questioned their hysteria. Could it be a bear? Was a tree ready to fall? Could it be a rattler? After a while, we ignored them and continued with our picnic.

"Maw-Maw, I have to go potty," my three-year-old grandson said as he squirmed out of the benched seat. This was an opportunity for all of us, including the dogs, to go inside for dessert.

My husband, Barry, and three others stayed by the campfire. It was finally quiet with the dogs inside. "Creeeeeak." Barry was curious with that familiar sound. A tree was about to fall. The sound came from far up the mountain where the dogs had been just minutes before. He turned his chair so he could watch. Suddenly he faced a large pine tree, ten inches in diameter, coming straight for him. "Run!" he cried.

He had a split second, a blink of an eye to roll over in a dive to get out of the way of the tree. Thank God the others heeded the warning and ran without hesitation. Several brush burns and scratches from flying branches were nothing compared to what could have been. Had we been trapped at that picnic table, had Barry not turned around, dove out of the way, then screamed a warning, we all might have been killed!

We praised God that night, knowing it was the Lord who warned Barry to turn around.

Dear Lord, thank You so much for Your warnings, Your protection and Your salvation.

Darla Garber enjoys her many retreats with her family and friends at their cabin. She and her husband, Barry, live in Manheim and attend Christ the King Church.

APRIL 12

Judge Not

"Do not judge, or you too will be judged. For in the same way you judge others, you will be judged, and with the measure you use, it will be measured to you." Matthew 7:1-2

One Thursday of each month, a group of church leaders and church planters gather together to eat, pray, read and discuss. The last few months we delved into the Sermon on the Mount. We looked at these passages in order to see how we can apply them to our local context and what they say about living missional and incarnational lives. During the last meeting, we finished our discussion on Matthew 7.

Earlier that day, before our gathering, I was walking from my car to one of my favorite coffeehouses where I work, pray, write and reflect. As I walked, I watched people walk by and cars drive by. I remember walking by some people and hearing their language. I remember thinking "Nice language, guy. What kind of person are you?" I also remember a car drove by with blaring music for the whole world to hear. I thought, "Dude, turn your music down. I don't really want to hear it and not everyone likes your kind of music."

As I got to the coffeehouse, I grabbed a table and a chai and then opened my Bible to reflect and prepare for the gathering. I came face-to-face with Matthew 7:1-2. How quick was I to judge someone based on language, music, dress and any other number of externals? I realized that every day I make snap judgments about people that I don't even know. When I judge them, I often come out feeling better about myself.

Jesus calls us not to judge or we will be judged. May our lives be filled with love and not judgment.

Jesus, forgive us for judging others.

Ryan Braught is the husband of Kim, father of Kaiden and Trinity, church planter of Veritas and a follower of Jesus.

APRIL 13

Miracles in Your Life?

"But without faith it is impossible to please Him; for he that cometh to God must believe that He is, and He is a rewarder of them that diligently seek Him." Hebrews 11:6 (King James Version)

A miracle is a sign of our Lord. It is a symbol of the divine covenant and a revelation from God. A miracle has been defined as "an act or event that does not follow the laws of nature and is believed to be caused by God."

In the parking lot of our church, a woman reminded me that I had prayed for her at the altar three months earlier. She informed me that now she no longer had breast cancer. I praised the Lord.

I received a telephone call and learned of a woman's hip pain problem. After praying for the Lord's healing, I learned the Lord healed her.

A man in the hospital was in a coma. After I learned from his family he was not saved, I touched his forehead and he awakened. He listened to the salvation message, accepted Jesus as his Savior and then went back into the coma. Later he went to heaven.

When Jesus ascended into heaven, He sent His Holy Spirit to empower His people with His gifts—including the gift of healing and to continue His ministry until He returns.

We have all of You, Jesus, in us. Lord, we know You want us to grow in You and to live the gifts of the Holy Spirit serving Your church. I ask You, Lord, to guide us to be closer to You.

Bob Burns, an ordained and licensed minister, serves as pastor and shepherd of Spiritual Growth Ministries. He is a member of the Potters House board of directors, Leola, a Bible teacher and serves the Spring Valley Church of God in the ministry of home visitation to the ill.

APRIL 14

Life-and-Death Issues

"He makes me lie down in green pastures, he leads me beside quiet waters." Psalm 23:2

The accident happened so quickly. I have no memory of the head-on collision, but I was reminded of the seriousness of my life-death moment as I lay for five hours in the trauma unit at Lancaster General Hospital. The elderly man in the collision was also dealing with injuries. Thankfully both of us healed. During my recovery, Psalm 23:4 had new meaning. "Though I walk through the valley of the shadow of death, I will fear no evil; for thou art with me, thy rod and thy staff they comfort me."

Accidents are uncertain, but nothing happens which first doesn't go through the eyes of God. I wonder how many times the Great Shepherd protects us from death and then comforts us as He leads us beside still waters and makes us to lie down in green pastures. Because my fractured ankle restricted my activities, my busy soul was restored, too.

Do you think about life-and-death issues? Are you allowing your Great Shepherd to lead you in the path of righteousness so you are prepared to die?

I praise Him for His goodness and mercy which follows me all the days of my life and I look forward to dwelling in the house of the Lord forever. Until then, each day is a cherished gift, and I find joy in serving my Master.

Og Mandino, author and motivational speaker, stated, "Beginning today, treat everyone you meet as if they were going to be dead by midnight. Extend to them all the care, kindness and understanding you can muster, and do it with no thought of any reward. Your life will never be the same!"

Thank You, Great Shepherd, for protecting me in life-or-death issues. Only You know when is my time to die. Meanwhile, I will live for You.

Dona Fisher is vice president of Friendship Foundation, founder of Change of Pace Bible Studies, correspondent for Lancaster Newspapers and serves as campaign chairperson for the annual National Day of Prayer event in Lancaster.

APRIL 15

Everyone You Meet

"Everywhere we go, we tell everyone about Christ. We warn them and teach them with all the wisdom God has given us, for we want to present them to God, perfect (mature), in their relationship to Christ. I work very hard at this, as I depend on Christ's mighty power that works within me." Colossians 1:28-29 (New Living Translation)

These verses could make us feel guilty. Paul says that everywhere he goes he tells everyone about Christ. I don't do that. Does the Holy Spirit want us to confront everyone? Jesus did not confront everyone he met.

I believe it is helpful to think in terms of heart's desire. All Christians should have a passion to see people come to Jesus and become His disciples. Paul was an extrovert. Sixty percent of people are introverts. Introverts usually need to have a relationship with people before it's natural for them to share Jesus with the unsaved. In fact, in our North American society few people will be open to listening to a presentation of the Gospel unless they have a relationship with the presenter. I understand in some countries where the Holy Spirit is moving in a powerful way, people come to Christ in great numbers as evangelists lead people to Jesus on their first encounter.

Here in the United States it usually takes many encounters. It is also helpful if these encounters come from more than one individual. Don't be discouraged when people do not respond as quickly as we like. Pray to be faithful. Loving perseverance is usually the way the Holy Spirit works in our context. Some studies say it takes on the average of nine contacts before people respond to the Good News. Let's be faithful so we can be fruitful.

Lord Jesus, I want to be a faithful witness. Help me to be persistent and to depend on Your Holy Spirit to work mightily through me to bring people to You and see them become disciples.

Dave Eshleman served as pastor and church planter for fifty years.

APRIL 16

Grazing versus Gazing

"But whoever looks intently into the perfect law that gives freedom … they will be blessed in what they do." James 1:25

"I meditate on Your precepts and consider Your ways." Psalm 119:15

"Christ loved the Church and gave Himself up for her to make her holy, cleansing her by the washing with water through the Word." Ephesians 5:25-26

After a season of free-spiriting my way through Scripture, I sensed God prompting me to commit verses to memory. In essence He was saying, "You can graze through my Word and not retain much, or you can gaze into it and be transformed."

I decided to look up the two words in the dictionary. No surprise there. Grazing is described as "touching, scratching, browsing." Is that what I'd been doing? Touching instead of embracing Scripture? Scratching the surface of it? Browsing through it like a magazine?

Gazing had a far different connotation: staring at something, poring over it, watching it intently.

And so the memorization began. First one Scripture passage. Then two. Now eight. I review them on my way to work, while I'm walking the dog, and when I need a new mind set.

Faithful to His Word and His instruction to me, God's perfect law is bringing freedom, order and a cleansing peace. I'm finding space in my mind that's producing order and organization in other aspects of my life as well.

Father, thank You for Your prodding that brings fresh revelation and change into my life. I want to keep gazing into Your face and into Your Word.

Lisa Hosler serves with Susquehanna Valley Pregnancy Services and the Regional Church of Lancaster County and worships with her husband, Ron, at Calvary Church, Lancaster.

APRIL 17

Memory Verses

"I have hidden your word in my heart that I might not sin against you." Psalm 119:11.

I love the kids' ministry at our church. The leaders make it so much fun and interesting. The kids sing, dance and play and do motions as they learn a Bible verse. And one other neat thing the teachers do is give the kids a passport, which is a yellow piece of paper that has a Bible lesson and a verse for them to learn at home. I enjoy reading the lesson and going over the Bible verse with my three-year-old son before bedtime.

I made an observation recently that made me smile. As I was trying to instill in my son those Bible verses from his class, I began to realize that I, too, was starting to remember those verses. And I thought how neat it was that my son and I were learning the same verses together.

I love the passage in Deuteronomy 6 that says, "These commandments that I give you today are to be upon your hearts. Impress them on your children. Talk about them when you sit at home and when you walk along the road, when you lie down and when you get up."

May we all be more diligent in studying God's Word and sharing it not only with our children but also those around us. And may we not hide it under a bushel, as the children's song goes, but let it shine.

Dear heavenly Father, may You help us to get into Your Word and begin to memorize more Scripture. And, as parents, may we begin to teach our children at an early age the importance of studying the Bible.

Jenn Paules Kanode is a part-time disc jockey for FM 90.3 WJTL and language instructor. More importantly she is a wife and mother and attends Lives Changed By Christ.

APRIL 18

Who Are the Evangelists?

"Some men came, bringing to him a paralytic, carried by four of them. Since they could not get him to Jesus because of the crowd, they made an opening in the roof above Jesus and, after digging through it, lowered the mat the paralyzed man was lying on. When Jesus saw their faith, he said to the paralytic, Son, your sins are forgiven." Mark 4:3-5

Were all four men evangelists? Perhaps. But one had to start by saying to the others, "This paralyzed man needs to meet Jesus. Will you help me get him to Jesus?" Perhaps the other three had the gift of mercy or the gift of service, or helps or maybe a mix of other gifts. Someone had to take the initiative to get this man to Jesus. We need people to take leadership—someone to get things moving.

Could the leader do it alone? No, he needed three others. Perhaps he also needed help to repair the roof. Maybe others beside the four repaired the room. To bring someone to Jesus often takes many gifts. God designed it so we frequently need to utilize others in the Body of Christ to bring people to Jesus. Others are needed in the discipling process.

We see many gifts in operation in this encounter with Jesus. Prayer is a vital gift that released the power of God. God gifts certain persons with the gift of intercession. Faith is a key. God gifts certain persons with the gift of faith. Leadership is a key and some have the gift of leadership. Mercy, service, helps, healing are also evident in this encounter.

As 1 Peter 1:10 states: "Each one should use whatever gift he has received to serve others, faithfully administering God's grace in its various forms." Let's always remember it's important to invite others to help us bring people to Jesus.

Lord, help me to use whatever gift(s) you have given me and to invite others to work with me so many can come to Jesus and be healed. Amen.

Dave Eshleman served as pastor and church planter for fifty years. Presently he is a church consultant.

APRIL 19

God Loves Every Creature

"The earnest (heartfelt, continued) prayer of a righteous man makes tremendous power available [dynamic in its working]." James 5:16 (Amplified Bible)

On January 8, 2010, at 2:30 a.m., my dad woke up abruptly thinking my mom had poked him. He immediately noticed the strong smell of smoke flooding into the bedroom. Thank God for angelic intervention as my dad became fully awake. He woke my mom and told her, "Get up and get out, there's a fire!" By God's grace and mercy both parents escaped safely along with their cat.

This was a traumatizing experience for all three of them. After my parents found lodging with family, my dad went to find Tony who had run away. Scared and confused, Tony was found crouched under the neighbor's car. After retrieving him, he was brought directly to my house.

Not surprisingly, Tony missed my parents. He tolerated this situation for about two weeks and then, he had enough of it. In an opportune moment, he slipped out. I called to him, but I could tell by the way he was moving—he was a cat on a mission. Call it discernment, but I knew he was going home, regardless of the snow and cold. Regrettably, I had to phone my mom and tell her the bad news. I looked for weeks, but found no trace of him.

Tony's challenges were huge. He had no front claws and finicky eating habits. He only liked dry cat food. To make matters worse, we had two of the largest snowstorms in ten years—two weeks apart and at least two feet deep. The faith of our family and friends praying for him was severely tested.

Miraculously, five weeks and one day later, Tony returned to me in the snow and cold, without a scratch on him. He was dehydrated and thinner, but otherwise, in good shape.

Dear Lord, thank You for being a good and merciful God. You got us through a trying time and blessed us by caring for everyone!

Dorinda Kaylor is a regional intercessor and director of Gateway Ministry Rooms.

APRIL 20

God Isn't Finished with Me

"God is our refuge and strength, an ever-present help in trouble. Therefore we will not fear, though the earth give way and the mountains fall into the heart of the sea…." Psalm 46:1-2

For nine years, I've worked in Haiti as a part-time missionary. After the devastating earthquake in 2010, I went to help with aid relief and to comfort my friends. Everyone I knew faced tremendous loss. No one was exempt.

One evening, my friend Zachary sat down to talk. He had been attending school in Port au Prince. One day, he simply did not go to school. He said he never, ever cut class like that and doesn't know why he stayed home. Later that day the earthquake hit.

A few days later his teacher called and told him they were the only two who survived the quake. All of his classmates died when the school building collapsed. As Zachary got to this point in his story, he was very emotional and asked some tough questions: "Why didn't I go to school that day? Why did all my classmates die? Why did I survive?"

After a while, he looked at me and said, "You know, I think God isn't finished with me yet; He has work for me to do." In the midst of all the loss and destruction, Zachary's faith in God shined brightly. Zachary has gone on to help provide aid to the refugees and minister to the children. God is using him in great ways.

Sometimes when we least expect it, devastation hits us right in the face: things like illness, broken relationships or wayward children. Zachary's example encourages me, over and over again, to be strong in my faith and trust God. God is not finished with me yet and He is not finished with you either.

Heavenly Father, thank You for the lessons that You teach us through difficulties. Open my heart to learn from them. Give me strength to endure and be strong so I may encourage others. Thank You for walking with me. In Jesus' name I pray.

Cynthia Zimmerman is a board member of Life Connection Mission in Montrouis Haiti and is married to Rick Zimmerman.

APRIL 21

Look and Love Like Jesus

"Jesus looked at him and loved him. 'One thing you lack,' he said. 'Go, sell everything you have and give to the poor, and you will have treasure in heaven. Then come, follow me.'" Mark 10:21

I have often wondered if Jesus walked the earth today, what electronic gadgetry He would use. Would Jesus email, text, Twitter and maintain his Facebook status via His well-worn I-phone, complete with its many apps? Would Jesus be ear-plugged, zoned in His own personal space listening to ITunes while reading his Kindle? One might do well to imagine this possibility. Based on what we do know about Jesus, He was really big on face-to-face relationships. The Gospels continually reveal Jesus engaging relationships at every turn. There are no written letters, as we have of Moses, the Prophets, or the Apostles, capturing the deep personal pen strokes of Christ. What we have from Jesus is in the form of spoken words and always spoken face-to-face.

Incredibly, words account for only 7 percent of human communication. A staggering 93 percent of communication occurs through body language and voice tone. It doesn't take a rocket scientist to understand why a faceless and relationless world operating through a world of sound bites, abbreviated texts and ear plugs often totally miss one another relationally.

This story of the rich young ruler reveals much of the person of Jesus. He looked at him and loved him. He met the young man right where he was. Jesus knew full well the young man along with his inhibitions. Yet Jesus invited him to let go and follow. Jesus was all about entering relationships. He communicated far beyond the 7 percent of words alone. Jesus looked and loved. We live in a world of peoples. Consider what opportunities we have to look and love like Jesus.

Lord, reveal to me the things which inhibit me from looking and loving like You.

Brian E. Martin serves as lead pastor at Weaverland Mennonite Church in East Earl. He and his wife, Shirley, are parents of three married children, one young adult at home and they have three grandchildren.

APRIL 22

Living Stones

"And you are living stones that God is building into his spiritual temple ..." 1 Peter 2:5

Last summer, we enjoyed a relaxing weekend at a cabin by the beautiful Loyalsock Creek in Sullivan County. We spent much time enjoying the creek, and my younger grandkids and I collected creek stones to take along home. We planned to paint the stones at a later time.

It was important to find just the right size, shape and a smooth surface for painting. We found the best stones were the ones still in the flowing water because they were smoother and had all their rough edges worn off—perfect to paint on. The exposed stones were too rough and porous from the elements of nature.

As I thought about those stones, I realized the importance of us, as living stones, to stay immersed in the Living Water. I don't know about you, but I get dry and rough edges sometimes. I can become sharp and hurtful to others and myself. If we immerse ourselves in Him on a daily basis, it will keep us seeing others through His eyes instead of being harsh and critical. To bless God and others, we must live constantly in the River of Life so we will truly be those living stones.

Now, when I look at those beautiful painted stones we collected, I am reminded to hang out in the River more often!

Lord, cause me to come to live by Your River so I will be a living stone that reflects You today.

Jeanette Weaver loves being a wife to Don, mom of two, G-ma of six and a living stone, who serves at DOVE Westgate Church, Ephrata.

APRIL 23

Deliverance Shall Be in the Church

"But on Mount Zion there shall be deliverance…." Obadiah 1:17 (New King James Version)

Many clients of counseling centers are Christians, but that is good because the church offers life and healing. According to the Scripture above, I believe it is God's desire that the church be the light that shines into a dark world. Jesus made it clear that we should preach deliverance to the captives. Sometimes you wonder who the captives are, the church or the world?

Prophet Isaiah says that the Lord's hand is not shortened, that it cannot save; nor His ear heavy, that it cannot hear. But your iniquities have separated you from your God; and your sins have hidden His face from you, so that He will not hear. I believe there are so many subtle iniquities that can be handed down through generations that can have an impact on our lives. We need to call sin what it is and learn how to recognize and deal with sins.

Recently we observed that our two youngest boys were constantly arguing. I asked the Lord to show me if there are any generational iniquities involved in their actions. I immediately recalled how my grandfather and my father used to argue. I also recalled how it was a part of my life. I took responsibility for this sin and repented of it. I also renounced this sin and broke it off my family forever. After about two days my wife asked me if I recognized the change in the boys, and I said I did. We are so excited to see the Lord work as we took responsibility for this sin that was recognized.

Lord, help me to walk in freedom as I allow the Holy Spirit to convict me of anything that is not pleasing to you. Bring me to a place where I am willing to humble myself and repent when I am convicted. Help me not to blame my fathers, but to be grateful for the grace you provide in my life to become free, in Jesus' Name.

Manny King is pastor of Harvest View Fellowship in Strasburg.

APRIL 24

Humility or Not

"We love because He first loved us…. Anyone who does not love his brother, whom he has seen, cannot love God, whom he has not seen. And He has given us this command: Whoever loves God must also love his brother." I John 4:19-21

Often as Christians we get humility and self-hatred tangled together. While we may not actually say we hate ourselves, this can be very subtly disguised in our hearts.

The brother that you can see is also in the mirror. We, ourselves, are part of the brotherhood of faith. Our ability to love others begins with first loving ourselves—love your neighbor as yourself.

God has convicted me that I must be able to receive His love for me in every part of myself if I am to be filled with His love. That includes my body, personality, skills and talents, my past and my childhood – the good, the bad and the ugly; the noisy, the messy and the sinful.

Being harder on ourselves than on others is not godly. Despising ourselves and loving others is not humility—it isn't even possible. You can't share what you don't have. If you don't receive His love, you don't have it! We love because He first loved us.

Dear heavenly Father, thank You for Your unconditional love. Encourage us to take the love You have freely given us so we may share it with others.

Doe Kopp is married to Dwight. They have two girls and two boys. She is a homemaker and homeschool mom. They meet as a church with families in various homes.

APRIL 25

Team Spirit

"The body is a unit, though it is made up of many parts; and though all its parts are many, they form one body. So it is with Christ."
1 Corinthians 12:12

Coach John Wooden, who coached high school and college sports for more than forty years and whose teams won more than 80 percent of their games, claims a key to success is team spirit. "Team spirit," says Wooden in his book *Coach Wooden's Pyramid of Success*, "is a genuine consideration for others … an eagerness to sacrifice personal interests of glory for the welfare of all."

For years, I believed that every person on ministry teams in which I participated possessed the same gifts that I had and thought like me. I was wrong! Now I recognize that each of us is unique with God-given gifts. I have learned to really appreciate others on the team who are different from me. Interdependence and being considerate of others is a key to experiencing a healthy team spirit. We really do need each other.

Organizational researchers reserve the term *team* for groups that have high interdependence—each individual task is dependent on what other team members are doing at the same time.

Dependent people need others to get what they want. Independent people try to get what they want through their own efforts. Interdependent people combine their own efforts with the efforts of others to achieve the greatest success.

Interdependence requires us to be convinced that God has called each person to be a member of our team. Also we need to be aware that each one has something unique to offer the team (1 Corinthians 12). Other people's gifts and personalities bring wholeness to our team. When we understand each other's strengths and weaknesses, we can build as a team, capitalizing on strengths and providing support where needed.

Lord God, empower us to work together as a team to enlarge your kingdom.

Larry Kreider loves being a husband, father and grandfather and serves the church as international director of DOVE International.

APRIL 26

Transitioning

"For I know the plans I have for you … to give you hope and a future." Jeremiah 29:11

Prayer is not just talking to God, but having conversations with Him. During a season of workplace transition, I captured this dialogue with the Lord:

"Son, I want you to work at a place that will bring you joy, for you will bring the best service there."

I replied, "But, which one, Lord? None of the open doors seems to offer joy. The pathways beyond the doors look ominous and like hard work."

I sensed God saying, "You must fight and win the battle in your mind. You can't do everything and you must commit to something. All paths will have struggles and obstacles. But these will not seem terrible when you are focused and committed to the goals and purposes I have for you."

"Father, which path should I choose—the one that looks easier or the one that seems more difficult? What are the benefits of choosing more difficulty for a longer time? I would normally choose the easiest and shortest route. But, does the longer and harder path result in more lasting lessons? My fear is that path is just longer and harder with no additional benefits."

"Son," I sensed the Lord reply, "that cannot be, because of My laws of faith and of sowing and reaping. The law of delayed gratification says that no effort goes unrewarded. My law of sowing and reaping says you will reap what you sow, after you sow and more than you sow. Are you planting vegetables for a season or fruit trees for the next generations? When there's a delay in receiving your investment, yields are larger and result in multiplied dividends and compound interest."

Lord, help us through transition. Thank You for Your plans, Your destiny for each one of us. Help us to build and to occupy until You come—for the praise of Your glory.

Bill Goodberlet is a member of the convening council for York Coalition for Transformation and an elder at Emmanuel Christian Fellowship.

APRIL 27

Making Peace with the Past

"If it is possible, as far as it depends on you, live at peace with everyone." Romans 12:18

I arranged to get away one weekend by myself for a well-needed retreat with God and headed for the Jersey shore. Prior to leaving, the Lord told me He wanted me to make a pit stop. He instructed me to stop along the way to my old hometown in New Jersey.

First stop was my parents' grave site. I sat in my car for over an hour and journaled, prayed and cried for all that seemed lost. Moments of unsaid forgiveness, missed "I love you's" and all that I held on to as a teen and never spoke, poured out in my journal. There was more inside of me than I ever knew, but God understood and that's why He had brought me there. I tore out the pages of my journal, went to the grave, fell upon it and cried for what seemed like forever. Right there, I forgave them and asked them for their forgiveness as well for all the years of pain and conflict I had caused as a teenager. I cried like never before in my life. I left the pages of my journal with them, and by the time I left, I felt like a new person.

Then I traveled to my hometown. I walked the neighborhood, visited my old schools and spoke out forgiveness to those who had hurt me. As the Lord led me, I gained victory and freedom every step of the way.

What a journey I was on, one that I could not have perceived prior to going. From there, I continued to the shore with less baggage than I had when I started my trip.

Thank You, Lord, for Your guidance, Your love and acceptance right where I am. Thank You that You know me better than I do, and You know just the right path I need to take to become whole—just like You.

Eileen Christiansen is a woman who walks in freedom and wholeness because of Jesus.

APRIL 28

God's Grace

"He will wipe away every tear from their eyes. There will be no more death or crying or pain, for the old order of things has passed away." Revelation 21:4

Who is like You Lord? There is none like You!

In disaster You give peace; in joy You give gladness; in sorrow You give grace. Without You life would be so hard to bear at times.

When tragedy strikes You are there to comfort me and bring me a peace that passes all understanding.

In joy, I have been able to praise You, oh God. You are the giver of life and when our time on earth is done, Father You take us home to be with You.

There truly is none like You! You give grace to get us through situations that would bring us down so low we could hardly get back up.

When we don't understand Your ways, You show us that we do not see the big picture, and one day we will understand as You do.

How can we neglect so great a salvation?

Father help us to see that there in none like You! You give life, and You take away. You are Holy and righteous. Thank You for the gift of eternal life.

Lord, our circumstances may seem random and unplanned, but someday we will see the order of Your hand! Help us to be faithful and to trust You.

Christine Harsh is married to Roger for forty years and the mother of Bonnie and Steve and grandmother to Zack, Tyler, Cody and Riley.

APRIL 29

The Joy of Grandchildren

"I have been reminded of your sincere faith, which first lived in your grandmother Lois and in your mother Eunice and, I am persuaded, now lives in you also." 2 Timothy 1:5

Our oldest daughter and our daughter-in-law each presented Bob and me with a beautiful new granddaughter within two months of each other. So, in little more than two years, we've gone from zero to three grandchildren. We enthusiastically embrace this quick math called Grandparenting 101.

Mackenzie Joy and Adelyn Jane have velvety-soft skin, rolls of adorable fat and big alert eyes that study "Opa" and "Oma." Smiling and rolling over are the beginnings of their many milestones we record with pleasure.

Also sharing the spotlight is Isaac, Mackenzie's older brother. His two-year-old mind quickly analyzes how things are put together. He associates different contexts, calling the parentheses on a keyboard "moons." Isaac decided we needed new names that more accurately described us. Bob chases Isaac around the house with a periodic loud and startling "Boo!" Thus, Isaac calls us "Boo-pa" and the rhyming "Moo-ma."

God intended for us to enjoy our grandchildren. Can you tell we delight in ours? How like God to give us the most motivating avenue to share our faith in Jesus with future generations—a time we will not see. Paul attributed his compliment to Timothy's genuine faith to the influence of his mom and grandmother.

Two months following Easter, Isaac spied a nail. He picked it up, and initially tried to communicate his excitement to his mom. Finally, he said "Easter egg!" "Jesus." He had remembered us telling him the account of the Passion Week and Easter through the objects he found in plastic Easter eggs. How fulfilling to mold impressionable minds with thoughts of our Savior.

Lord, thank You for the joy of teaching our grandchildren and reminding us how they teach us about approaching the kingdom of God like a little child.

Tamalyn Jo Heim is proud to be called sweetheart to Bob, mom to Bobbi and Steve, Josh and Kari, Kendralyn and Josh and Bekah; Moo-ma to Isaac; and Oma to Kenzie and Ady.

APRIL 30

Transformation

"Be alert, be present. I'm about to do something brand-new. It's bursting out! Don't you see it?" Isaiah 43:19 (The Message)

Transformation: we've talked about it, looked for it, planned for it and organized for it. But how much have we really prayed for it? And as we've prayed, have we waited and listened and committed ourselves to follow whatever direction we receive by the Spirit?

Transformation comes when God invades lives that in turn affect the places where people live and work and go to school. God only comes by invitation—their invitation or our invitation on their behalf.

Transformation is when everything is changed.

It's an impossible task that takes a God bigger than our impossibilities. How do we begin to bring that about? Practically, how do we see everything transformed?

Look for an impossible situation, the person or place that seems like it could never change and invite God into that place by speaking peace and declaring blessing, then watch what God will do. One person may impact one person, and that person will affect a family, a neighborhood, a school, a business or a government office. That affect, empowered by the Holy Spirit, changes things making a way for transformation.

We are seeing God do that very thing in a local business where a man has faithfully prayed for his company and its managers. God is touching every aspect of that business and bringing transformation that will impact a community and beyond.

Lancaster County can be transformed street by street and this is the kairos time. God is inviting each of us, all of us, to take part in what He is doing. We invite you to join us by adopting your street, school or place of employment in prayer.

For more information, visit www.lancastertransformed.org.

Father, help us to take our responsibility for transformation right where You've placed us. May we cry out to You with an expectation that You will show us our part and that You will come and do what only You can do.

Lauren Charles serves with Lancaster Transformed Street by Street.

May

MAY 1

Light of the World

"You are the light of the world. . . let your light shine before men, that they may see your good deeds and praise your Father in heaven." Matthew 5:14-16

We were going on a field trip to the bathroom. We had turned off all the lights in the house and the kids held flashlights in their hands excited to find out what we were going to do with our small lights.

I was embarking on my first year of homeschool for my daughter who was starting Kindergarten. My preschool age son was joining us on the adventure as well. Our lesson was based on the letter *M* for moon. Single file, we marched up the stairs and entered the bathroom because it was equipped with a large mirror.

The previous week they learned about the sun and that Jesus is the light of the world. The moon, unlike the sun, does not have any light of its own. The moon is a light only because the sun shines on it. We pointed our flashlights into the mirror and marveled at the reflection. I explained that we are like the moon, and Jesus is like the sun. If we know Jesus, then his light shines on us. I told my kids that other people need to see our light shining so they can know the light of the world, Jesus. Then I challenged them to act like Jesus and when they do, they are like the moon.

The kids accepted this challenge like it was gummy candy. My son would run up to me shouting, "Sissy was a moon to me Mommy!" My daughter would brag on my son, displaying a knowing grin. "Seth was just a moon, Mommy. He was showing me love."

God challenged me through the enthusiasm of my children that this is a lesson I needed to learn as well. Was I being a moon? What selfish thoughts, unholy behavior or self-righteous pride was eclipsing the brightness of the Son of God on me? What needed to be transformed into his likeness, so that I may reflect the fullness of His glory?

Lord, like my children, I want to be a full moon. I pray that others would be able to know You, because I am being a moon and reflecting Your glory. Transform me into Your likeness with ever-increasing glory.

Sonya Lanford is a homeschooling mother of two and homemaker. She attends Ephrata Bible Fellowship Church where she serves in a life group and on the worship team.

Photo by Jennifer Raff

MAY 2

Lift Up Jesus

"But I, when I am lifted up from the earth, will draw all men to myself." John 12:32

When we lift up Jesus Christ, His Spirit often creates an awareness of need in people who do not know him. Jesus said, "The Spirit gives life; the flesh counts for nothing. The words I have spoken to you are spirit and they are life" (John 6:63). The sharing of my personal testimony must always point directly to Jesus so the listeners see Jesus more than me.

Lost people may see your passion, your love, your sympathy—but this will never save them. It is only Jesus. No matter how much human love or elegance of speech, we can save no one. When we focus on our disappointments and trials, we often detract from Jesus and His redemptive work.

Paul writes, "My message and my preaching were not with wise and persuasive words, but with a demonstration of the Spirit's power. So that your faith might not rest on men's wisdom, but on God's power" (1 Corinthians 2:4-5). "We are … Christ's ambassadors, as though God were making his appeal through us" (2 Corinthians 5:20). Anything that draws attention to myself makes me a conspirator to Jesus' work. When others see me instead of Jesus, they see what I can do but too often do not grasp what Jesus can do.

When Jesus is lifted up, the Holy Spirit creates a need in the person for Jesus. Lift Jesus higher. "He must increase and I must decrease." (John 3:30).

Lord Jesus, I choose to lift You up in all I do and say. All my accomplishments are only because of You. Help me to always point to You, for apart from You I am nothing.

Dave Eshleman served as pastor/church planter for fifty years. Presently he is a church consultant.

MAY 3

National Day of Prayer

"Do to others whatever you would like them to do to you." Matthew 7:12 (New Living Translation)

"Where is God?" has been asked many times throughout world wars, tsunamis, earthquakes, tornadoes and terrorist attacks. God hasn't moved or changed. He is the same yesterday, today and tomorrow. He created life and allows death. He created the earth with all its tumultuous effects. The suffering season can be a time to bow to the absolute sovereignty of God. Pain can be a fresh incentive to grow in grace.

Who doesn't respond warmly when someone offers to pray for you? Be sure to return the favor. Healing comes when we humble ourselves to lovingly pray for our families, neighbors and our country. Love generates energy and is enjoyed from God's heart to our souls.

In a Thanksgiving Day proclamation during the Civil War, Abraham Lincoln proclaimed, "It has seemed to me fit and proper that God should be solemnly, reverently and gratefully acknowledged, as with one heart and one voice by the whole American people."

As we pray corporately on the National Day of Prayer, I am amazed by how the awesome, transcending communication from earth to heaven awakens God's people. It is a glorious, spontaneous embrace of the sweet fragrance of God's Holy Spirit touching each of us who desire His presence. What a stirring sight when thousands, representing different denominations, assemble under the open skies to pray in one accord. Some pray like a mighty rushing wind while others respond in quietness on bended knees, but all agree for God's will to be done.

Come. Join the multitudes as your community gathers together the first Thursday of May for corporate prayer.

Oh God, I ask that praying becomes our lifestyle as we pray without ceasing throughout the year.

Dona Fisher is vice president of Friendship Foundation, founder of Change of Pace Bible Studies, correspondent for Lancaster Newspapers and serves as campaign chairperson for the annual National Day of Prayer event in Lancaster.

MAY 4

Milestones or Millstones

"O God, from my youth you have taught me, and I still proclaim your wondrous deeds. So even to old age and gray hairs, O God, do not forsake me, until I proclaim your might to another generation, your power to all those to come." Psalm 71:17-18 (English Standard Version)

Recently, I was honored by my family with a weeklong vacation in Roatan, an island off the coast of mainland Honduras. There, we celebrated my major milestone—my seventieth birthday. Neither of my parents had lived past their sixties so I do not take making it this far for granted. Now I have vision for at least another ten years of healthy and fruitful life with my family and in serving the God that I love. He has extended so much grace to me all these years, so I'm trusting Him for a few more.

Our culture increasingly views our aging population as an economic burden and social problem. Older people are often marginalized and viewed as baggage and burdens to younger generations. I want to challenge those views by life example as well as words. I don't want to be a millstone around the necks of younger people or someone to be patronized and indulged. Millstones have had a good use, but can also be deadweights that drag things down. Instead, at this milestone, I am profoundly grateful that God has given my wife of forty-six years and me the opportunity to partner in ministry to ignite fresh purpose, passion and power in those coming along after us. I desire to drive on until the last milestone in the road, wherever and whenever it shows up.

Father, I thank You that You are not through shaping me and conforming me more to the character of Your Son, nor in using me to advance Your purposes and plans in these days.

Bruce Boydell and his wife, Joan, are leaders of the Haft, Inc., a Christ-centered community, whose mission is the development of emerging ministry and marketplace leaders who are in need of refreshing, retooling and rebuilding.

MAY 5

Greasepaint and Smiles

"A joyful heart is good medicine." Proverbs 17:22
(English Standard Version)

Outline the smile, put on the bright red wig and I'm ready. Walk the few blocks to the hospital waving and smiling at drivers and walkers who are amused to see a clown on the streets of Lancaster City. Check in at the hospital desk, find the room where the church member is and smile at nurses, doctors and fellow visitors as I walk down the hallways.

The church member is asleep. I gently say, "Hello," hoping that the older man is just taking a light nap and will be happy to wake up to see a member from Fools of Faith in his room. He does not awaken. I gingerly touch his shoulder and see that he is deeply asleep.

To think that I had taken time that I didn't really have to put on makeup and a clown costume just to bring a smile to this man who I didn't even know and now isn't even awake. Sighing, I leave the card that I prepared for him and tell a nurse to mention that a clown from First United Methodist Church had been to see him.

I retrace my steps down the hallway. Then almost to the elevator I hear, "Hello! Can you come here?"

I turn to the room and ask permission to enter. A young man with natural red hair is lying in the bed and older friends and relatives surround him. Everyone smiles. I chat with them, find out the young man's name and ask if I can say a prayer. He agrees. Then I ask if I can give him a sticker. When he nods, I search through my huge pockets and find a sticker that I attach to his water bottle. Then I leave with a wave of my gloved hand and a big smile.

Dear Lord, help me remember that Your ways are higher than my ways. Thank You for the opportunity to bring cheer to whom You choose.

Ellen Campbell participates in Fools of Faith at First United Methodist Church.

MAY 6

God, Use My Anguish

"I will be glad and rejoice in your love for you saw my affliction and knew the anguish of my soul." Psalm 31:7

"You have to be strong, Karen, you can't cry, you have to be strong and keep going." I still remember those words spoken by my mother when I was a child. My mother was only fourteen when she gave birth to me. By the age of eighteen, my mother had two more children. I grew up watching my mother being physically and verbally abused by my stepfather. I was physically, verbally and sexually abused and wanted to escape. At age eleven, I began a vicious cycle of foster homes, running away, detention centers and eventually at age seventeen being sent to prison. For the next twenty-three years I was in and out of prison, selling drugs, living in abusive relationships and suffering addictions.

On the outside, I appeared to be a very hard and violent person, but inside I was dying. I felt empty, like a black hole was consuming me cell by cell. All I could ever envision was a void of darkness. I was certain that it would always be inside me—an empty sadness that would never go away. Beneath the surface, beneath all my false fronts, all my walls, all my protecting, all my years of being unable to speak what is inside me, I was afraid there was no "me" left.

In prison, God opened a door for me one day and led me to the Lydia Center. When I was a child, I had prayed for God to send an angel to save me. Now at age forty, God has sent me seven of them through the staff at Lydia Center. Although it's been rough, my black hole is slowly being filled with God's love.

Thank You, Father, that wisdom is gained through life experience. Help me share my strengths and struggles and become the person You created me to be.

Karen McLaughlin is a Lydia Center resident.

MAY 7

How He Loves Us

"Look at the birds of the air; they do not sow or reap or store away in barns, and yet your heavenly Father feeds them. Are you not much more valuable than they?" Matthew 6:26

It was the call we all dread, a voice on the phone saying "I have some bad news...." I was at a beach campsite with my family. It was 6:30 a.m. when my father, in London, called my cell phone in the USA—something he never does. He told me that my mother had suddenly and unexpectedly died of a heart attack. Stunned, I groped for words. Thoughts of her flooded into my mind and with them, the overwhelming sense that I had to leave as soon as possible to be with my dad in England.

In shock, we packed our things to travel back to Lititz. My children were upset at losing their grandma. Should they and my wife make the trip too? But how was it even possible? It was midsummer. Last-minute flights were hard to find and even more expensive than usual.

As we prayed, my wife and I had a growing sense that all four of us should indeed go, but it was becoming clear that we would need thousands of dollars, and not at some unspecified time, but straight away. I prayed to the Lord: "You are my provider. Lord, I need your provision and need it quickly." Within about twenty-four hours of first hearing this sad news, we received the promise of a substantial donation, which covered the majority of the need. My tears now were not those of grief but those of gratitude. God really did know every detail about my life—and He moved swiftly to provide an emergency need. In fact, within a few days we had received financial gifts that covered all four last-minute flights to London.

Thank You, God, that You know everything about us. We do not need to worry. May we all rest knowing that You will always provide what is needed.

Peter Bunton, originally from England, serves as the director of DOVE Mission International, part of DOVE Christian Fellowship International. He lives in Lititz with his wife and children.

MAY 8

God's Light

"In the same way, let your light shine before others, that they may see your good deeds and glorify your Father in heaven."
Matthew 5:16

Whenever I was disobedient as a child, not only did my conscience bother me but also the lights in my bedroom would flicker on and off. Even though I would try to hide under the covers thinking that I had gotten away with my sin, God was reminding me that He saw it all. When I could take my guilt no more, I would run to my parents and confess my wrongdoing.

My father tried to convince me that there was a short in the wiring, but I knew better. God was letting me know that He was disappointed in my choices. After every confession, the lights would go back to their constant brightness. Was this just a coincidence?

For fourteen years the lights fluttered in my room when I was sad, lonely or in trouble. Finally, after a home renovation, I moved out and my little sister moved in. I was anxious to see how she would react to God's nudges, but to my surprise nothing happened. My sister never once saw the lights blink.

Years later when my childhood home was sold, I walked through each room for one last time. Stopping at my old bedroom, I looked around. The room was bare except for my memories. As if on cue, the lights once again started to flicker.

I felt a strange peace wash over me. Whether this was God or not, those lights had changed my life. As a small child I learned that the things I did in secret couldn't be hidden from God. As an adult I realized that no matter where I was or what I was going through, I could always be confident that I never walked my path alone.

Thank You, Lord, for being with me through all my trials and loving me despite my shortcomings.

Karen Helm is records coordinator at Messiah College.

MAY 9

Remember the Ant

"You lazy fool! Look at an ant.... Let it teach you a thing.... How long are you going to lazy around doing nothing? A nap here, nap there.... a day off there. Sit back, take it easy—Do you know what comes next? You can look forward to a dirt poor life. Poverty your permanent houseguest." Proverbs 6:6-11 (The Message)

"I'm tired." "My back hurts." "I have a headache." Whatever the excuse is I always found a reason to stay in bed. It interfered with my job, family and church life. I got severely depressed. I turned to drugs, alcohol, and men to deal with my depression. I turned my back on everyone and everything. My life spiraled out of control. I never understood how everyone in the world was able to keep it together.

My mentor would tell me to get out of bed, talk to God. Do something for someone else. "The more time you spend being lazy, the worse it gets." Finally I enrolled in rehabilitation. One day after entering treatment for my addictions, a friend gave me the Scripture of Proverbs 6:6-11 (Message Remix). This Scripture would end up changing my entire outlook on life. I realized I could not spend my life lying in bed being lazy. God expected me to be out working for Him. I was able to "remember the ant" and get out there and live for God.

Every morning when I awake and am plagued with one of these former thoughts, I give it to God and get up anyway and dedicate my day to Him. My day is always full of wonderful people and blessings.

Heavenly Father, I thank You so much for giving us another day to serve You. I ask that You help us "remember the ant" today and keep us busy for Your glory Lord. You are an awesome God.

Rachel McKay moved from Jacksonville, Florida, to live at the Lydia Center and attend Community Fellowship Church.

MAY 10

No Kidneys

"Be still, and know that I am God; I will be exalted among the nations, I will be exalted in the earth." Psalm 46:10

I do not have any kidneys. I first heard about the deterioration to my kidneys on a bright sunny day five years ago. At that time I passed blood in my urine and was treated for a bladder infection. A week later, my doctor wanted to do a CAT scan.

"Why?" I argued. "I feel good. There is nothing wrong."

But the scan showed I had large tumors on both kidneys and I was diagnosed with kidney cancer. My kidneys needed to be removed.

"How will I live?" I questioned.

I was told I needed dialysis. What a life-changing shock for my wife and I as we adjusted to daily dialysis and a radical diet. I was limited to drinking twenty-four-ounces of liquid daily. I had been accustomed to drinking one and a half gallons of water daily. The limitation made me feel like I was burning up, but I learned to cope.

Five years later, I am on home dialysis every night for nine hours. I have been trained to manage the process myself.

Because of the mercy and grace of the Lord Jesus Christ, I am a living miracle. I work. I preach. I travel. I am staff chaplain for Dutch Valley Food Distributors. It's amazing how normal I can live when nothing is normal.

Here are some principles that help my family and I to adjust to living normally in a non-normal situation:

1. Accept whatever happens to you.
2. Do not pity yourself.
3. Be very thankful for everything.
4. Be a blessing to others, not a blister.
5. Do kind acts of service for others.
6. Live life to the fullest today (tomorrow isn't here yet).
7. Give all praise and glory to the Lord Jesus Christ.

God, help us find a place of joy and obedience to Your will regardless of the circumstances.

C. B. Horst is chaplain for Dutch Valley Food Distributors and retired senior pastor of Blue Ball Church of the Brethren.

MAY 11

He Is Who He Is

"Moses said to God, 'Suppose I go to the Israelites and say to them, "The God of your fathers has sent me to you," and they ask me, "What is his name?" Then what shall I tell them?' God said to Moses, 'I Am Who I Am. This is what you are to say to the Israelites: "I Am has sent me to you."'" Exodus 3:13–14

We're familiar with this name of God that describes His self-sustenance, His eternal existence and His active presence: "I Am Who I Am."

We're probably also familiar with this phrase that's crept into our lingo—"It is what it is." We use it to describe a not-so-great situation that won't be resolved instantly and is going to roll out in its own predetermined way.

It's a bit like the old song, "Que Sera, Sera" (Whatever Will Be, Will Be).

Recently, I found myself facing a difficult scenario with no easy end in sight. As I shared it with a friend I said to her, "Well, it is what it is." I immediately felt unrest in my spirit and asked God what was wrong with it. "I Am Who I Am" came to mind, and I realized the superiority of viewing the hardship from that perspective. God is Lord over every situation, is actively involved in it, is with us in the midst of it and will display His goodness through it.

So when a tough situation comes my way, instead of saying, "It is what it is," I now say, "He is who He is." No matter how complicated it is, how long it drags on or how painful it is, God is Lord over it and will bring glory to Himself through it.

Father, help me not to slide into the pattern of the world, but to choose Your high road in my thoughts, actions and words.

Lisa Hosler serves with Susquehanna Valley Pregnancy Services and the Regional Church of Lancaster County, and worships with her husband, Ron, at Calvary Church, Lancaster.

MAY 12

It's Not Easy Being a Mom

"Pour out your heart like water before the presence of the Lord; lift up your hands to Him for the life of your little ones." Lamentations 2:19 (New American Standard Bible)

While at a wedding last night, I watched as the mother of the groom danced with her son and due to the premature death of her husband, the mother of the bride danced with her daughter. It was like an explosion in my heart.

I sensed years of pouring into their lives being celebrated in a single dance. Time to release and let go, and trust God to carry on what both mothers so greatly invested in. Deep sigh.

It's difficult to imagine how encompassing having children is. From the moment of conception, a mother's heart is permanently tied to the life growing within her. And then she's expected to train that little one toward independence.

The tough part is that we can't shield them from life's deepest disappointments and it's crushing to stand by unable to change their circumstances. Unfortunately, children don't always make the choices we hope they will. It's not easy being a mom, but it's worth every tear.

On this day, remember the countless hours and unspoken heart cries poured out by your mother on your behalf. In some small way touch her heart and bring salve to the places that ache in her, and you will have honored her more than you can imagine.

Lord, would You please touch my mother's heart this day with Your tender Love. You are well acquainted with her grief and able to comfort her in ways that no one else can. I pray that You would affirm and strengthen her as she presses in to know You. Carry her in Your arms of Love, Jesus, and be the lifter of her head. Amen.

Kathi Wilson and her husband, Mark, are co-authors of *Tired of Playing Church*, co-founders of Body Life Ministries and serve as church planters for the Lancaster Mennonite Conference in Lancaster.

MAY 13

Mother in Deed

"She speaks with wisdom, and faithful instruction is on her tongue." Proverbs 31:26

"Happy Mother's Day!" There it was in print, the very first Mother's Day card I ever received. The words brought tears to my eyes. I felt completely overwhelmed!

I am old enough to be a grandmother, but I am not a mother. Circumstances have provided no children for me. Each Mother's Day, as friends gather to celebrate with their children, I've been reminded of that void. With a little sadness, a little emptiness, I sense the missing out on one of the most important joys of life. Now, I know I may be making Mother's Day a larger-than-life deal, and I know it's really not that grand of a day for many mothers, yet the feelings still are real for me. Have I missed out by not being a mother?

The card read: "God often shows His love through you—His tender care is felt in all the warmth and thoughtfulness you always share with others."

I have mothered others. I've cared for and supported many back to health through my work, discipled women through life-to-life groups and loved little ones through children's ministry. I have mothered many. Likewise, many have mothered me. My kind and caring friend who sent the card was one life I was able to touch, and her gratefulness was sent through the message in this Mother's Day card.

Mothers come to us with many faces, in many places. We have opportunities to care for others every day. Each time we share God's love through gentle words or acts of kindness is a mothering opportunity. I am forever grateful for that card and the reminder that I am and will forever be a mother!

Thank You, God, for being my heavenly mother and father. Thank You for awakening me to Your overflowing love and teaching me how to bless others through actions and words. Thank You for the reminder that I can and will mother others in Your name.

Laurie Sabol serves as a life-to-life leader and in children's ministry at Tapestry Church, Lancaster.

MAY 14

My Mama's Prayers

"The effective, fervent prayer of a righteous man avails much."
James 5:16 (New King James Version)

I was not always aware of my mother's prayers, but I'm sure she prayed for me even before my birth. When I was a tearful four-year-old, she tried to comfort me. I felt lonely in the other room I had to sleep in because I had a new baby sister. Her prayers brought me peace.

As a teenager, I was tempted to go out with an ungodly boy and suddenly realized I had a dislike for him and woke up to his true character. It dawned on me that my mother was fervently praying for me and my safety in this situation. Praise God, her prayers were effective!

As a young mother, I had many frustrations and it seemed each day brought new challenges, with our family of three sons and five daughters. My mother always encouraged me and helped when she could. Her daily and often nightly prayers for me were effective, fervent and availed much! They caused me to have hope for each new day.

Thank you, Mother!

I lay in bed, tears flowing freely, after getting the news of her "home-going."

I miss her terribly and the pain is deep, but I realize the one thing I miss the most is her prayers for me and my family. I need to pick up the baton and carry on for the coming generations.

Lord, help me to be faithful in prayer. Be exalted in my life.

Mary Ruth Lehman attends ACTS Covenant Fellowship and is involved in various prayer groups in the region.

MAY 15

A Gift of Puzzles

"For now we see in a mirror dimly, but then face to face. Now I know in part; then I shall know fully, even as I have been fully known." 1 Corinthians 13:12 (English Standard Version)

I called my sister to discuss plans for our mother's surprise ninetieth birthday party. About a dozen family members planned to gather at the adult day care center she attends and where my sister is the director. Laden with cake, balloons and musical treats, we planned to surprise and delight her.

After our conversation, my sister handed the phone to Mom, who was tucked into bed doing crossword puzzles. "I am really enjoying these puzzles," she said. "I don't know who gave them to me, but they are great and there are so many of them."

My sister chuckled in the background and reminded her that I had ordered the jumbo box of puzzles for her for Mother's Day. Mom and I chatted briefly about her great-grandchildren, discussed their ages once again and agreed that "someone around here is getting old."

Then Mom said with enthusiasm, "I have a wonderful box of puzzles. I don't know where they came from, but they are great."

Mom cannot remember the source of all her blessings, but she knows that she is blessed and gives thanks. She moves from day to day with an attitude of gratitude for even the simplest things. Before too many years pass, Mom will undoubtedly be in the presence of her heavenly Father, the giver of life and of all good things. Someday soon she will see His face and know Him fully. I think I know one thing she will say: "Thank You, Lord. You gave me those puzzles. There were so many and I really enjoyed them."

Lord, help me to be grateful for every puzzle that passes my way, for each one is a gift from You.

Joan Boydell and her husband, Bruce, direct the ministry of the Haft, Inc. They are members of Covenant Fellowship in Chester County.

MAY 16

Make the Most of Every Opportunity

"Be very careful … how you live—not as unwise but as wise, making the most of every opportunity, because the days are evil." Ephesians 5:15-16

"Be wise in the way you act toward outsiders; make the most of every opportunity." Colossians 4:5 (NIV)

"I consider my life worth nothing to me, if only I may finish the race and complete the task the Lord Jesus has given me—the task of testifying to the gospel of God's grace" (Acts 20:14).

"Teach us to number our days aright, that we may gain a heart of wisdom" (Psalm 90:12).

"Show me, O Lord, my life's end and the number of my days; let me know how fleeting is my life. You have made my days a mere handbreadth; the span of my years is as nothing before you. Each man's life is but a breath." (Psalm 39:5 (NIV).

Life is so very short. Time is a precious gift from God. I pray daily for the Lord to help me not to waste time. Each day brings us one day closer home. Paul mentions the days are evil implying that is the reason we need to take advantage of the opportunities. In evil days, the opportunities are not as frequent. People may not be as open to hearing the Good News. Noah preached for one hundred twenty years with no response. In Revelation the people who did not die in the plagues still refused to turn from their evil deeds. (See Revelation 9:20.)

Opportunities are often not repeated. When we miss an opportunity to witness for Jesus, we feel badly. We feel guilty and rightly so. Tell Jesus you blew it. Ask Him to forgive you. He will. Ask Him to give you another opportunity. He will. When that opportunity comes, allow Him to speak through you in a gentle but confident manner. He will. You will be surprised and exceedingly grateful. You are growing!

Lord, help me to make the most of every opportunity.

Dave Eshleman served as pastor/church planter for fifty years. Presently he is a church consultant.

MAY 17

My Mother, My Mentor, My Friend

"Her children rise up and call her blessed...." Proverbs 31:28 (New King James Version)

My mother went to heaven quite a few years ago, at age forty four. I will always remember her with fondness and admiration. She was a godly woman whose legacy lives on. Her number one desire was to serve and glorify God. She prayed, from the age of fourteen, for her husband, children and grandchildren that they all would love and serve the Lord. She mentored and led many to Christ. She was willing to die to her own desires so many more would come to know Jesus in a personal way. What an awesome woman.

When I was a girl, sometimes the bedroom door would be shut. I would think she should be doing housework so I wouldn't have so much to do, but she was spending time with her Lord and Savior. What a testimony to a young girl. It's a precious memory and gives me the desire to do the same.

I could tell my mother everything and know it would be kept confidential. She answered my many questions often going to the Word of the God for her answers. She not only prayed for me but she prayed with me. If I didn't agree on matters dear to her heart, she still loved me. What a precious example of unconditional love as I worked my way through the questioning doubting times. She loved and accepted me in a beautiful way.

She was an amazing encourager. She told me she was thankful that I was spiritually minded—a great motivation to get to know Jesus even better. Her encouragement told me that I was a valuable person and that I could do whatever the Lord called me to do.

Lord, help me to be a godly woman like my mother.

Yvonne Zeiset is a financial counselor (consumer credit and default mortgage) with Tabor Community Services in Lancaster. She is also a prayer intercessor.

MAY 18

If I Had Only Known

"I pray that your hearts will be flooded with light so that you can see something of the future he has called you to share. I want you to realize that God has been made rich because we who are Christ's have been given to him." Ephesians 1:18 (The Living Bible)

- If I had only known that a few extra hugs and kisses would have reassured him that he was my God-given husband, I would have shown him more affection.
- If I had only known that "you can't take it with you," I would have encouraged him to buy that extra auto part he really wanted.
- If I had only known how deeply he hurt inside because he had been abandoned as a child, I would have been more sensitive when he was silent.
- If I had only known he needed someone to talk to, I would have listened more and talked less.
- If I had only known I would never touch him again, I would have rubbed his neck when he complained about his pain.
- BUT I DO KNOW that nothing ever separates us from God's perfect, unconditional love.
- BUT I DO KNOW that the Lord has forgiven me for all my past mistakes and blunders.
- BUT I DO KNOW my heavenly Father loves me perfectly despite my human faults.
- BUT I DO KNOW that I have more compassion because of my loss.
- BUT I DO KNOW that my husband is in perfect peace with the Lord—that he no longer feels his hurts; he no longer has aches and pains; he is whole, praising the Lord and he will greet me with love and compassion when we meet again in Glory.

Thank You, Lord, that You are God of the past, present and future. You have accomplished what was best in the past, and I can count on Your love and direction in the future.

Jan Dorward is a Messianic Jew attending DOVE Westgate Church, Ephrata. She's grateful for all the opportunities God has laid before her—including writing, editing and presenting Messianic Passover teachings.

MAY 19

God in Our Midst

"The helpless call to Him, and He answers; He saves them from all their troubles." Psalm 34:6 (Good News Translation)

It was a Friday afternoon at my workplace and an employee whose work I managed was still on the premises after his shift had ended. He had been told several times that he could not expect overtime wages. His personality was volatile under normal circumstances, and I was informed that he was really upset because he couldn't find his car keys.

As a Christian, I had been forewarned when I accepted this management position that I was to be "politically correct" and careful not to mention anything about the Lord. Up to this point in my employment, I had complied; however, as I was leaving the room where he had just rooted through the trash can for the second time, the Lord prompted me to say, "When I can't find something, I say, 'Lord, you saw where I put that. Can you please show me?'"

As I finished that prayer, he suddenly spotted the car keys on top of the microwave. Shaking his head, he insisted the keys had not been there a minute ago. He ran down the hall, waving the keys over his head.

One of his co-workers asked me if I had prayed to Saint Anthony, and I said, "No. I went straight to the top." The coworker replied, "God showed up at work today!" From that time forth, our team of ten worked better than ever, because God was now in our midst.

Dear Father, thank You for meeting us in our time of need, and for revealing Yourself to those who are far off. Thank You for making Yourself known in our midst in everyday circumstances. When we are thwarted, thank You for the creative way in which you reveal Your glory.

Denise Colvin served in several life-affirming ministries, directed a deaf and hard-of-hearing agency and worked in various secular settings. She is blessed with four daughters and ten grandchildren.

MAY 20

God Wants Me

"You will seek me and find me when you seek me with all your heart." Jeremiah 29:13

God has used the staff and the community at the Lydia Center to set me apart from my old lifestyle. I came to the Lydia Center with no purpose, no desire and no dreams. I just existed. I had this empty spot deep in my soul. I hated myself and was unable to show love to anyone, let alone myself. If I had a man in my life, I was happy for a time, until the man I was with did not want me any longer. What was so wrong with me that no one wanted a relationship with me, let alone I did not want a relationship with myself?

I found out God wants a relationship with me and loves me. God has used staff and sisters in the Lord to show me what love is. I had held on to resentment from my childhood and blamed others for my choices, but I needed to ask God for forgiveness for decisions that I made. God has shown me what it is to forgive my family and others. I am a new person today because of God. With hard work, I am a freed woman. It has not been easy. It is the hardest thing to forgive others but I would do it again. I see the good in others with God's help. My dream is to have an intimate relationship with Jesus Christ and to be able to love others the way God loves me.

Dear Heavenly Father, I want to thank You for this day and for the work that You have done in me. I want to thank You for the persons who You placed in my life. I know You will meet my desire in Your time. I will wait for You to present it to me.

Abbie Knopp attends Community Fellowship Church.

MAY 21

Sing to the Lord

"Speak to one another with psalms, hymns and spiritual songs. Sing and make music in your heart to the Lord, always giving thanks to God the Father for everything, in the name of our Lord Jesus Christ." Ephesians 5:19-20

When a twenty-year member of our choir became ill with brain cancer, we began praying. We wanted to include Bill as much as we could, and he wanted to remain in contact with his choir family. Around the same time our beloved choir director and organist announced he was leaving for a job at a university out of state. We recorded a CD so the choir director could remember us by the anthems he had taught us to sing so beautifully. The CD ended up being a gift for Bill who played it over and over.

Following the academic year, the music director returned to our area. Since Bill was getting weaker, the organist offered to play favorite hymns for him. The choir also was thinking of singing anthems for Bill. The organist's wife heard all this planning going on in the church office where she worked, so she told them what was being considered. Bill's family was able to bring him to the church on Sunday evening. We had a wonderful evening focusing not on Bill's illness, but on God's goodness and his mercy toward us. It was a joyous time not only singing for Bill but watching him tap his feet to the beat of the music. The sorrow of his situation was removed as the words of Scripture in the hymns lifted his spirit.

By the next Saturday, Bill had gone to his eternal rest. We were so blessed by acting on our intentions immediately. The choir sang at Bill's Life Celebration Memorial Service.

Dear God, Your timing is perfect. We always want our calendar to be open when You have something You want us to do. Help us to be sensitive to Your plans for our time.

Marilyn Erb is a member of the choir at Lititz Moravian Church. She lives with her husband and son in Ephrata. They have three grown children.

MAY 22

The Bigger Picture

"Now you are the body of Christ, and each one of you is a part of it." 1 Corinthians 12:27 (New American Standard Bible)

One of my greatest joys is singing in a choir of voices raised to God.

The thrill of being part of something so beautiful and so much bigger than I am is indescribable.

A couple of years ago, I was slogging my way through the novel *War and Peace* by Leo Tolstoy, and I came upon a passage that struck me with its similarities to what I experience being part of a choir.

It reads, "Every general and soldier felt his own insignificance, was conscious of being a grain of sand in that sea of men, and at the same time felt his own might, being conscious of himself as part of that great whole."

God has invited us to share in the great and glorious masterpiece He is creating and the kingdom He is building. We are all members of it, being caught up in the bigger picture.

I especially love being surrounded by voices that are so much better than my own. They inspire me to sing better, higher, more gloriously.

I am so thankful for the great and awesome privilege God gives us each day to share in what He is doing in the hearts of men and women all over the world.

Father, thank You so much for creating each one of us and inviting us to share in Your kingdom work.

Dolores Walker is a member of Dove Westgate Church.

MAY 23

Battles Can Make Us Stronger

"I will never leave you nor forsake you." Hebrews 13:5 (New King James Version)

My eighth-grade history took a four-day and three-night camping trip to learn all about the Battle of Gettysburg. On the first day, each group set up a tent. It started to rain really hard so we hid under the pavilion to eat lunch. When we went back to our tents, I walked inside and stepped right in a puddle. Our tent got flooded so we needed to build another one.

We biked around the area to learn history, but a rain downpour caused classmates to slip and fall off their bikes. Some students got lost because it was raining so hard they couldn't see to follow the bikers ahead of them and ended up making wrong turns. It rained and thundered and stormed all night.

The second day it was thundering and hailing so badly that we had to stop biking and take cover. Did I mention it was freezing? The bugs? The food? Getting sick? Having everything soaked and smelly was overwhelming for me. I slept badly all three nights so that caused me to be overly dramatic and have an extra bad attitude like everyone else in our class.

My whole class had a lot of bad moments and we didn't think we could make it through, but we did.

On the trip I learned that I am a lot stronger than I thought I was. I learned teamwork. I learned that if a hard situation comes up, I don't have to be scared and quit … I can keep going. Although bad things were happening throughout the trip, I sensed God's care and help. I learned that I don't have to have Him answer right away or have everything perfect. I just need God to make me strong. God taught me that I will always have Him to lean on no matter how old I get.

God, thank You for teaching me important messages that I'm going to remember for the rest of my life. I know I will have lots of hard times in my life, but I know I can get through it with Your help.

Becca Good, daughter of Brent and Traci Good, is a student at Lancaster County Christian School.

MAY 24

God Moment

"Daughter, be of good comfort; thy faith hath made thee whole."
Matthew 9:22 (King James Version)

For a long time in my life, I suffered from psoriasis, an ongoing miserable skin problem. One Tuesday morning my hands were so swollen and sore, that I knew there was no way I could work at Root's Market where my husband and I operated a stand. After my husband left to attend to the market stand, I turned on the little TV in our family room. The words of a guest speaker on one of the stations caught my attention. He said, "The Lord has told me someone in the viewing audience has sore hands, hindering their work. I would like to pray for that person now."

I gasped! Could it be me? The speaker instructed the person with the illness to lay hands on someone while he prays. I was hit with a surge of self-pity. I was alone in the house. I had no one to touch while the speaker prayed. Instead I touched the TV while he prayed for the person's healing.

After the prayer I told the Lord I'm accepting the healing of my hands by faith and I thanked Him for doing it. I added, "But Lord, You will have to give me the faith to believe it!"

Opening my Bible at random I was amazed at the verse that caught my attention! "Daughter, thy faith hath made thee whole."

I sat there completely stunned, thinking about that verse. I realized if the Lord was healing my hands, I could go to market, which I did. That day, many customers made comments about my sore hands, but I let customers know my hands were going to be healed. The healing process took about a week, but the amazing thing is that I never again had sore hands. This experience happened years ago, but I remember it as an awesome God moment!

You are an amazing God! Awesome!

Grace Graybill and husband, Paul, formerly operated Fireside Crafts near Lititz. The Graybills have four children, ten grandchildren and six great-grandchildren.

MAY 25

Breakthrough Promised

"Look at the birds of the air…. Your heavenly Father feeds them. Are you not worth much more than they?" Matthew 6:26

I had a dream in which two situations continued to get messier, more confusing and frustrating until a breakthrough came that resolved the dilemma. In my journaling, I sensed the Lord say, "Keep on moving, looking and searching. Ask, seek and knock. At the right time the answer will be revealed or discovered. The right person will arise or arrive with the breakthrough."

In the predawn morning, I observed a fly circling the lightbulb of my reading lamp and I wrote: Lord, I sometimes feel like this fly buzzing around looking for a way out—but he's just going in circles, tiring himself out and focused on the wrong solution.

The Lord replied, "Eventually the dawn arrives and draws him to a door with the true solution to his dilemma.You are much more valuable and wiser than he. You won't die seeking the true light you crave. I AM the light and I AM drawing you into Myself and there is no danger I have not foreseen or prepared for in My paths and plans for you. Keep walking in and toward the light. I have solutions to every problem that you cannot yet see. The answers will become obvious at the proper time. Continue to be faithful and true. Be My witness and walk in the light and be obedient to the opportunity to be light for others. Remember, this is not just about you but affects multitudes."

Lord, keep my eyes focused on You, the true Light, and give me eyes to see what You are about to do. Help me be patient for Your timing in every situation.

Bill Goodberlet is a member of the convening council for York Coalition for Transformation and an elder at Emmanuel Christian Fellowship.

MAY 26

Impressing Others

"Be careful not to practice your righteousness in front of others to be seen by them. If you do, you will have no reward from your Father in heaven." Matthew 6:1

From the hospital, my daughter and son-in-law took me to their home. The warm and loving care I received there was appreciated, but the loss of control was hard to bear. A prescription kept the pain in check, but I looked and felt awful. The large stitches over my eye rendered me a monster lookalike, and a colorful cast kept my arm immobile and useless. A pity party ensued. It was at this low point that my pastor called. When Chuck asked how I was doing, the misery and complaining poured from me. He listened, said the church would pray for me and the call ended.

Suddenly it occurred to me that I had made myself vulnerable and had not appeared in the least bit spiritual. Didn't everyone know about dear Brother John who, while on his deathbed, kept a smile on his face and a praise to God on his lips? And what about Mary who refused to talk about herself or to complain, in spite of the pain of terminal cancer? And here I was with injuries that would heal, and nothing but grumbling to the pastor. What would Chuck think of me? I had blown my cover, for now it was obvious that I was not as godly as other Christians. My embarrassment was great.

Years later I recall my reaction and laugh aloud. Why had I been so concerned about what people thought of me? God alone is worthy of my attempts to please. I remain imperfect, but there is no need to impress men. My goal is to be transparent, to be honest before God and men. And God is faithful to work that in me.

Lord, thank You for growth.

Sally K. Owens lives with her husband, Don, in Lancaster, where they participate in two home fellowship groups. They share many children and oodles of amazing grandchildren.

MAY 27

A Blade of Grass

"Little children, you are from God, and have conquered them, for the one who is in you is greater than the one who is in the world."
1 John 4:4

I remember the sunny day when my dad and I, still a little child, headed to the beach. Thick concrete blocks paved a lovely avenue that led to the beach. As much as I tried to see some beauty in those gray and heavy squares of concrete, there was absolutely nothing attractive in them—they all looked monotonously the same.

But at some point, my eye did catch a glimpse of a big spider-web type crack in one of those boring blocks. Being careful, I stooped over the crack to make sure that it was not hiding any serious danger. No, it wasn't. What it did hide, though, was a tiny blade of green, growing grass, almost invisible behind the concrete crumbs.

"What a power!" I said, staring at the little piece of grass.

"Isn't it amazing that it could break through such thickness?" my dad whispered in awe.

Jesus after His crucifixion and death on the cross was also "hidden" in the grave. The guards even placed a heavy stone on the tomb to make sure that nobody would steal the body. But nothing—even death—could hold Jesus, for the Spirit of God was at work. It is hard to believe that nowadays Christians still carry the same power of the Holy Spirit inside of them. But they do. Therefore, no matter how thick or heavy their circumstances are, God's power is still greater to break through in victory for their well-being and His glory.

God Almighty, we bring to You our heavy burdens, knowing that there is nothing impossible for You to overcome.

Yulia Bagwell, Beth Yeshua, a housewife-caregiver, a writer and a translator for *The Upper Room* devotional magazine.

MAY 28

Missing In Action?

"... he had deserted them in Pamphylia and not continued with them in the work." Acts 15:38

Down through the centuries, wars between nations have resulted in the death of many in the military. Still, a number of other soldiers were classified as "missing in action."

In Scripture, there are many stories told of people set apart for God's service who became missing in action. People such as the following:

- Adam and Eve, who hid behind enemy lines,
- David, who should have been on the battlefield but was in bed with someone else's bed,
- Jonah, who booked a passage on the wrong ship for the wrong destination,
- Judas, who played the role of a disciple while deceiving others.

It's a sad day when one gets the bad news that a friend, colleague or family member has forsaken the Good News. One should heed such a warning and make sure that Jesus possesses them, and they are positioned in Him.

I cannot forget the words of my grandfather, who with tears in his eyes, said to me, "I missed God's first call on my life to be a missionary in India." As a result, for years, he wandered in a "no man's life" of just existing. Later on in life God did reclaim him, and he was a real "mission in action" for his Lord.

God has called us apart, so we don't come apart. There is a purpose for our lives. Daily there is a mission for us to accomplish. Christ affirmed our mission in Matthew 28:18-20:

- Go.
- Make disciples.
- Teach them to follow Christ.
- Enjoy my companionship.

Dear Commander of my soul, may I not drift in the sea of a missionless, self-centered life, but rather be found in the surging channel of Your mission, fully dedicated and focused on the One who is the finisher of the faith.

Dr. Sandy M. Outlar is the liaison to Christian Schools out of Lancaster Bible College. He lives in Landisville, with his wife, Joye. They attend Wheatland Presbyterian Church.

MAY 29

Relational or Friendship Evangelism

"Jesus saw a tax collector by the name of Levi sitting at his tax booth. 'Follow Me,' Jesus said to him, and Levi got up, left everything and followed him. Then Levi held a great banquet for Jesus at his house, and a large crowd of tax collectors and others were eating with them. But the Pharisees and teachers of the law who belonged to their sect complained to his disciples, 'Why do you eat and drink with tax collectors and 'sinners?'" Luke 5:28-29 (New Living Translation)

A relational style is often referred to as friendship evangelism. After leaving his lucrative business to follow Jesus, Levi invited his peers to a banquet to meet Jesus. The Pharisees were turned off with Jesus associating with tax-collector Levi. They were concerned about keeping the church pure and did everything to give the impression that they were sinless. Jesus spent time with people who sensed their need for God, not the Pharisees.

Let's not neglect those with a poor reputation. They might be the very ones who are open to hearing the invitation of God's love.

If you're an impatient extrovert you will need to exercise patience because relationship building usually happens over a period of time. You don't make a friendship in one encounter. It's easy to be friendly but being a friend demands sacrifice. It will affect your schedule, your priorities and your finances. There is a million miles between being friendly and being a friend. How many new friends have you made this past year?

Audrey, an example of a relational evangelist and a beauty salon stylist, shares with her clients how Jesus is transforming her life. She has invited many to church and some have come. Audrey also built a friendship with her neighbor who eventually came to church and brought others with her. New people bring new people and the Kingdom of God grows.

Lord Jesus, help me to love those who need a friend and to lead them to Yourself.

Dave Eshleman served as pastor/church planter for fifty years and is a church consultant.

MAY 30

Put Your Own Air Mask on First

"… then the Lord God formed the man of dust from the ground and breathed into his nostrils the breath of life, and the man became a living creature." Genesis 2, 7 (English Standard Version)

During any flight attendant's opening informational speech, the instruction is given that upon depressurization of the cabin, air masks will drop out of the ceiling. He or she will then instruct you to put on your own air mask first before helping those around you in order to accomplish this same life-saving task.

This illustrates a key spiritual principle of regional transformation: regional transformation begins with personal spiritual renewal. If I, as an individual, am not rooted in my sonship in Christ and not taken with the beauty of Christ, seeking His supremacy and glory in all things, then I cannot be an agent of transformation in the world around me.

Many Christians are caught up in ministry and/or the life of their church, trying to offer the life-giving breath of God to others while themselves suffocating on the poisonous gases of sin or the stench of stagnant religious air. God blew into Adam's nostrils the breath of life. This puts God in the posture of a kiss, or the giver of CPR. It is a position of intimacy, right there at Adam's face blowing into him that which without, he dies.

Do not neglect your need for the breath of life, given to you through an intimate relationship with your Maker, the Lover of your soul. From that intimate relationship, enjoy your calling as a channel of His goodness to others, leading them and showing them by your words and life the source of their breath.

Dear Lord God, we need Your help to open our eyes to the goodness of Your Word.

Jay McCumber serves as lead pastor at Cornerstone Christian Fellowship in Lebanon and as president of the Lebanon 222 team.

MAY 31

God's Banquet

"Why spend money on what is not bread, and your labor on what does not satisfy? Listen, listen to me, and eat what is good, and your soul will delight in the richest of fare." Isaiah 55:2

As a hopeless romantic, I dreamed of being married. I often prayed about my heart's desires and put myself in situations where I could meet new people. Although I thought it was okay to attend singles' events, one day the Lord challenged me in a way I never expected.

I was on a Christian singles retreat, sitting by the ocean and reading Isaiah 55:1-2. After reading the verses several times, the Lord gave me a vision of a banquet hall with long tables full of the most delectable foods and beautiful flowers. Then I saw myself outside the banquet room, in the hallway. Every time a waiter came into the hallway and dropped a crumb, I would enthusiastically gather it up to eat it. I felt as though the Lord said to me, "You are settling for crumbs but I have an entire banquet to give to you."

At that moment, I realized that God had a husband for me. My job was to stop seeking out a husband for myself and start trusting. I began praying not for God to bring me a husband, but praising God for the husband He had for me.

Several years later, when I was thirty-six years old, the Lord provided a husband for me. Indeed, he is my banquet. God orchestrated our entire love story and His amazing wisdom and grace is so evident in placing us together!

Dear Lord, help me to surrender every area of my life to You on a daily basis, remembering that You always know what is best for me. Help me to give my "crumbs" to You in exchange for Your banquet.

Joy Fisher is a wife and homemaker in Lancaster. She sings on a worship team and is a member of Calvary Church.

June

JUNE 1

Love Never Gives Up

"What marvelous love the Father has extended to us! Just look at it—we're called children of God!" 1 John 3:1 (The Message)

One Friday I really flubbed up. I got angry, using heated words while my children listened. Time-pressured, I had forgotten things for the trip. Returning home to retrieve the needed items made us unbearably late for our rendezvous.

I tried to maintain composure, saying alternately, "It won't matter ten years from now," and "Jesus, please help!" but tears spilled over. After regaining control, I glanced in the rearview mirror catching a view of my daughter Erika's eyes. My five-year-old's face was sunshine—she smiled with love in her eyes. She held my gaze accepting me and my tears. There I saw a glimpse of my Father's love—His complete, "I-love-you-no-matter-what" love.

This is God's love: meeting us where we are, not only in the joyful moments but also in the stormy, messy ones. He is there. He embraces us in that place, and by His touch, we experience acceptance, the beginning of healing.

Do you, like me, want to be "perfect," to be godly in all your responses, whether to a family member, an annoying colleague at work or a slow bagger at the grocery store? That is as impossible as a one-month-old baby eating a steak dinner!

Yet, God doesn't ask us to do everything perfect; He wants us to allow Him into our lives. He wants to be present, to demonstrate His love with a smile full of acceptance—no matter what. His love is lavished on us, not in dribs and drabs, but gushing forth flowing over us like a refreshing shower.

It's our choice to step away, or to stand in it.

O Father, thank You for pouring out Your love on me, Your child. Help me to soak in it, delight in it, to run and play in the sprinkler of Your love today and every day.

Renita Gerlach home educates her children and teaches writing to high school homeschoolers. She's been meeting with a home church for fourteen years.

JUNE 2

How Big Is Your Faith?

"Ask of me, and I will make the nations your inheritance, the ends of the earth your possession." Psalm 2:8

"Ask for the nations—some people don't even ask God for the salvation of their next-door neighbor. Few Christians feel little responsibility for their neighbors or peers. When we get to the judgment day and see our friends who have not given their life to Jesus can you picture them turning to you, as they cry in desperation, "Why didn't you tell me I needed to be born into God's Kingdom? I saw you and talked with you hundreds of times. You never once told me about Jesus?" What will we say?

Jesus said, "As the Father sent me I am sending you into the world" (John 17:18 and 20:21). Why did the Father send Jesus? "To seek and save the lost" (Luke 19:10). Just as Jesus was sent we are sent.

You are sent to your office, to your classroom, to your neighbors. How is it that we can work at the same place, live beside the same neighbors for years and go to school for a whole semester, sit beside or work beside these people and not pray for them or share the Good News with them?

Ask God to give you a compassion for your unchurched friends. He will open the door for you to share the Good News if you earnestly ask Him to do so. The apostles were bold. They went everywhere preaching the Word. The Holy Spirit will give you the same boldness if you cry out to God for a fresh anointing of His Spirit. Don't let guilt overwhelm you for not sharing Jesus. He will forgive you. However, repentance means we will change our ways. We can't change except through His power. Trust Him. He will surprise you today as you seek to be a witness for Him.

Lord, forgive me for not proclaiming Your Good News to my neighbor. Empower me by Your Holy Spirit to witness for You today.

Dave Eshleman served as pastor and church planter for fifty years.

JUNE 3

God's Painted Sky

"Be still and know that I am God …" Psalm 46:10 (King James Version)

I attended a very special and unusual worship service at Dolly Sods, West Virginia. There was an air of expectancy. We did not sit on chairs or wooden pews but on the randomly placed boulders. Not one person complained. There was no sound system or musical instruments. There was no need for them. While a waning gibbous moon slowly set behind us, a thin line of cadmium orange appeared over the last visible mountain to the east. The clouds came into view colored with different shades of pastel grays, blues and violets. The only speaking at this time was done with a whisper, but for the most part everyone was silent while our Creator produced a celestial masterpiece. Some of the clouds turned a pastel pink while the visible sky was tinted a very light shade of ultramarine blue. Some clouds became decorated with rose and yellow colors, and then an orange vermilion sun slowly peeped above the distant horizon until a dark cloud dissected it.

Finally very bright gold and yellows became the dominant colors of the clouds while the mountains took on the color of Windsor blue. As beams of sunrays burst through the clouds in all directions, a friend could no longer contain herself and started singing, "This is the day, this is the day that the Lord has made…." The birds sang with her as the sunrise completely enveloped the entire sky.

Several minutes later as we slowly walked back to our campsites, I said to another friend, "Many people who live in cities never see a sunrise as beautiful as this." He replied, "Perhaps the world would be a more peaceful place if they did."

Father, You gave us two eyes to see and two ears to hear. May we be still to witness Your glory that is all around us.

Jim Shaner lives in Honeybrook and is the founder of One Nation Under God—Walk Across America.

JUNE 4

Spiritual Giants

"And they sang a new song, saying: 'You are worthy to take the scroll and to open its seals, because you were slain, and with your blood you purchased for God persons from every tribe and language and people and nation. You have made them to be a kingdom and priests to serve our God, and they will reign on the earth.'"
Revelation 5:9-10

Each summer for the past four decades, my wife and I have taken our children and grandchildren on a pilgrimage to Iowa to visit our extended families. The Midwest is where we both grew up, living out childhood dreams as our worldviews were formed and nurtured by godly parents. Returning home every year forged close ties between our children and grandparents, aunts, uncles and cousins.

One recent summer I did something I had not done before. I found myself in the graveyard of the tiny town where I lived my boyhood years. I spent time strolling through the cemetery, looking for the resting places of people who had a profound influence on me. Among the many names I recognized was a man whose grass I mowed, the garage owner who loaned me money for my first lawn mower, the shopkeeper who gave me my first job and one of my favorite teachers.

The faces of our past are so important. We each have a history filled with names inscribed on our memories. Many of us are blessed to have histories filled with spiritual giants standing on the truthfulness of God's Word. We recount stories to our children and grandchildren of God's hand on our lives, just as did the people of Israel.

Revelation 5:9-10 tells us God is preparing His children to be a people of gratitude. The worship of the redeemed in the age to come includes a shout of thanksgiving! Let us celebrate the people who helped shape our spiritual legacy by showing gratitude each day of our lives.

Thank You for the people who influenced us and helped shape our worldview. Truly, we are blessed. Not only as a people testifying to God's faithfulness, but as the redeemed Bride of Christ testifying to His glory.

Peter W. Teague, Ed.D., is president of Lancaster Bible College.

JUNE 5

Put on the Yoke of Christ

"Come to me, all you who labor and are heavy laden, and I will give you rest. Take my yoke upon you and learn from me, for I am gentle and lowly in heart, and you will find rest for your souls. For my yoke is easy and my burden is light." Matthew 11:28 (New King James Version)

Many people cling to the first verse of this passage saying, "Come to Jesus, all you who are weary and tired, and He will give you rest." But I believe the second sentence is the most important one. "Take [His] yoke upon you and learn from [Him], for [He is] gentle and lowly in heart, and then you will find rest for your souls."

Jesus calls us to walk with Him in obedience and surrender, allowing Him to lead us. He invites us to learn what He is like—gentle and humble—and walk with Him in His Spirit of humility and lowliness of mind.

I have practiced putting on Jesus' yoke whenever I have felt proud, too proud to admit someone else was right, and I was wrong. And it worked!

When I deliberately put on the yoke of Christ and remember that He is gentle and humble, I am empowered to lay aside my pride and walk with Jesus in His humility. It brings such rest and contentment to my soul! It frees me from having to be right all of the time. It takes my focus off of me and on to Christ.

Father, thank You for Jesus. He is the exact representation of Your tender and compassionate nature, Your complete selflessness and willingness to become as nothing to lift us up. Thank You!

Dolores Walker is a wife, mother and grandmother and lives in Lititz.

JUNE 6

Say Yes to God

"Do not conform any longer to the pattern of this world, but be transformed by the renewing of your mind." Romans 12:2

I had the privilege of growing up in a Christian family that attended church regularly. From a young age, I was taught Bible stories and biblical principles. I received Jesus as my Savior when I was nine years old.

As a teenager, I got the impression that being a Christian was a lot of "don'ts." If I could just avoid certain things and not look like the rest of the world, I could be a good Christian. When I asked why I couldn't dress like some of my friends or do some things they did, I was told that the Bible says we should not conform to the world. Most of the emphasis was on outward appearance, looking different from "worldly people" on the outside. So this was my early idea of what it meant to be set apart for God.

It wasn't until later in my twenties that I realized there was more to Romans 12:2 than not being conformed to the world. The second part of the verse says we should be transformed by the renewing of our minds. There has to be an inward work by the Spirit of God to transform our minds. I discovered that being a Christian is about saying yes to God. It's focusing on doing the things God asks us and empowers us to do, rather than focusing on trying to avoid certain things. As we focus on saying yes to God and obeying His Word, saying no to wrong things (or even second-best things) will become almost second nature. Then we will truly be set apart for God.

Lord, thank You for helping me to discover that being set apart for God is a positive, not a negative thing. Help me say yes to You in every aspect of my life today.

Jane Nicholas lives in Elizabethtown is a part of Hershey Evangelical Free Church. She serves as an intercessor for various missionaries and ministries.

JUNE 7

Life Choices

"He who has begun a good life in you will complete it until the day of Jesus Christ!" Philippians 1:6

Life is full of joys and sorrows. I find the time I grow the most is when something is going on. Whether it is something at work, at home or in my family's lives, how I react is always my choice. I can choose to bring Jesus glory in the situation or I can choose to do things my own way.

I wish I could say I always handle life well, but that isn't the truth. I do find, however, that as I mature in Christ I look at life differently. I find things that happened to me earlier in life do not need to control my life now. It took me a long time to learn that lesson.

Who I am in Christ does not depend on who I was as a child or how I was treated as a child. Those things can influence me for bad or good, but when I choose to let God be in control, He can change me.

I can use my past to help other people who may have had similar situations, or I can let it rule me. It's up to me to respond to God or wallow in self-pity over what happened in the past. I choose to allow Jesus to make me a new person in Christ.

We may not be able to control events, but we can control our attitude and response to them.

Father, help me always to seek You for everything in my life. Let me see that You are good all the time.

Christine Harsh is married to Roger for forty years, is the mother of Bonnie and Steve and grandmother to Zack, Tyler, Cody and Riley.

JUNE 8

Two for One Special!

"I can do everything through him who gives me strength."
Philippians 4:13

I am a survivor of fourteen years of being bound by panic attacks. Although the Lord healed me of this gripping terror, I had by-products of the attacks: being afraid of traffic jams and of bridges.

One day I had to travel to Pensacola, Florida, with my two children. Our flight left first thing in the morning. I packed the kids and our suitcases and prayed that our travel would be uneventful—no traffic was my main prayer request. As most of you know, it would require a miracle to encounter no traffic jams to Philadelphia during the morning rush hour.

Sure enough, on the way to the airport, there was total gridlock merging onto Interstate 95. My heart pounded. The lies in my head that insisted my fears were greater than Jesus' healing overwhelmed me. I repeated the above verse over and over to counteract those lies. The more I focused on the Lord and His promise, the better mentally I became. I asked the Lord to get the traffic moving so we wouldn't miss our flight, not because of fear. The traffic started moving and we flew to Florida, but that wasn't the end of my struggles.

Once in Pensacola, my next feat required crossing the bridge to get us to the island where we were staying. There wasn't just one bridge but two. I was so unnerved and not sure what to do, but remembering my time with the Lord on Interstate 95 caused me to rely on that verse again to sustain me in my time of need. That day I was totally healed of my fear of bridges and traffic jams.

Thank You, Lord, for healing me completely. Help us to remember that sometimes You do not answer our prayers exactly as we desire, but You use situations to bring complete healing within.

Eileen Christiansen, once and for all, is completely healed of panic attacks and the by-products of them as well.

JUNE 9

On Being a Philadelphian

"If one falls down, his friend can help him up." Ecclesiastes 4:10

I love coffee. In fact, a little corner of Starbucks is my second office. When I enter, the employees lovingly call out my nickname—"Big Daddy."

Together, we've gone to baseball games and on bus trips. I was even invited to a manager's baby shower.

It is nice to have a place where we are recognized, a place where everyone knows our name, a place where they know how we take our coffee. Places like this are important to our well-being because we live in an increasingly alienated society that replaces front porches with fenced-in patios. We may not know our neighbors. We can feel all alone in a crowd. It is not the quantity of people in our life that matters, it is the quality of the relationships we enjoy that counts.

King Solomon said in Ecclesiastes: "There was a man all alone; he had neither son nor brother. There was no end to his toil, yet his eyes were not content with his wealth. 'For whom am I toiling?'" he asked, 'And why am I depriving myself of enjoyment?' This too is meaningless—a miserable business!

Two are better than one, because they have a good return for their work: If one falls down, his friend can help him up; but pity the man who falls and has no one to help him up!

Solomon depicts our need for deep, lasting friendships. More than money, we need friends. More than entertainment, we need friends. More than career advancement and recognition, we need life-giving relationships. Even if you live in Bird-in-Hand, I challenge you to be a Philadelphian. *Philia* means the love of a good friend and brother. When someone cares about you, includes you or helps you, they are a true Philadelphian. So, who can you treat with brotherly love today?

Dear Lord, You love us by extending grace and mercy. Help us to be true Philadelphians by extending brotherly love to friends and strangers alike.

Dan Houck is a member of the Table Community Church, Lancaster.

JUNE 10

Children Bring Pleasure

"His unchanging plan has always been to adopt us into His own family by bringing us to Himself through Jesus Christ. And this gave Him great pleasure." Ephesians 1:5 (New Living Translation)

After grieving the sudden death of my husband in 2005, eventually I sensed that God wanted me to marry again. Given my age and the likely age of my future husband, I thought any children he had might be in their upper teens or twenties.

When Todd, a widower, and I met, we began to see that God brought our lives together. But I had one concern. Todd had four children. They were twenty-four, twenty-three, eighteen and seven. "A seven-year-old!" I thought. "My four kids are adults and I'm a grandmother now. Do I have what it takes to be a mother to a young girl again? Do I have enough love—the love that Becky needs from a mom?" I repeatedly submitted my fears to the truth that if God wanted Todd and me to be husband and wife, then God must also want me to be Becky's mom.

After a year and a half of marriage, I'm so thankful for the gift of Todd in my life. And I am repeatedly surprised and delighted by the joy and pleasure that Becky—and being her mom—brings. God asked me to embrace her as part of my family, and He gave us deep love for each other.

Our heavenly Father set the example of welcoming new members into a family. Sin separated us from Him and, essentially, made us orphans. But even before Adam sinned, God had already established an adoption plan that would bring us back to Him. Through Jesus, we become God's children. And this gives God great pleasure.

Father, thank You for the love You have lavished on us, that we might be called Your children. We desire to bring You pleasure.

Kati Swisher serves with Susquehanna Valley Pregnancy Services and attends Cornerstone Christian Fellowship with Todd and Becky.

JUNE 11

Paying It Forward

"My times are in your hands; deliver me from my enemies and from those who pursue me. Let your face shine on your servant; save me in your unfailing love." Psalm 31:15-16

According to the footnote in my study Bible, all the events and circumstances of my life are in God's hands. That means He's sovereign. It means that He doesn't forget about me. I'm always held by Him. No matter what happens, good or bad, He never lets go of me. That makes me smile peacefully, because He pulled me out of the miry clay of sin and guided me to an understanding that all my guilt and shame were taken on by Christ at the cross. Because of that, I have His righteousness. I'm not guilty. At times, I sure felt guilty and satan accuses me of being guilty. Since I've learned the truth, I've lived in freedom. I am now free to be Christ's servant, and that means coming alongside other sinners and letting them know what Christ has done for me. I have to admit that I wish I did that more often than I do.

Do you know this same freedom? Are you looking for opportunities to help others understand that they too can be free? We are forgiven. Why withhold that news from others who can have the same forgiveness? No matter what has happened to us or what we've done, God blesses us with the same wonderful benefits. I'm amazed at the times that He uses the knowledge of my past sins to help someone else and rewards me at the same time. That is the loving God we serve. He wants me to have the joy of seeing others set free from their shameful past. God uses a broken vessel because I understand brokenness. I've felt shame and been redeemed. He wants to renew, transform and heal you too. Then He wants you to pass it on.

Father, thank You that You save us in Your unfailing love and allow us to be a part of Your kingdom work. Help us be Your messengers. Amen.

Sharon Neal attends Lancaster Evangelical Free Church in Lititz, where she serves on the Shepherding team, teaches kindergarten and women's Bible studies, and volunteers with Susquehanna Valley Pregnancy Services in post-abortion Bible studies.

JUNE 12

Give the Gift of Prayer

"And pray in the Spirit on all occasions with all kinds of prayers and requests. With this in mind, be alert and always keep on praying for all the saints." Ephesians 6:18

This past February, I had the incredible opportunity to join my husband and six other team members on a medical mission trip to Uganda, Africa. I spent several days helping the Ugandan people see better with glasses donated by Lion's Club members. What a joy it was to see the smiles on their faces when the correct prescription was found for them. Young and old alike were blessed with improved vision.

After traveling ten hours to a mountain village, we stayed in tents and had medical clinic for two days. This was when I had the privilege to pray for each patient after they saw the doctor and received needed medication. I was encouraged by the strength God gave me to persevere in prayer. The Ugandans would express so much appreciation for the prayer they received and I felt like I was giving them a precious gift. There is so much power in prayer!

A woman came for prayer requesting deliverance from demons. As I began to speak the Name of Jesus, she shook violently. After a while, I asked for God's peace to come upon her and she immediately was still. As we share our hearts with God, His love showers down upon us and those to whom we minister. We may not know all the Lord has done in the lives of these people, but we can rest assured He is working in them to do good because He has compassion on all He has made (Psalm 145:9).

Lord, help us to be alert and always willing to pray for those in need. May we be mindful of this gift we can give to others which has the power to change their lives for eternity.

Karen Jackson assists her husband, Scott, coordinator of DMI Medical Missions and volunteers with DMI and Transforming Leaders International. She is on the elder team at Oasis Fellowship.

JUNE 13

Where Are Our Evangelists?

When Jesus ascended he gave gifts to the church: "apostles, prophets, evangelists, pastors and teachers." Ephesians 4:11

Unless God turns things around many churches will become extinct as many young adults are dropping out of church.

Questionnaires designed to reveal our spiritual gifts indicate that 10 percent of Christians have the gift of evangelism. We affirm librarians, ushers, secretaries, administrative assistants, Sunday school teachers, small group leaders, pastors and so forth. Why don't we call and affirm evangelists? The Ethiopian Church calls evangelists before they call pastors. What would happen if we empower 10 percent of our members as evangelists? Let's pray, affirm and empower them for the ministry of evangelism. This change will be a major step in turning our churches from decline to growth.

You may say, "Shouldn't everyone be a witness not just a certain few?" Of course. Acts 1:8 says that God gives us power when the Holy Spirit comes upon us to be witnesses in Jerusalem—that means we witness to those we rub shoulders with. It's helpful to ask, "Shouldn't everyone be a teacher, a giver or an intercessor?" Of course, but some have the gift of teaching, the gift of giving, or the gift of intercession. To some God has given the gift of evangelism even though everyone is to be a witness for the Lord.

I believe if you have a sister in your congregation who has a special gift of relating to her unchurched neighbors, and you free her by taking care of her children from time to time or clean her house so she can minister to her neighbors, you will receive the same reward she will receive for witnessing to her neighbors. Let's recognize and empower our evangelists.

Lord Jesus, thank You for the gift of evangelism in our churches. Help me to encourage them. Empower me to use my gift of evangelism as a faithful and fruitful witness for You.

Dave Eshleman served as pastor and church planter for fifty years.

JUNE 14

Folding Our Nation's Flag

"Blessed is the nation, whose God is the Lord…." Psalm 33:12 (The Living Bible)

"God-devotion makes a country strong; God avoidance leaves people weak." Proverbs 14:34 (The Message)

This summer I was surprised and inspired one Friday evening when Ephrata orough was celebrating "Hometown Heroes," service men and women, firefighters, first responders, police officers and even a next-door neighbor.

During the celebration, I learned one of the meanings associated with the thirteen folds of the American flag when it is lowered from a flag pole or given to the grieving next of kin at a veteran's burial ceremony.

The first fold symbolizes life, the second one represents our belief in eternal life and the third honors veterans who died defending our country. The fourth fold reminds us of our weaker nature and how we are to turn to God in times of peace as well as asking for His divine guidance during wartime. The fifth fold represents a tribute to our country and the sixth admonishes us to keep our hearts true to our country and God. A tribute to the Armed Forces is the seventh fold, while the eighth honors the One who entered the "valley of the shadow of death" so that we might see the light of day. This fold also esteems mothers. The ninth fold is a tribute to womanhood and the tenth salutes fathers. The eleventh fold glorifies the God of Abraham, Isaac and Jacob while the twelfth represents eternity and exalts the Father, Son and Holy Spirit. The final fold of the flag leaves the stars prominently visible calling us to always be mindful of our nation's motto, "In God We Trust."

We need not fear that politicians can "legislate" God out of our lives, for His Holy Spirit abides within us when we ask Him to permanently reside in our hearts. Even a simple "Hometown Heroes" celebration reminded me that God is still glorified in our nation.

Lord, enable me to bring You glory in everything I do … taking a walk, showing gratitude to a person in uniform, serving my community and even in properly folding our nation's flag.

Susan Kulka is a writer, wife, mother and grandmother. She and her husband, Michael, attend the Worship Center.

JUNE 15

Keep Your Eyes to the Skies

"The arrival of the Son of Man isn't something that you go to see. He comes like swift lightning to you!" Matthew 24:27 (The Message)

Those who go camping regularly have their stories to tell. Our stories have delighted many and prompted much laughter over the years. On some occasions the experiences were not funny at the time. But as many avid RV'ers would agree, the joys of camping outweigh the occasional unpleasant experiences. We learned the importance of "keeping your eyes to the skies" during a recent camping outing in western Pennsylvania. Our RV was set up at an ideal wooded spot near the base of a mountain alongside a river.

While sitting in our chairs, enjoying the sunny warm weather, reading and dozing, we did not realize that a violent summer rainstorm was approaching on the horizon. The ominous clouds and thunderheads were obscured by the mountain. Even though we responded as quickly as possible and had things secured as best as we could, the driving rain accompanied by severe wind gusts got the best of us and whipped up our large awning ... ripping apart one of the awning arms. We were saddened that the awning supports were damaged, yet grateful that the damage was limited and that we were not hurt when the top portion of a huge tree fell twenty-five yards from our campsite.

I love how the Holy Spirit uses the occurrences that we experience as practical life lessons. After a sudden repeat storm the following day, I was reminded of Matthew 24:30, 31: "... the sign that the Son of Man is coming will appear in the sky and there will be deep mourning among all the peoples of the earth. And they will see the Son of Man coming on the clouds of heaven with power and great glory ... And He will send out His angels with the mighty blast of a trumpet, and they will gather his chosen ones from all over the world ... from the farthest ends of the earth and heaven." It is crucial no matter what our activities that we need to be aware of the signs of the times and to "keep our eyes to the skies."

Lord, thank You for empowering us to live ever mindfully of the Holy Spirit's indwelling presence and that You are returning to gather Your chosen ones to live with You for eternity.

Reyna Britton relies on God's wisdom and delights in encouraging, exhorting and praying for others.

JUNE 16

The Three O'Clock Wake-up Call

"He, the Holy Spirit, will guide you into all truth …" John 16:13

My wife, Rose, and I had gone to bed, but I was having one of those nights I just couldn't get to sleep. It seemed the harder I tried to sleep the less I did. I remember looking at Rose sleeping contentedly beside me and then looking at the clock which read three in the morning.

We had to get up at 6:00 a.m. so I was telling myself, sleep. All of a sudden Rose sat straight up and said, "Pray for Marion," and then went right back to sleep. Wow! I got out of bed, took the few steps to our living room and starting praying for Marion. I didn't know what time I went back to bed, but it seemed like I just fell asleep when the alarm went off. I asked Rose how she slept and if she had any dreams. She said she slept well, and she had no dream or any recollection of sitting up in bed.

We waited until 7:00 a.m. and called the only Marion we knew. I asked how she was and if anything happened lately. She's a nurse, and she worked last night. A man had come into the hospital on drugs, and the doctors had hand restraints on him as they sedated him. After he fell asleep they had removed the restraints. Marion went into his room to check his pulse when all of a sudden he rose up from the bed, put his hands around her neck and started choking her. Suddenly, the man's eyes got large as if he had seen something in the room. He let go of Marion and fell back into bed. I asked Marion if she knew what time that was. Yes, I was taking his pulse at 3:00 a.m. The Holy Spirit certainly will guide us!

Father God, thank You for Your Holy Spirit who guides, protects and talks to us for the sake of our own good ... even three o'clock in the morning.

Steve Shank is a strategic coach for Eastern Mennonite Missions.

JUNE 17

Father's Delight

"And the Holy Spirit descended upon him in bodily form like a dove. And a voice came from heaven, 'You are my Son, the Beloved; with You I am well pleased.'" Luke 3:21-22 (New Revised Standard)

It was an amazing concert of a Jewish troubadour, whose love for Jesus truly captured the audience. But when his daughter appeared on the stage, an electric charge rushed through my body. I knew that fragile girl was a powerful worshipper.

As the child began to sing, the beauty of her voice overwhelmed me. To hide my tears I closed my eyes. "I wonder what her father feels right now," I asked myself and opened my eyes. I saw an expression of delight on her father's face. Playing the piano in accompaniment to his daughter's singing, the father was pleasingly absorbing every high and every low key of his child's voice. How tenderly he was observing her moving on the stage and pouring out her heart both before the audience and the Lord. How proud he was of what his daughter was doing for God's glory.

Is this the way God the Father felt when His Son came onto the stage of our world history? How pleased our heavenly Father must have been watching every move of his Beloved Son.

When the divine music ceased to flow, we the audience also witnessed sincere love of the human father for his daughter, as well as the daughter's appreciation of what her dad meant to and had done for her.

We all have our unique purposes in life. We do not all need to be musicians in order to please God. But we can glorify Him by believing in His Son's life, death and resurrection; by loving Jesus and the ones He brings into our life; and by fulfilling our own mission assigned to us by our heavenly Father, through His Son Jesus, in the power of the Holy Spirit.

Lord, bless us to be a delight to Your heart and to others.

Yulia Bagwell, Beth Yeshua, a housewife-caregiver, a writer and a translator for *The Upper Room* devotional magazine.

JUNE 18

I Missed Out

"For I know the plans I have for you, declares the Lord, plans to prosper you and not to harm you, plans to give you hope and a future." Jeremiah 29:11

When I was twenty-one, let me rephrase. When I was a firm, slender, dare I say, beautiful, twenty-one-year-old, I thought God's command to stay sexually pure until marriage was the worst thing He could ever ask a person to do. Now, I'm a sagging, widening, unmarried, thirty-something virgin. My days of sexual appeal are far behind me and all my friends are married and gone. I wonder if I have missed out. After careful consideration and prayer, I realize, I did.

I missed out on throwing away what I could never give back. I've had an impenetrable shield against men who say whatever they must to get what they want. I missed out on heartbroken morning afters filled with shocking disappointment. Not all of my friends were that lucky.

Where I once thought God was cruelly mocking my feelings, I now know He was protecting me like a loving Father. Knowing I am under His care has kept me from growing bitter. There are good men out there and as long as I stay close to my loving protector, I will not miss out.

Dear Lord, I am so thankful that Your ways are higher than my ways and Your thoughts higher than my thoughts. Please give me the courage to have faith and trust You in all things.

Amy Swanson is a Bible college graduate. She lives with her one true love, her dog, in Downingtown. In her spare time, she is a horseback riding instructor and aspiring writer.

JUNE 19

God's Protection

"He who dwells in the secret place of the Most High shall abide under the shadow of the Almighty. I will say of the Lord, 'He is my refuge and my fortress; my God, in Him will I trust.'" Psalm 91:1, 2 (New King James Version)

Our medical team headed to Uganda where we set up a clinic in Kampala for two days, treating people with malaria, eye problems, asthma, STD's and skin diseases. A group of Ugandans served tirelessly beside us in each area of the clinic, translating for us and making our efforts effective. Our pharmacist got sick for twenty-four hours but his wife carried on for him without missing a beat.

Day three found us driving ten hours to the Congo border to a mountain village that had no running water or electricity. Our doctor became very sick and I found myself begging God to heal him and keep the rest of us well so that clinics could be held. We arrived after dark and the village children lined the road to greet us, clapping and cheering for our arrival. What a humbling reminder that we were there to do God's work and He would make a way for us. We set up tents in the dark, blowing up air mattresses by flashlight, which proved to be huge entertainment for the entire village. Some had never seen white people, so we provided lots of laughs for them.

We had two days of treating long lines of patients, eating food cooked over an outside fire, sleeping and washing up in tiny tents, hand painting hundreds of beautiful children and praying with villagers. Then we were off for the long ride back to the city. Riding shotgun in the van beside our Ugandan driver on the trip home proved to be the ride of my life: children dashed out in front of us, motorcycles spun off the berm, vehicles challenged us for the road. Nonetheless, we arrived safely back at our guesthouse late that night.

As I reflect on the trip, I see God's protection, provision and divine help to our entire team. He truly is my refuge and fortress.

Thank You, Most High that we can dwell in Your secret place and under Your shadow every day, not just in extraordinary times.

Mary Prokopchak leads a small group for DOVE Christian Fellowship in Elizabethtown.

JUNE 20

Sweet and Sour Summer

"Taste and see that the Lord is good." Psalm 34:8

Each year as the countdown to the end of the school year begins, a taste of summer is in the air. Each summer has its own expectations of fun flavors to anticipate.

As I write this devotional, another summer has just passed. It was a summer that sizzled back and forth between sweet and sour moments.

In the prophet Ezekiel's vision, Ezekiel ate God's message—His Word. Ezekiel found that God's digested Word was good for him as well as "sweet as honey." James' epistle contrasts the sweet with the sour when he says, "consider it pure joy, my brothers, whenever you face trials of many kinds...." The trials can be described as those sour experiences we taste in life. Ezekiel's vision was a reminder that we need to digest God's Word to prepare us and strengthen us for the trials that James says will come.

Whether you are served lemonade with or without sugar on a hot summer day, may you taste and see that the Lord is good!

Father God, help me to savor each moment You give to me—whether sweet or sour. May I stay conscious of You in every situation that I encounter today and everyday.

Rosene Hertzler and her husband, Ken, lives in York with their four children and is a part of the Valley View Alliance church family.

JUNE 21

Ordinary Days

"The thief comes only to steal and kill and destroy. I have come that they may have life, and have it to the full." John 10:10

Ask me about the highlights of my life and I'd probably spout off my wedding day, Bob's and my college graduations and air force commissions, travels to Israel and Egypt, Italy and Greece, and the births of our four children and three grandchildren.

But those occasions only add up to several weeks out of fifty-four years. What about the other fifty-three years and forty-six weeks of my life?

Those were the "ordinary" days—filled with small, commonplace, seemingly insignificant events that form the brick and mortar in the building of our lives.

We're often reminded of the wonder of simple things when we no longer can enjoy them. Red beet eggs, Lebanon bologna and shoo-fly pie are items that one can order only in eastern Pennsylvania without odd looks. Barn silos, mountains, four seasons and lightning bugs are "a few of my favorite things" after residing several years in west Texas and Louisiana.

Not often enough do we ponder the most gentle details … our children's excitement for a "love" note in their packed school lunches, or hugs going out the door, or reading bedtime stories, sharing the happenings of the day at the evening family meal, learning what our children are thinking during myriad drives to soccer practice, giving baths and blowing bubbles, exchanging conversations of both fears and dreams.

Perhaps it's these ordinary days that residents in assisted-living homes miss the most. I believe when we are received into Glory, God will ease us into His wonder, not with His heavenly throne, but with our familiar blessed ordinary of barn silos, mountains and fields of green corn.

Lord, help us to live life to Your definition of fullness, to appreciate each moment, object or person so we are in awe of all the simple, gentle wonderments You provide for us.

Tamalyn Jo Heim enjoys the wonderment of over eighteen barn silos from her back porch in Willow Street.

JUNE 22

God's Plans

"In Him we were also chosen, having been predestined according to the plan of Him who works out everything in conformity with the purpose of His will, in order that we, who were the first to hope in Christ, might be for the praise of His glory." Ephesians 1:11-12

It has been nearly fifty years since an experience happened that I was too young to remember, but I can picture it through the eyes of my mother. I was three, my older brother Dave was five and my little sister was just one. We were visiting my grandparents' farm south of Erie. My grandparents and my Uncle Homer were going for a ride in their Studebaker, and my grandmother was going to take my brother and me along.

This was in the days before seat belts, much less car seats, but my grandpa was a careful driver and they were not going far, so my mother did not give it a second thought. We walked to the end of the long concrete porch, with Dave and I each holding one of Grandma's work-worn hands. She got to the end of the porch and hesitated. Then she turned around and resolutely came back down the porch and returned us to my mother.

Then she spun again and climbed into the passenger seat next to my Grandpa. On a sharp curve in the road, a few miles from the farm, a drunk driver crossed over the center line in his pickup truck and struck my grandparents' car head-on. They were killed instantly and my uncle was severely injured. (Ironically, at the same spot that Grandpa's father had been killed years before.) God had other plans for my brother and me.

Lord, may we consider each day the specific way You called us to glorify You!

Chip Mershon is a family physician at Cornerstone Family Health and attends Lancaster Evangelical Free Church.

JUNE 23

Enthusiasm Not Limited by Imperfections

"Work with enthusiasm, as though working for the Lord."
Ephesians 6:7 (New Living Translation)

Two years ago I was given an opportunity to raise a puppy handicapped from birth. Born with three strong legs but with only half of one of his front legs, it was obvious that what most dogs did with ease would require much more effort on his part.

Watching Tre's response to his handicap has given me a whole new perspective about what it means to do those things which we were created to do, and to do so with enthusiasm for the glory of God in spite of any handicap or imperfection we may perceive we have.

Learning to "heel" and "lie down" was not easy for him, but what I did notice was the zeal with which he would try. With gusto, I watched him tackle any obstacle presented to the dogs in his obedience class, and to my surprise, overcome each one.

He showed me that with determination even a dog with only one full front leg can learn to "doggie paddle," and now he nearly outswims other dogs in the pool. His enthusiasm and zeal for living in spite of his imperfection is contagious. He doesn't appear to allow anything to hold him back from living the life for which he was created. Today he carries this enthusiasm to the elderly in retirement homes, and is being trained to minister to children, especially those with special needs.

Each day I observe Tre giving his all. No one told Tre he's handicapped or explained to him that he's not perfect. I'm glad he wouldn't understand it even if someone did. Tre just goes about his day doing the best he can with what he is blessed with and because of this, can be used to bring glory to God by being a blessing.

Lord, may we always look to You and not our shortcomings as we enthusiastically live out the plans and purposes you have for our lives.

Anita Wolfe is affiliated with KPETS and attends the Worship Center with her husband, Gregg.

JUNE 24

Gain from Loss

"And we know that in all things God works for the good of those who love him, who have been called according to his purpose." Romans 8:28

We adopted Johnna when she was eight years old. She had moved seven times, experiencing neglect and abuse in various forms before landing in our home. She had classic Reactive Attachment Disorder and had no intention of making the "mistake" of attaching to yet another adult(s) who would betray her or let her down.

Just before Johnna's junior year, she decided to leave our home and move in with members of her birth family. She had the false notion that they would be less strict with her than we had been.

In September of Johnna's senior year, she became pregnant. Her birth family kicked her out and she returned to live with us.

I was laid off from my job at the end of January. Day after day Johnna came home from school and talked with me because I was there. I wasn't judging. I was listening. We were laughing together.

Unemployment provided me with plenty of time to hang out with the kids and get to know Henry (father of Johnna's baby). I had encouraged the idea of adoption from the beginning, acknowledging that the final decision was theirs. In the final month of pregnancy, these two incredible young people made the decision to gift their son for adoption and change the lives of another family forever.

It was a beautiful choice, and the right one for all concerned. Johnna may have "lost" a baby in the process, but God gave her an entire family in return. She has become fully attached to me, her dad, her three sisters and her two brothers. God allowed Johnna to experience the loss of one, for the gain of many!

Oh Lord, thank You for being our Beginning and our End. Thank You for setting us apart and blessing our socks off as we watch You turn ashes into beauty.

Kristin Williams Balla is a member of the Praise Team of Upper Octorara Presbyterian Church in Parkesburg.

JUNE 25

Find Your Style

"I know this, I was blind, and now I can see!" John 9:25 (New Living Translation)

In John 9, Jesus healed a blind beggar. The Pharisees were upset that Jesus would heal on the Sabbath. They asked the beggar what he thought of the man who healed him. His answer was straightforward: "I was blind, now I see!"

connecting with our community

This experience applies not only to physical blindness but to spiritual blindness. All of us were blind spiritually until Jesus gave us sight. We too can say, "I was blind but now I see! Messiah Jesus changed my life. He can change yours too."

Testimonial evangelists usually are not people who became Christians as children and followed a steady path to spiritual maturity. Often they will say they thought they were Christians. They say, "I went to church and tried to live a good moral life. Then I turned control of my life over to Jesus and began to trust Jesus as my personal Savior. That decision made all the difference in the world. It was the best decision I ever made. If you are interested, I would love to tell you more."

A testimony is not preaching; it is basically giving facts about how Jesus has impacted your life. Paul used this approach in Acts 22 and 26 before the multitude in Jerusalem and before King Agrippa. You will find the following questions Paul asked in Acts 26 helpful as you think through your own testimony: Where were you spiritually before receiving Jesus? How did that affect you in your relationships? What caused you to consider Jesus as the solution to your needs? Specifically, how did you receive Christ? How did your life begin to change after you trusted Jesus? What other benefits have you experienced since becoming a Christian? Most of these questions can be answered in a sentence or two.

You have a testimony. Most seekers don't need to hear a sermon: they need a Christian like yourself to share with them how Jesus made a difference in your life. Your testimony will be one more step the Holy Spirit uses to bring them closer to kingdom citizenship.

Lord, loosen my tongue. I will share what You are doing for me.

Dave Eshleman served as pastor and church planter for fifty years.

JUNE 26

God, the Proud Parent

"See what great love the Father has lavished on us, that we should be called children of God! And that is what we are!" 1 John 3:1

When I volunteered to help with a group of three-year-olds, I noticed most kids, including mine, were scribbling in straight lines. But two kids were drawing with arcs and circles, creating faces. I remembered a preschool art teacher explaining this move from straight lines to curved ones was the expected progression in their development.

A few weeks later, I saw my son leap from drawing circles to drawing faces. I was thrilled to see his artistic ability bloom. Amazement and pride filled me.

I wonder if God feels the same when we reach a developmental milestone or finally "get" a lesson He'd been trying to teach. Until this moment, my thoughts of God as parent were often limited to wondering how God contends with us and our shortcomings. We can be so stubborn, reluctant to trust, thinking we know a way better than obeying Him. Imagining God getting excited when we grow is new to me ... but I think He must.

I wonder, too, if my "extra" sense of pride of seeing my child develop a talent or characteristic I have is something God experiences. It's an extra window between parent and child to really see and know each other. When we begin to do or be things that give us something in common with God, does God feel a deepening layer of kinship?

Now I have a new picture of God: like a soccer mom proud to see her child do what she always knew he was capable of accomplishing.

Dear Lord, help grow my desire to mature into the likeness of Christ, deepening the sense of belonging between us.

Renee Lannan, New Cumberland Church of the Nazarene, writes and cares for her family.

JUNE 27

The Apocalypse

"This calls for patient endurance and faithfulness on the part of God's people." Revelation 13:10

In recent years, a new wave of apocalyptic interest has been sparked. Movies like *2012*, books like *Left Behind* and Harold Camping's predicted rapture have all aroused debate. Amidst all of the end-times hype, it seems like a tsunami of confusion has washed into our churches. Many have turned to the pages of Revelation with hopes of sorting out the timeline of events and nail down answers to the confounding questions. Depending on how one reads this unveiling of Jesus Christ, it's easy to overlook the encouraging messages to the church.

As John writes down what he is seeing in this revelation, it's important to remember he's writing with a heavy heart of concern for the church. The churches in Asia, of which he was overseer, were suffering intense persecution for their faith. How could they stand strong in the midst of evil, war, famine, deception and death? What are the people of God to do amidst the growing wave of wickedness?

The answers to these relevant questions are found within the symbolic vision given to John. Images like Jesus walking among the lampstands, the church (Revelation 1:13), keeping Jesus centered in our daily lives. Worshipping God (chapter 4) and the Lamb (chapter 5) focuses our allegiance on Christ. Even though spiritual warfare abounds (chapter 12), satan has been overpowered by the blood of the Lamb. No matter how dark the world may become, only the believer has a song in his heart (chapter 14) because the best is yet to come (chapters 21, 22).

Do the messages of the Apocalypse scare you? Try rereading the book of Revelation. Instead of reading it as a timeline, look instead for the encouraging messages to the Church. In the midst of much uncertainty, I've found encouragement from God's vision given to John. It encourages me to be a faithful witness for Christ no matter what happens.

Lord, we acknowledge that we live in a culture that is more intrigued by the antichrist and his actions than in Jesus Christ. Increase our love for You and our passion to share the Gospel messages of hope. Enable Your church to be faithful witnesses today.

Wesley D. Siegrist pastors Erb Mennonite Church, Lititz.

JUNE 28

Generational Changes

"Let us therefore make every effort to do what leads to peace." Romans 14:19

While raising my children, I never suspected how their lives would influence others, especially my own. My two sons and I did things opposite of most other families when it came to who leads whom to God. They were in their late teens when they decided to become members of Petra Christian Fellowship. The pastor explained what it meant to become a member. When the pastor asked my sons if they were saved and had prayed to have God come into their lives, they answered that they had not. That day the pastor led them in a prayer and they asked Jesus to come into their hearts.

Little did my sons know that their becoming saved was the beginning of leading a family filled with generations of atheists to the Lord. As my sons grew up, married godly women and began to raise their children—my grandbabies—in the Lord, I watched how they handled life. Despite events that occurred and caused pain or difficulty in their lives, my sons persevered with peace and confidence in God that all would be handled. I watched my adult children and longed for the peace they demonstrated.

I, too, met with a pastor who explained how I could be saved. But I had so many unanswered questions about God, that I left without asking Jesus to come into my heart. However on the way home from that meeting, I had to pull my car to the side of the road and pray. I could not wait any longer to become a part of God's family. As soon as I was saved, I thought "it is finished." Little did I know that prayer was only the beginning of leading me into a new way of living. God was just getting started in changing our family's legacy.

Heavenly Father, I thank You for bringing my family closer to You. May each generation bring honor and glory to Your name and influence others to become part of the kingdom of God.

Connie Martin provides lay prayer ministry/counseling to women at her home and attends Petra Christian Fellowship.

JUNE 29

Walking in the SONshine

"I will lift up my eyes to the hills from whence comes my help. My help comes from the Lord who made heaven and earth."
Psalm 121:1-2

The majesty of the mountains called out to me on a beautiful morning in the Poconos of Pennsylvania. Summer had taken a long time getting here with a "longer than usual" winter full of challenges and stress. I had come to the mountains to take a fresh breath and gain new perspective while renewing my relationship with God. With the hectic schedule I had kept up during the winter months, I found it difficult to set aside the time to concentrate on Him. I knew that time spent focusing on Him meant spiritual strength for difficult days, and that without that consistent focus, my heart would feel restless and weak.

On this morning, the sun was shining brilliantly and the beauty of the river stretching through the hills made me eager to be outside. As I walked, I put my thoughts on the Lord, not on the circumstances of my life and every pressing need. A butterfly fluttered past me and sat very still on a nearby branch. Beautiful wings were spread to catch the warm sunlight. It stayed there as if gaining strength by basking in that warmth, then took off with vibrant energy soaring into the air. It seemed it had gained strength just by sitting in the sunshine. With my own heart feeling the need for strength, I realized that Christians are often like that butterfly. The pressures of our lives can sap our energies and cause us to forget that our strength comes from the one who can supply all our needs. Allowing ourselves the time to stop and sit still in the warmth of His love gives refreshing new strength to our "wings." When we are walking in the SONshine, His help is there and our hearts are renewed!

Precious Father, You made us for fellowship with You. Slow us down, Lord, to live each day in the warmth of Your presence.

Karen Knight is a former actress with Sight & Sound Theaters. She is an inspirational speaker, dramatist and concert artist for Heartsongs Ministries, Inc., Lancaster.

JUNE 30

Be Still

"Let be and be still, and know—recognize and understand—that I am God. I will be exalted among the nations! I will be exalted in the earth!" Psalm 46:10 (The Amplified Bible)

Viewed from my back porch, sunset is such a beautiful and peaceful time of day. God puts on such a gorgeous nightly show whether I pause to breathe in its beauty or not. Too many times I choose earthly pursuits or even a television program over the breathtaking scene which closes each day. Oh, how my elderly dad used to love sitting on our porch to meditatively end his day's activities.

However on one summer evening, I paused from cleaning the house to allow God's artwork to feed my soul. As I sat in my comfortable porch chair, I noticed the day was coming to a close with a clear western sky framed in a few high fluffy white clouds, which would shortly become a deep pink as the sun disappeared over the horizon. My eyes soon followed the rabbits peacefully feeding on a bedtime snack of clover, not worrying about tomorrow's provision. A robin was searching for a final worm to satisfy her hungry babies back in the nest before they all settled in for the night secure in the Father's care. My ears heard the gentle singing of other birds as they raised their final praise to God before sleep overtook them as well.

As daylight gave way to darkness, the fireflies began their evening ballet of gracefully rising from the grass and magically floating over the cornfield. A sight that always thrills my inner child, but also reminds me of the promise of resurrection in our lives.

Why does it take me so long to pause, sit with my Heavenly Father and listen to His whispers as He speaks to me through the beauty of His earthly creation?

Dear Father, enable me to choose You over all that tends so easily to distract me from seeking Your Presence in my daily life.

Susan Kulka is a writer, wife, mother and grandmother. She and her husband, Michael, attend the Worship Center.

Photo by Mark Van Scyoc

July

JULY 1

What's for Supper?

"His divine power has given us everything we need for life and godliness through our knowledge of him who called us by his own glory and goodness." 2 Peter 1:3

Sitting down at the table called "life," I realized I had an increased appetite to understand the circumstances I was in. In front of me was a concocted casserole dish that looked like limp leftovers. The dish represented a plethora of my problems. I was tired of coming to this same unappealing table of problems. Staring at the same old casserole, my appetite to sit at a different kind of table suddenly increased. I wanted to dine among linens, china and fresh flowers accompanied with served foods of my choosing that pleased my palate and satisfied me.

As I continued to stare at the table before me, I discovered that I was indeed sitting at a different table. Just like Psalm 23:5 reads "You prepare a table before me in the presence of my enemies," I recognized the table prepared for me was anointed by God. God Almighty was serving me exactly what I needed for "life and godliness" as described in 2 Peter 1:3. At the table God had called me, I could learn to live above my circumstances, even while eating concocted casserole dishes.

Oh, Father God, whatever table that You have prepared for me, I know that You will anoint for my good and Your glory. When I want to complain about leftovers or go to a finer restaurant, enable and equip me to savor the meal You have prepared for me. Thank You for limp leftovers to strengthen me for Your higher purposes.

Rosene Hertzler lives in York with her husband and four children and attends Valley View Alliance Church.

JULY 2

The Impossible Dream Came True

"Call unto me and I will answer thee, and show thee great and mighty things, which thou knowest not." Jeremiah 33:3 (King James Version)

Early in my life, at a Bible camp, I decided that I would like to become a missionary. I knew very little about the Bible or about God except that He loved me as well as He loved the whole world. But I was a small, shy, poor little girl from Kentucky. What could I do? I kept praying that God would show me what He wanted me to do and to guide me to do it. He definitely answered.

With God's help I went to two schools where I studied the Bible and to another where I learned a little about medical work. There were several setbacks and discouragement, but God kept nudging me along. Eventually, He gave me a husband who had the same goals that I had. Together we kept reminding ourselves of Jeremiah 33:3. My husband leaned on John 10:4: "When he putteth forth His own sheep, He goeth before them, and the sheep follow him: for they know His voice." In 1959 we arrived in Dutch New Guinea and served the Lord for sixteen years.

None of the many tribal languages in New Guinea were written at that time, so we had to begin listening, writing it down and trying to discern its meaning. As soon as we learned enough, we began telling the people about God and His son Jesus who died for them. Previously they had believed in evil spirits who sought to harm them. So, when they understood that the True God loved them and wanted to help them, they readily accepted our message.

By the time we came home, about twenty churches had been planted and some of the Bible had been translated. Today the whole Bible is translated. Those twenty churches, and many more, are thriving. God has indeed done "great and mighty" things.

Our Father, I thank You for those who will be in Heaven because You made it possible for me to become a missionary. Help us all to do Your will each day, and to remember that You can do great and mighty things.

Lorrie Lockhart, a retired missionary, attends Calvary Church in Lancaster.

JULY 3

Comfortable or Crazy?

"Whatever you do, do all to the glory of God." 1 Corinthians 10:31

A customer called to tell my husband that their air conditioner needed to be fixed. Steve asked the customer, "Mrs. G. doesn't like to be uncomfortable, right?" Mr. G. responded, "Yep. That's right."

I began thinking how that applies to our lives as believers. How many times do we just want to be comfortable? We don't like getting hot and sweaty. We just want a nice cool ride.

In *Crazy Love*, Frances Chan challenges us: "Having faith often means doing what others see as crazy. Something is wrong when our lives make sense to unbelievers."

Do our lives seem crazy to those around us or are we doing the "status quo"? God can use each of us. Everyone has a different story. Everyone has a different gifting. The most important thing is, "Are we using what God has given us (our talents, time and so forth) to honor and glorify Him and bring people to the kingdom?" Are we stepping out in faith and doing something "crazy"?

"Don't think you need to be some great preacher or have theological training to share the gospel. To be a preacher, all you have to do is obey Jesus.

"Simply share those things from God's Word that He has placed in your heart. If you can tell another person about what Jesus has done in your life, you will be surprised how interested people are."

According to Brother Yun's wise words in "Living Waters": Your testimony is a powerful weapon.

Dear Lord, reveal to us how we can be "crazier" and less comfortable in this life. Thank You for the giftings and abilities You give us to carry out our call. May we be obedient.

Lynnea Hameloth is wife to the best mechanic around, who also fixes her air conditioner, and mama to six awesome kids. The Hameloths attend DOVE E-town.

JULY 4

Freedom

"If the Son makes you free, you will be free indeed." John 8:36

Today throughout our nation, we celebrate our country's independence from England and the oppression of King George. It is important to have these moments where we celebrate. Sometimes we forget that we are free. We get comfortable with our freedom and forget the price that was paid and of the bondage in which people once lived. When that first day of freedom is so long ago, we may forget the past.

People, who are deep in bondage to wrong behaviors and attitudes, can usually recall those first days of freedom. They will say things such as; "It was one year ago today that I took my last drink and had my last sniff of crack."

We generally remember the feelings from oppression of injustice and the bondage of hatred if we have experienced it recently, but in time the memory becomes distant.

Scripture is clear that God hates oppression and injustice. He loves freedom. In Isaiah 63, Christ is revealed as the One coming to deliver us from oppression and to bring freedom to those whose hearts are held in captivity. We can honor those that paid a price for our freedom, because Christ modeled for us the reality that freedom is costly. As Christians, we can celebrate our nation's freedom from oppression because our God is the author of freedom.

Father, we thank You for being the author of all freedom. Thank You for hating injustice and oppression. We are grateful for our nation's the freedom. Thank You for the courage and perseverance our founding fathers paid for freedom. Grant our nation the strength and courage to continue to stand for freedom and fight against injustices.

Jere Shertzer is president/CEO of Water Street Ministries, serves on the executive team of the Regional Church of Lancaster County and attends Ephrata Community Church.

JULY 5

New Hope

"The Lord is good to those whose hope is in Him, to the one who seeks Him; it is good to wait quietly for the salvation of the Lord." Lamentations 3:25-26

I was on a forty-minute lunch break from my part-time position at the chiropractor's office. I took advantage of the warm and windy spring day to walk around the path through the adjoining community. In the center was a playground.

I was chatting with the Lord as I walked, wondering again how I would survive on the limited hours I was working, how much longer until I would see restoration in my family and other general feelings of loneliness and discouragement. I said I trusted Him, yet could not "see" how His plan was going to unfold. So, I asked Him to give me new hope for the day.

On the second trip through the neighborhood, I had an urge to stop and swing for a bit at the playground. A little girl waved to me from the sliding board. She was with her daddy. She took his hand and led him over to the swing next to me. With such sweet innocence, she told me that she was almost three and a half. I showed her how to pump her legs so we could reach the sky together. When we did, I felt free and like a little girl again myself.

Soon, it was time for me to get back to the office. Before I left, she asked my name.

I answered, "My name is Marti, but my grandkids call me Grandma MJ. What's your name?"

"My name is Hope," she replied.

And so it was that at the very moment I needed it, God sent me "new" hope.

Father, You are so good ... just when I need it, You manifest Your presence in my life. You fill me with new hope for the future. I submit my life to You for Your honor and Your glory.

Marti Evans attends Water's Edge Community Church in Annville and is on the board of directors for Lebanon Valley Youth for Christ.

JULY 6

Results of Choices

"Love suffers long [and] is kind; love does not envy; love does not parade itself, is not puffed up; does not behave rudely, does not seek its own, is not provoked, thinks no evil." 1 Corinthians 13:4-5 (New King James Version)

Life is a series of choices. As I look back over my years and assess choices I have made, I realize that more often than not the options available each time either were an opportunity to show a reflection of self-centeredness or a reflection of love for another.

Day-to-day living has shown me that to choose on the side of love brings life. One particular time loudly stands out and opens my eyes to this simple but monumental concept. To some people, what might have seemed like a simple act of foregoing a long-awaited opportunity in order to be able to do something for someone else, instead, resulted in that person recognizing and being so appreciative of this selfless act that it opened the door for them to understand and receive the love that God has for them. Such a softening of the heart, resulting from the right choice that I had made, allowed this person to be open to being ushered into the Kingdom of Heaven in a way that changed a life forever.

Dear Lord, help me to put myself aside in such a way that allows me to be an expression of such a pure love that I continually put others before myself. I pray, Lord, that as this love touches another's life that it opens the door for them to receive all that You have for them, beyond anything they could ever imagine.

Wendy S. Domkoski is restored to wholeness through understanding her identity in Christ. She attends Harvest Chapel in Abbottstown.

JULY 7

Confrontational

"You followed God's prearranged plan. With the help of lawless Gentiles, you nailed him to the cross and murdered him.... So let it be clearly known by everyone in Israel that God has made this Jesus whom you crucified to be both Lord and Messiah! Peter's word convicted them deeply, and they said to him and to the other apostles, 'Brothers, what should we do?' Peter replied, 'Each of you must turn from your sins and turn to God, and be baptized in the name of Jesus Christ for the forgiveness of your sins. Then you will receive the gift of the Holy Spirit.'" Acts 2:23, 36-38 (New Living Translation)

Peter laid it on the line and three thousand responded. Some people must be confronted directly for the Holy Spirit to get through to them. Maybe you have the personality, temperament and the ability to confront under the guidance of the Holy Spirit so people are faced with their sin and their need of the Savior.

Billy Graham often used the phrase: "You must be born again!" My friend Joe used the confrontational approach. There were times when I was embarrassed as we walked into a home and he abruptly asked, "Is your dog saved yet?" He then shared what Jesus did for him and asked them if they wanted to receive Jesus into their life? When Joe suddenly died because of a heart attack, I preached at his funeral and gave opportunity for persons to share how Joe touched their lives. For more than an hour one person after another spoke of Joe's boldness and how they appreciated his witness. One person from another state flew in to attend the funeral and thank Joe's family for his witness.

Acts 4:13, 19-20: "The members of the council were amazed when they saw the boldness of Peter and John, for they could see that they were ordinary men who had had no special training.... Peter and John replied, 'Do you think God wants us to obey you rather than him? We cannot stop telling about the wonderful things we have seen and heard.'"

Lord Jesus, help me to be a bold witness for You today.

Dave Eshleman served as pastor and church planter for fifty years.

JULY 8

Bridges and Detours

"We know that God is always at work for the good of everyone who loves him." Romans 8:28 (Contemporary English Version)

Tomatoes, check. Sweet bell peppers, check. Jalapeos, check. I was almost ready to can pizza sauce, but I still needed fresh basil and extra onions. I dashed out to a local farm market, using the longer way around since a bridge on my usual route was under construction.

A few hundred yards from the market a quaint covered bridge stands guard. That day on the road approaching the bridge I saw signs: "Road closed." What? Sure enough, trucks blocked the way and, annoyed, I jumped out to question the men. Did they realize this is the second area bridge closed? What was I supposed to do, hike the last quarter mile?

That final question spewed out, surprising me, but it turned out to be a solution. Upset but determined, I threw my cloth grocery bags and purse over one shoulder and then strode across the bridge.

Funny thing was, halfway down the road the exasperated feeling changed into thanksgiving as I began to notice the world around me. A flock of birds rose from the grass in a whirlwind of wings. Virginia creeper climbed a fencepost with graceful curves. A pair of greenhouses peeped out from behind cornstalks which made me wonder what might have grown there. Amish children skipped from the barn to their house. Varied leaf textures drew my eye in a flower bed near the road. God's beauty was everywhere!

Telling the clerk, "This is the first time I hiked to Hoovers!" I thought about the story I'd have to tell my children later. I realized again that only conflict makes a story. Closed bridges can generate gratefulness. God had reached into my heart to make a difference.

All-knowing Father, thank You that nothing ever surprises You. Help me to see my detours, both small and big, as gifts that You can use to change me.

Renita Gerlach home educates her children and teaches writing to high school homeschoolers. She's been meeting with a home church for fourteen years.

JULY 9

For Whom Do You Work?

"Whatever you do, work at it with all your heart, as working for the Lord, not for men, since you know that you will receive an inheritance from the Lord as a reward. It is the Lord Christ you are serving." Colossians 3:23-24

I have remembered these important verses and applied them to my life.

After having a number of health and nursing aides in our home to care for my wife, since I am unable to do so, I have experienced a number of things. These include: Some aides do not respond immediately to the needs of the patient; some are not gentle and kind in their way of caring; most are on time to take over from another aide at the end of a shift; some are not dressed appropriately; one lied to us; some computer and phone items were missing from our home and then replaced by the nursing firm.

I have talked to the individuals and also the management about these work-related items. I question: who do they work for? Do you realize that Jesus provides all the jobs for us and the ministries to live with Him in His way?

Lord Jesus, help us to serve You faithfully in all we do each moment of each day. Thank You Lord. In Your name, I pray Jesus.

Bob Burns serves as an ordained and licensed minister and as pastor and shepherd of Spiritual Growth Ministries. He is a member of the Potter's House board of directors, Leola, a Bible teacher and serves the Spring Valley Church of God in the ministry of home visitation to the ill.

JULY 10

Improved Picture

"… He who began a good work in you will carry it on to completion until the day of Christ Jesus." Philippians 1:6

I've learned from painting the rooms in my house that the word "paint" propagates into several other "p" words:

- **Perseverance and Process** Three years seems like a long time to endure the process of painting the walls, ceiling, trim and moldings one room at a time.
- **Patience and Precision** I'm a messy painter. Even with a drop cloth, the paint found fondness with the carpeted, wood and tile floors. Peeling off the tape around the door and window frames frequently left jagged edges. My perfectionism prompted the patient repainting of straighter lines with a much smaller brush.
- **Preparation** This process required much greater time than the actual painting.
- **Picking** the color fulfilled my "creativity."
- **Patching** nail holes and cracks was part of the necessary, but boring work. Removing knickknacks and furniture, laying down drop cloths, wiping down the walls, buying and stirring paint, collecting brushes, rollers and ladder, and patching up drywall seemed to rival heaven's length of existence.
- **Performance** The actual "doing" of rolling on paint flew by quickly. It was exciting to "feel" the ambiance of new color.
- **Pleasure** Finally seeing the results of the mind's plan made the long painting process all worthwhile.

The analogy to God's process in our preparation toward a purpose is implied. Joseph spent long years in prison before his palace days of saving Egypt and Israel from famine. Esther prepared herself for pageants before saving her Jewish people from certain death. David spent numerous hours protecting sheep before proving His reliance on God in slaying Goliath. They willingly trusted God for a better picture than they could presently see. And then they experienced the joy of completing a good work, having fulfilled God's purpose in their lives.

Lord, help us to focus on You and the good work You are patiently doing in us.

Tamalyn Jo Heim enjoys her "improved" home with her husband, Bob, and sharing it with her visiting family.

JULY 11

Rainstorm

"But he was pierced for our transgressions, he was crushed for our iniquities; the punishment that brought us peace was upon him, and by his wounds we are healed." Isaiah 53:5

As I grow older, life doesn't seem as carefree and sometimes I feel like I'm in a constant rainstorm. During the past two years, my rainstorm was Lyme disease. In the fall of 2009, I began to have achy joints. At first I thought I was running too much. But the pain became worse until my knees became swollen to the point that I couldn't even bend them. I also felt extremely tired all the time.

I became very discouraged because I didn't know what was wrong and neither did the doctor.

After a year of pain, I was at the place of brokenness and giving up on ever being healed. Then I went to see a different doctor, who Jesus gave wisdom to find that I had Lyme disease and prescribed antibiotics. After one round of antibiotics I didn't feel much difference. However, after the second round of antibiotics, Jesus brought complete healing. I was able to fully bend my knees again. I had no swelling and restored energy just in time so that I could start the basketball season. Thanks to Jesus' healing, I participated in running a half marathon, something that I would never have dreamed possible a year ago.

Through my experience with Lyme disease, Jesus showed me that even when I feel alone in the trials of life, He is still there. Jesus is like a wonderful daddy, who stands by our side through whatever trials come our way. Just when we think we can't handle another drop of rain, Jesus pops up a big umbrella and comes to our rescue.

Thank You, Jesus, that it doesn't matter whether or not we are having a two- or twenty-five-year rainstorm, You will pop open the umbrella to protect us and bring full restoration. With You, nothing is impossible.

Heather Hoffman attends ECC church and is a freshman at Reading Hospital School for nursing.

JULY 12

Imagine ...

"God determined the times set for them and the exact place where they should live. He did this so that men would seek Him and perhaps reach out for Him and find Him." Acts 17:26-27

What would Lancaster County look like if every person on every street were prayed for by name? What would happen in neighborhoods, business, education and government if people prayed in those places every day? Lancaster Transformed Street by Street is a prayer initiative committed to see that become a reality.

The concept is simple: talk to God about your neighbors before you talk to your neighbors about God. The strategy is effective: speak peace, look for opportunities to interact, ask God to meet their needs supernaturally, then when God directs you, tell them the Good News about Jesus. This lifestyle of evangelism makes a way for Him to change people's lives, and when lives change, whole communities change.

People of every age, denomination and culture are taking responsibility by praying for neighbors, co-workers, fellow students, business owners, employees, government officials and others. Participants are adopting streets, businesses and schools by stepping out of their comfort zones and getting involved in the lives of others.

Lancaster Transformed Street by Street is set on the historic foundations of prayer that are part of this county's heritage. Through the years, many groups and individuals have recognized prayer as the key to revival and transformation. Today, people are taking their place of privilege and responsibility to pray for those around them. Through a lifestyle of prayer evangelism, we will see long-awaited breakthrough in Lancaster County, and all of society will be affected.

Dear Lord, our vision is to see sustained transformation across Lancaster County; but the goal is to see You receive Your inheritance as individuals of every ethnic background across this region and beyond encounter You and come to know Jesus as Lord and Savior.

Lauren Charles and Bonita Keener lead the initiative Lancaster Transformed Street by Street. To adopt your street, workplace or school, visit the Website www.lancastertransformed.org. Or contact lancastertransformed@windstream.net.

JULY 13

Despair to Dependence

"We do not want you to be uninformed brothers, about the hardships we suffered in the province of Asia. We were under great pressure, far beyond our ability to endure, so that we despaired even of life." 2 Corinthians 2:8

I don't know about you but like Paul, sometimes I feel like "I'm despaired even of life." Life itself is a daily challenge and I sometimes question "where is God in all of this?"

Recently my husband and I stepped out in faith and sold our home and moved to Florida. Things didn't work out the way we planned it. I need to emphasize the part about "how we planned it." I can hear some of you saying "been there, done that." However as hard as things got at times, God still proved Himself faithful.

Through that experience, God taught me a very valuable and necessary lesson. I consider it a lesson I would not have learned any other way. I learned complete dependence on God. Today, everything in my life is not wonderful and not the way I wanted it, but the freedom I now have from my dependence on the Lord is priceless and I wouldn't have it any other way.

So when things don't "go your way" ask God what He's trying to teach you and believe me He will.

Thank You, Father, for not letting me have my way. Thank You for taking my burdens and teaching me dependence on You.

Jean Henry and her husband attend Living Stones in Newmanstown.

JULY 14

God and Nail Polish

"Jesus called the children to him and said, 'Let the little children come to me, and do not hinder them, for the kingdom of God belongs to such as these.'" Luke 18:16

One day my husband accidentally spilled half a bottle of bright red nail polish on our kitchen floor. We tried to clean it up with a dry paper towel, then a wet paper towel and various cleaners, but all we ended up doing was smearing the red stain farther.

Finally, we used nail polish remover and were able to remove the nail polish completely off the tile floor, not even a faint stain remained.

That night as I tucked my ten-year-old daughter into bed, she looked at me and said, "Mom, you know sin is like nail polish and God is like the nail polish remover. The only thing that can take nail polish off is the remover and the only thing that can take our sins away is God."

Wow, I thought how simple and yet how profound. I was amazed to see how God can take a mishap in our lives and use it to teach a young child a biblical truth.

I shut the door and walked down the stairs thanking God for the simple ways He talks to us. God loves us so much He takes the time to show us who He is in simple everyday examples. We just have to make sure we are not too busy to see them.

Dear Jesus, give us the eyes of a child to see the simple love that You have for us. May we never get too busy that we forget to listen to Your voice.

Marie Good and her husband, Todd, have four children and are youth leaders at DOVE Newport.

JULY 15

Illumination

"Your word is a lamp to my feet and a light to my path."
Psalm 119:105

When I was legally blind I used to wear thick glasses through which even in the daytime enabled me to see only shapes and colors. How much harder it was to function at night, especially in poor illumination. Yet I never fell, even at night. The Lord always provided the light to my feet literally.

God illuminated my path in different ways. Sometimes it would be the light of a passing car, or of a rare lantern or of a window in the house I walked by. Sometimes it would be just a reflection of the light in the puddle or on any other object on the road. And sometimes the Lord would directly speak to my spirit, warning me about the potential dangers along my way.

In the Old Testament we read that King David has experienced much darkness in his life. That's why from early days of his life, he learned to trust the Lord with all his heart and mind. Later in life, his confidence and standing in God only grew stronger. Moreover, the darker his circumstances seemed to become, the more he would depend on God to illuminate his path. God's word of encouragement and guidance was truly the lamp to David's living.

We also need God's Word to be the lamp to our feet physically and spiritually, especially when we don't know where we are going, or when the going is tough. The good news is as long as we cling to the Lord, step-by-step He illuminates our path so that we won't stumble or fall in the world full of darkness.

Jesus, You are the Light to the World. Bless us to walk in Your light.

Yulia Bagwell, Beth Yeshua, a housewife-caregiver, a writer and a translator for *The Upper Room* devotional magazine.

JULY 16

Intellectual Quest

"He (Paul) was explaining and proving the prophecies about the sufferings of the Messiah and his rising from the dead. He said, 'This Jesus I'm telling you about is the Messiah.'" Acts 17:3 (New Living Translation)

If you like to wrestle with intellectual questions, you may find it natural to use this style to witness. In this approach, you refer seekers to books and other resources. You spend time studying with them.

Invite people to follow Jesus in spite of their doubts and questions. All of us have questions. Questions are good except when asked in defiance about God. Seeking evidence of our humanity and humility are both necessary attitudes for us to discover God. We must recognize we never have all the answers. We need to make a commitment to Christ before we have everything figured out.

In Acts 19:9 we learn that Paul went to the lecture hall of Tyranus and debated daily for two years. He conversed with the intelligentsia and debated with the philosophers of Athens. In his sermon on Mars Hill, he ingeniously used the Athenians' altar to an unknown god as an introduction to his presentation of the true God.

Don't let persons with a high intellect intimidate you. Often their questions are a smoke screen to hide a guilty conscience. They intuitively know they need salvation. Only the Holy Spirit can break their wall of resistance. On the other hand we need to discern that honest questions need honest answers.

Lee Strobel, once a skeptical journalist, freely recognizes the difficult questions and exposes them, revealing that faith in Christ is an answer very much worth considering. Josh McDowell, known worldwide for his ministry to university students, uses this approach very effectively. My friend Mike goes on the Internet and debates with those of other faiths. He uses his gift of intellect to invite people to encounter Jesus.

In using this approach, always remember that we are not called to win an argument but to show God's love with gentleness and respect.

Lord, help me to diligently study and present the best answers to those who have sincere questions concerning Christianity.

Dave Eshleman served as pastor and church planter for fifty years.

JULY 17

Hidden Treasures

"They will be nourished by the abundance from the sea and the treasures hidden in the sand." Deuteronomy 33:19 (God's Word Translation)

My husband and I were under a lot of stress about our businesses. A trip to Charleston, South Carolina, seemed like a good place to get away to relax and draw near to God.

As we walked along the beach, we were asking the Lord to let us know that He was with us. I also specifically prayed we would find a perfect sand dollar. After we had walked a distance, we decided to turn back because it was cold and windy. We turned and walked about ten feet and there was a perfect sand dollar lying on the sand we had just walked over seconds earlier. We were so excited and then we spotted another one only a few feet away.

The true treasure wasn't finding the sand dollars, but the reminder that God was truly with us and that He really cares and has everything under His control. Yes, God gives us hidden treasures to make us more aware of Him.

Father, thank You for Your presence in our lives every day. Have us be aware of those hidden treasures You prepare for us all along the way.

Faye Good is a wife, mother and grandmother.

JULY 18

Calibrated to Him

"Now the Lord is the Spirit, and where the Spirit of the Lord is, there is liberty. But we all, with unveiled faces, beholding as in a mirror the glory of the Lord, are being transformed into the same image from glory to glory, just as from the Lord, the Spirit." 2 Corinthians 3:17-18 (New American Standard Bible)

Recently, our children and grandchildren contributed to an electronic game system that would be enjoyed by all generations in our house at any given time. Admittedly, it has proven to provide mutual participation and healthy competition between the three generations. One of the required steps in the process of beginning a game is for all players to lay their remote on a flat surface facing the screen so that the remotes can be calibrated.

We once had a friend whose only job was traveling to atomic power plants to calibrate instruments.

Webster's definition of *calibrate* indicates that the standardization process of calibration involves correction of any deviation from a standard.

One morning as I sat in quiet worship, for periods of time I was seemingly not doing anything. Then the Lord reminded me of the process game remotes need to calibrate with the game system and one another. The remote must be still, doing absolutely nothing but receiving input and being adjusted.

Praise God for His ability to calibrate us to His image as we wait quietly before Him. Corrections, adjustments can occur with almost no conscious participation. Just being with Him in yieldedness produces calibrated change into His image.

Father, You are altogether true and righteous in all Your ways. As I wait before You, adjust my heart to Your holiness and glory by Your Holy Spirit.

Ruth Ann Stauffer lives in Lititz with her husband, Al. They are members of Ephrata Community Church.

JULY 19

Empty Stable, Empty Heart

"An empty stable stays clean, but no income comes from an empty stable." Proverbs 14:4

How convenient when we can use scripture to accomplish our own goals instead of allowing scripture to change us so that we can accomplish God's.

Years ago when one of our sons was an adolescent, he usually got the job of cleaning up the shop. When he complained about it, I would quote the above verse to him.

We laugh about it now, but I must admit, I used that scripture to accomplish my own goal of getting some needed work completed. That situation makes me question how often we quote scriptures to satisfy our own needs.

How about when a husband uses a verse on submission when his real desire is to control? How effective is a verse on submission when a wife does not see her husband submitting to His Lord Jesus or to a policeman and others in authority?

We need to see a new generation of men who allow scripture to remake them instead of using scripture to mold others for their own satisfaction.

Father, send Your Holy Spirit to raise up a new generation of godly men.

LaMarr Sensenig serves as an elder at Lancaster Evangelical Free Church in Lititz. He and his wife, Naomi, are counselors at Abundant Living Ministries in Lititz.

JULY 20

Nothing Plus God

"You shall love the Lord your God with all your heart, with all your soul and with all your mind. This is the first and greatest commandment." Matthew 22:37-38 (New Living Translation)

Being a grandmother of twenty-nine grandchildren, I enjoy observing the development of their reading skills. One of my granddaughters was overjoyed last Christmas when we gave her a book that had chapters. She had reached the level of reading that was exciting and pleasurable.

Growing up as a middle child in a family of eleven, my personal possessions were few, but they were treasured. Among these items was a book given to me by my Sunday school teacher for Christmas titled, *Nothing + God = Susie*. I was eight years old and the book stayed by my bed for many years. Even though I no longer remember the details and plot of the story, I do know the main theme was how Susie learned at an early age to always love and keep God first in her life. This helped her decide at many decision points throughout her youth to choose what was good, right and true.

So at age eight when I gave my heart to the Lord, I had a strong desire to serve God, follow His instruction and live my life to honor and please the Lord. I also grew in love for those around me as He instructed and guided me all these years. There were times of testing and trial throughout my life when philosophies were presented as plausible and good, but in reality were false teachings contrary to the Word of God.

I cannot estimate the impact that simple little book had on my life during my growing years. Even to this day, the message of that book is a tool that directs me to "Nothing + God." He is sufficient for me.

Father God, how wonderful You are. You are all we need! Thank You for Your great love and for leading us into life that is abundant.

Naomi Sensenig serves as deaconess and husband, LaMarr, as an elder at Lancaster Evangelical Free Church in Lititz. Both also enjoy serving at Abundant Living Ministries in Lititz.

JULY 21

Adrenaline Junkie

"I am come that they might have life, and that they might have it more abundantly." John 10:10b (King James Version)

I used to be an adrenaline junkie with insatiable need for speed, thrills and spills, which led me across the entire country looking for the most extreme rides.

In Wildwood, New Jersey, I was spinning in a freewheeling cage on one end of an arm that was one hundred and sixty feet across, which was also spinning in a circle at sixty miles per hour.

I'd already ridden the ride twice before, but this time I wasn't having fun. When I got off the ride, I promised I would never do it again. Then I realized I had one more extreme ride ticket to use, which I didn't really desire to use but I wouldn't have gotten a refund if I didn't. I decided to ride the "Sky Coaster," which is a big swing with a ripcord that when pulled releases you into a free fall flying position.

While I was waiting to go on the ride, a quiet voice started speaking. "Why are you doing this? Why do you seek out these rides? What can you gain from them? Don't you know that I can provide all you will ever need? Trust in and seek out Me."

I wanted to cry, which was so out of character for me, because I had never reacted like that ever. I ignored the voice that was speaking to me and proceeded with the ride. A hundred feet in the air, I pulled the ripcord, went free flying and was scared to death. It occurred to me that the voice that was speaking to me had the answer I had always been looking for. It wasn't an extreme ride I needed. It is Jesus. No longer do I need to risk life and limbs to find happiness and joy. Jesus "fills my senses" more abundantly than any ride.

Lord, You do fill my senses to overflowing. Thank You for fulfilling my every need.

Carol Denson, ex-adrenaline junkie, attends Church of the Open Bible in Parkesburg.

JULY 22

Just a Few Words

"The one who calls you is faithful and he will do it."
1 Thessalonians 5:24

As I reflect back over my life, I am reminded of some of the smallest things that had some of the greatest impact. It is not always through the dynamic or the spectacular that life's greatest experiences occur.

As a young man in my early teens I was asked to exercise leadership in a very small role in an event in the church that my family called "theirs." After the event an older gentleman in his senior years came to me and spoke one statement to me and walked away. He said, "Someday I see you standing tall as a leader in this church." Although this happened more than forty years ago, I remember the exact place I was standing as though it was yesterday. It took, at the most, fifteen seconds of one person's time in order to make a powerful impact on the life of another. I consider this my call to church leadership as every aspect of those few words became a wonderful reality in my life.

Our words are very powerful and influence the future of others in ways that can either be positive or negative beyond our imagination. I wonder how many people pass on from this earth never fulfilling their life's purpose because nobody ever affirmed them in the area of their potential. I am eternally grateful for the fifteen quick seconds someone took to affirm my potential and I am watching for the opportunities to do likewise for others.

Lord Jesus, thank You for the simple ways You have communicated Your love and acceptance through the words and actions of others that have had a positive impact on my life. Fill me with the inspiration of Your Spirit to deposit seeds in the lives of others that will bring forth the awesomeness of Your love and grow into the fulfillment of Your divine purposes.

Lloyd Hoover serves as a bishop in Lancaster Mennonite Conference, on the executive team of the Regional Church of Lancaster County, executive director of Transition to Community and with other transformational and healing ministries.

JULY 23

A Patch Apart

"Listen to what the parable of the sower means...." Matthew 13:18

I have a very small patch of front lawn and probably spend more time thinking about its vitality than its size warrants. Yet the Lord has used my relationship with that patch to encourage His truth in many ways. When I moved to the home this area was weed ridden. But I saw its potential and set it apart as a manageable place to focus my attention.

My first step was to remove the weeds. Since it was all weeds my lawn became a patch of dirt. Next I prepared the soil, seeded, fertilized and watered. Over time the grassy lawn I had envisioned began to emerge.

Yet the maintenance process continues. I battle dry spells, winter debris and the endless onslaught from "invaders." Recently my sons and I removed some patches of weeds and reseeded. Over the next few days we watched the miraculous emergence of new life. In spots where the ground had been best prepared the seeds sprang up quickly. In places where the ground was not prepared the seeds lay dormant. The other morning I even caught a bird picking at the new plants!

The imagery in Matthew is richly organic and the parallel between caring for my set-apart place and the kingdom Jesus describes is illuminating. Those who have set apart a special place in their heart for Christ can realize the personal analogy there. New believers can gain wisdom about what to expect in walking with the Lord. There are also lessons for those who have labored together to bring to life a kingdom vision for our regions.

God You created all things, even the Earth and its people, and in Your mercy permitted us to know Your invisible qualities even through that which was made. Thank You for that gift and may You encourage us today to use what we observe of this creation as a tool to help others see your eternal power and divine nature.

Bill Shaw is executive director of Life Transforming Ministries in Coatesville.

JULY 24

The Power of Kingdom Partnership

"And with great power the apostles were giving testimony to the re surrection of the Lord Jesus Christ and abundant grace was upon them all." Acts 4:33 (New American Standard Bible)

Partnership happens when we agree to work together for a specific purpose because we can achieve more together than we can achieve alone. Partnership for the sake of partnership is sure to fail, but partnership with a focused purpose will produce great fruit. Partnership in the Body of Christ is a reflection of the unity we already possess in Christ. We will not see our kingdom transformation on a macro-community level without the body of Christ choosing to partner together around the common purpose of the gospel.

Christ calls us to live as "one heart and soul" with no regard for our own interests, and to serve only the glory of Christ. The idea of kingdom partnership presupposes that we view ourselves as stewards of Christ and that ideal kingdom purposes are preeminent. In Acts 4:32-35 believers lived as "one heart and soul" to the extent that no one claimed anything for his/her own.

Partnership requires humility. Humility ushers in grace and gives life to unity, which when fully mature, erupts in a mighty display of God's adundant grace. The partnership of believers in the early church in caring for those in need resulted in social transformation in that there was "no needy person among them" and opened the doorways of heaven for a mighty outpouring of the power and grace of God.

Father, I lay aside my own interests and choose to live as a steward in Your Kingdom. I surrender to the Holy Spirit's work of cultivating a humble spirit within me. Manifest, in my life and actions, the unity that You have provided through Christ. Lead me into partnership with others so that Your love is revealed to the world around me and Your kingdom comes.

Jere Shertzer is president/CEO of Water Street Ministries, serves on the executive team of the RCOLC and attends Ephrata Community Church.

JULY 25

Limited and Limitless

"The fruit of righteousness will be peace; the effect of righteousness will be quietness and confidence forever." Isaiah 32:17b

As I sat down to write today, my mind went blank. I didn't know what I should write. I feel so limited in the amount of wisdom or insight I could give to whoever happened to read this devotional.

Some days are like that. We feel wordless. We don't know what to say. As a counselor, I feel powerless and incompetent when that happens.

I'm supposed to be wise and capable, able to ask the right question in the right timing and with great perception. Most days I'm pretty good at that, but not every day. Some days, I am advice-less. It's not that I'm temporarily stupid, just … not sharp. And when that happens, I have a choice to make. Do I allow myself to sit in my lack of astuteness and wallow in a "woe-is-me" mind set of uselessness or do I choose a better path?

The better path is one of being available. Whether I have the right words to write or say is not the only thing that helps others; important, yes, but not all. I have found some of the most meaningful and healing sessions have been when there was little said. But I was present and with my clients in the middle of their pain. Those quiet moments are sacred and rich.

I am reminded of Psalm 85:10-13:

"Love and faithfulness meet together; righteousness and peace kiss each other.

Faithfulness springs forth from the earth, and righteousness looks down from heaven.

The Lord will indeed give what is good, and our land will yield its harvest.

Righteousness goes before him and prepares the way for his steps."

Thank You, Lord, that You can use anyone (even those of us with limited vocabularies) to minister Your love, righteousness and peace.

Shannon Shertzer is a counselor at New Hope Community Life Ministry in Quarryville. She is married to Jere. They live in Lititz and are members of Ephrata Community Church.

JULY 26

Dirty Windows

“The eye is the lamp of the body; so then, if your eye is clear, your whole body will be full of light.” Matthew 6:22

The windows in our apartment looked alright if the days were overcast. But when a bright ray of the sunshine touched them, the dirt was distinctive. “They’re fine,” my husband stated, not even looking at them. “You’re just exaggerating,” he added. But I was not! How could they be fine when they distorted the reality of the outside life: its true colors, shapes and forms?

Refusing to argue with my husband, I filled up a bucket of water to wash those windows. Surprisingly, a bucket of clean water made them look worse. I needed more water. Actually, I needed quite a few buckets of water to accomplish my task. “You were right,” my husband finally admitted. “Now they do look different. It’s amazing once we get used to dirt, we don’t even pay attention to it anymore.”

Someone said that our eyes are windows to our souls. Originally, in the Garden of Eden, our ancestors’ souls were clean, but sin made them dirty. When we come into this world, sooner or later we face sin too. At first, we dislike it. Then we try to resist it. Then we may feel uncomfortable hiding our filthy thoughts or actions. Overall, if we don’t deal with the sin of our lives, it will look alright to us.

In Luke 11:34 Jesus warns us: if your eye isn’t clean or healthy, then your whole body is full of darkness. Isn’t it nice that Jesus sees us through? He knows how sin can distort or disfigure our perspective and life. Best of all, Jesus knows how to make us clean again. He knows, and He does it even if it takes Him much work and many “buckets” of the living water: the Holy Spirit.

Jesus, take care of our eyes so that our souls could be full of Your light.

Yulia Bagwell, Beth Yeshua, is a housewife-caregiver, a writer and a translator for *The Upper Room* devotional magazine.

JULY 27

Kiss Is Worth a Thousand Words

"Who is able to open the seal?" Revelation 5:5

There I was with a short-term mission team in a field somewhere in the bush country outside of Gulu, northern Uganda. A beautiful countryside ravaged by fear and raped of freedom by a terrorist group called the LRA.

The Word was being proclaimed and orphans were seated on the laps of my teammates. As my eyes scanned through the multitudes sitting on the grass, compassion raised in my heart, but with it, sad awareness that I could do nothing in the face of all the woundedness and loss here.

When the call was given for salvation prayer, curiously only a few stood. When the call for healing prayer came, the multitude lined up. Instantly an interpreter was before me with a small-framed mama with a baby nursing at her breast. Her face was contorted in an unusually painful fashion. The interpreter relayed to me that the LRA soldiers had padlocked her mouth shut because she screamed at their horrific indignities. I was sickened and within me raised this commissioning to be the Lord's ambassador to give a kiss to that torn mouth. Just a kiss—that's the prayer that the Lord ordered for healing.

And so with all the Father's love behind it He moved me past my comfort to deliver that kiss of grace and mercy and tell her she was loved with an everlasting love and that He would continue to love her like a devout husband and tender Father. Prayers of forgiveness followed and a new countenance on that face.

Had someone photographed my face in that moment surely there would have been a look of awe and wonder!

Set apart in a moment's time for a moment of unusual healing, I pondered the thought of many voiceless who have had their mouths "padlocked shut" in other ways.

Some of us need a heavenly kiss. Some are the ones who will deliver that kiss. Father God's kisses of grace "open the seals" to the treasure that remains locked and hidden in earthen vessels.

Lord, empower us to be vessels for use and vessels to receive Your love.

Nancy Clegg is His child and vessel.

JULY 28

Recognize "the Spot"

"When Jesus reached the spot, He looked up, and said, 'Zacchaeus, come down immediately, I must stay at your house today.'" Luke 19:5

What was "the spot" that Jesus reached? How did Jesus know He had reached it? Was it a literal, physical place or can we conclude that it is much more than that? Jesus was quite busy in mission—places to go and things to do, implementing important life-changing ministry as the surrounding text reveals. However, there is an incredible pause in the narrative as Jesus reaches "the spot." The original Greek word "topos" identifies this as meaning a condition or opportunity. What a profound description which paints a powerful word picture. The Spirit definitively speaks and boldly interrupts Jesus' incredibly busy day as He reaches "the spot." Jesus, being sensitive and attentive to these "Spirit spots," stops. He looks up and engages with the "topos," which dangled from the tree in the form of Zacchaeus. What a model for recognizing a human condition and embracing a spirit-led opportunity. I marvel at how Jesus flowed and hummed with the Holy Spirit recognizing "the spot" of a condition or opportunity.

The same Holy Spirit which directed Jesus to this "spot" is now given to us. This should instill comfort, yet this reality also calls for much attentiveness to the Spirit. How easy it is to become self-absorbed and consumed in our own mission and blow by the "spot" the Lord has already arranged in our day. The outcome of Jesus humming with the Spirit is amazing. The entire condition of Zacchaeus is transformed personally, ethically and relationally as Jesus seizes the opportunity in stopping at the "spot" in the path.

God still places "Spirit spots" in the form of people in our pathways. Stop, and look up.

Lord, may I be living fully in "the spot" where You would have me be Your hands and feet today.

Brian E. Martin serves as lead pastor at Weaverland Mennonite Church in East Earl. He and his wife, Shirley, are parents of three married children, one young adult at home and have three grandchildren.

JULY 29

Opening Doors

"But I will stay on at Ephesus until Pentecost, because a great door for effective work has opened to me, and there are many who oppose me." 1 Corinthians 16:8-9

One of our residents has been amazing to watch in her growth as she searches the Scriptures and asks penetrating questions, few with easy answers. She also deals with damage from her past and questions about the current workings of God in her life.

One day we were discussing her frustrations with her job: her boss, her fellow employees, the wages. She muttered, "I just don't understand why God leaves me in this job and doesn't give me a new one."

I asked, "Have you put in any job applications?" She stopped and looked at me. "Oh. Good point."

It is not only baby Christians who are guilty of that mistake. We serve a God of miracles, but he does not automatically move in and fix all of our problems while we prop our feet up and wait for him to act. If the blind man had not washed in the pool of Siloam (John 9:11), he would have remained blind. If Naaman (2 Kings 5) had chosen to not wash seven times in the Jordan River, he would have remained a leper. If the man with the withered hand (Luke 6:10) had held his hand by his side, he would have remained one-handed.

God would much rather redirect a moving object than to prod and coax a stationary object into motion. Saul of Tarsus was running full speed in the wrong direction until God laid him low and turned him around to put the same energy into the cause of Christ.

In Acts 16:6-10, the open door to Macedonia was discovered by trying the closed doors to Asia and to Mysia. Open doors are discovered by testing closed doors. Open doors do not always remain open and closed doors do not always remain closed.

Father, this day open the doors where I can be effective in Your work.

Steve Hershey is a teacher and speaker at White Oak Church of the Brethren. Steve and his wife, Brenda, have opened their home to young adults.

JULY 30

Invitational Approach

"Andrew, Simon Peter's brother, was one of the two who heard what John had said and who had followed Jesus. The first thing Andrew did was to find his brother Simon and tell him, 'We have found the Messiah' (that is, the Christ). And he brought him to Jesus." John 1:40-41

George Barna says, "One out of four" will come to church if a friend invites them." I believe the key word here is "friend." If you first have a relationship with the unchurched people and invite them, perhaps Barna's findings are true.

Some studies conclude that more than half the people who come to Jesus in the United States come through this style. This has certainly been true in my ministry. Jesus built a relationship with people. They heard about him and observed him.

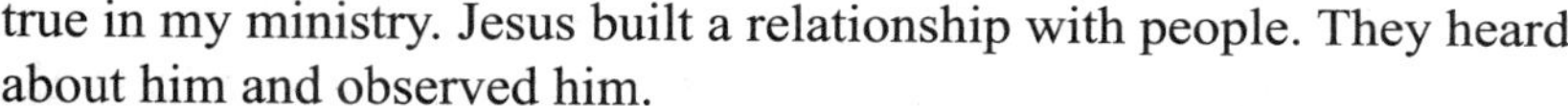

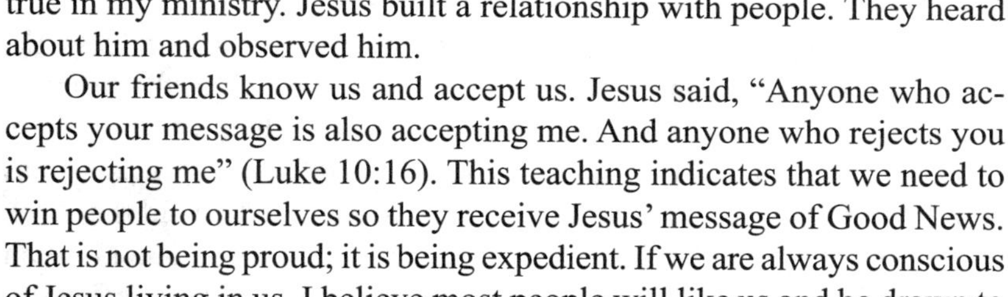

Our friends know us and accept us. Jesus said, "Anyone who accepts your message is also accepting me. And anyone who rejects you is rejecting me" (Luke 10:16). This teaching indicates that we need to win people to ourselves so they receive Jesus' message of Good News. That is not being proud; it is being expedient. If we are always conscious of Jesus living in us, I believe most people will like us and be drawn to him who lives his life through us (Galatians 2:20).

For the invitational approach to be effective, churches need to conduct services at which the unchurched feel comfortable and the gospel is presented in a way they can understand. Unchurched friends should not sense that they will be put on the spot or in some way embarrassed.

Gentle persistence in a loving manner communicates to the unchurched that we care. When Elwood, a new believer, went to a church conference, someone asked him why he started coming to church. He said, "Because Pastor Dave kept inviting me, He wouldn't give up." I had gone to his home and visited with him and his family many times. I called occasionally and prompted others in the church to do the same. This is how we "compel" them to come (Luke 14:23).

Lord, give me eyes to see those people today who are open to an invitation to come to You. Give me gentle boldness to extend that invitation.

Dave Eshleman served as pastor and church planter for fifty years.

JULY 31

Timing

"As the heavens are higher than the earth, so my ways are higher than your ways…." Isaiah 55:9

The first time we saw the house, we were overwhelmed by the amount of work it needed. There was no heat, plumbing leaked and electricity was minimal. The rooms were bare, floors had holes, windows were broken and plaster walls were cracked.

Five years ago, with a sense in our hearts that we were to move into the city, we began looking at properties online. We visited a few with a realtor, but came away feeling that it was not the right time or place. But now we couldn't get this run-down house out of our minds.

We were faced with a choice. Do we continue to live out our lives in a comfortable predictable way, or do we want to take a risk and trust God with the details? Our faith was being stretched.

After purchasing the house, we spent the next five months working hard on renovations. Each time there was a glitch in the process, God amazed us and used it to put us ahead of schedule. Even a family vacation planned two years prior gave us rest in the midst of the stress and labor of the project. Our other house unexpectedly sold the week we put it on the market so our moving day came more quickly than planned. Moving day was timed perfectly by God as we were officially granted occupancy the very hour we finished loading all our possessions onto the truck.

Today, we continue to trust God for His perfect timing and provision as we continue to care for this house that is His. Trusting Him is worth the risk.

Father God, Your ways are not my ways. Your plans are much higher than mine. Teach me to live with Your perfect timing in my sight. I want to live a life full of faith rather than choosing the comfortable way ... for Your glory. Amen.

Keith and Brenda Blank live in Lancaster City. Keith is lead pastor at Mountville Mennonite Church.

Photo by Amy Mishler

August

AUGUST 1

Power Washing

"And He has said to me, 'My grace is sufficient for you, for power is perfected in weakness.'" 2 Corinthians 12:9
(New American Standard Bible)

I am a squeamish person. I am afraid of dirt. Either I attack it with a vengeance or I deny its existence.

Last year, my husband and I needed to clean a couple of cement porches and remove mud that had been left behind by Lee, a tropical storm.

From a distance the job didn't look too bad, but when I got closer and started sweeping and attempting to remove the quarter-inch-thick, dried-on mud with a garden hose, which had very weak water pressure, I began to feel discouraged and overwhelmed in a hurry.

All I could accomplish was moving muddy water around in circles and not getting anything clean. I was exhausted. Then, along came my husband with a power washer and "voila!" My job suddenly got a whole lot easier and more fun.

The mud began to disappear as the cement floor turned colors right before my eyes!

What a difference the power washer made. In my own strength and with ineffective tools, I was tired and unproductive, but with the power washer, I was able to accomplish much and had fun in the process.

In the same way, when we try to do things in our own strength we will surely fail, but when we rely on God's power, He gives us supernatural ability to do whatever He has called us to do.

Father, thank You for giving us Your power when we are weak and forgive us when we attempt to do things in our own strength rather than trusting in You.

Dolores Walker and her husband, Dave, are members of DOVE Westgate Church and live in Lititz.

AUGUST 2

The Priority of Prayer

"Ask of me, and I will make the nations your inheritance, the ends of the earth your possession." Psalm 2:8

The first and most important action we can do as Christians is pray. People can reject our kindness but they cannot reject our prayers. We can reach our next-door neighbor or those who are halfway around the world through prayer.

We must pray for the following:

connecting with our community

1. Workers: Jesus said, "The harvest is plentiful, but the workers are few. Ask the Lord of the harvest to send out workers into his harvest field" (Luke 10:2).
2. Favorable circumstances to witness: "Pray for us that God may open a door for our message, so that we may proclaim the mystery of Christ, for which I am in chains" (Colossians 4:3).
3. Courage to speak up: "For our struggle is not against flesh and blood, but against the rulers, against the authorities, against the power of this dark world and against the spiritual forces of evil in the heavenly realms" (Ephesians 6:12).
4. Those who will believe: "My prayer is not for them alone. I pray also for those who will believe in me through their message, that all of them may be one, Father, just as you are in me and I am in you. May they also be in us so that the world may believe that you have sent me" (John 17:20-21).
5. The rapid spread of the message: "Pray for us. Pray that the Master's Word will simply take off and race through the country to a groundswell of response, just as it did among you. And pray that we'll be rescued from these scoundrels who are trying to do us in. I'm finding that not all 'believers' are believers. But the Master never lets us down. He'll stick by you and protect you from evil" (2 Thessalonians 3:1-3).

Lord, help me to be faithful in prayer.

Dave Eshleman served as pastor and church planter for fifty years.

AUGUST 3

Consequences

"Nathan replied, 'The Lord has taken away your sin.... But because by doing this you have made the enemies of the Lord show utter contempt, the son born to you will die.'" 2 Samuel 12:13-14

One of the most difficult things to teach the children that God brings into our home is financial management. Often they do odd jobs for me to earn spending money for themselves. One of the girls, who had done some work for me, no sooner had she completed her job than she was on her cell phone asking me for her check. "I earned fifty dollars and I need it now. When can you give me my check?"

I asked her if she remembered that she needed to pay her fine, so I would need to hold out twenty dollars. She reluctantly agreed. I told her that she also owed another twenty that she had borrowed to buy cigarettes. She was shocked. "But that only leaves ten dollars." She bargained. She complained. She threatened. Finally she took her ten dollars.

I wanted so badly to give her the fifty so she could enjoy an evening with her friends, but I knew that I would do her no favors by not allowing her to suffer the consequences of past crimes and current bad habits. As the conversation ended, I pondered that this must be how God feels when we pray. Much of what we suffer from and wish to escape from is consequences of our past actions. We beg God to take away the consequences. A child burns his fingers on a stove. A teen is caught cheating on a test. An adult is fired for insubordination. Consequences are the things in life that teach us to walk closer to the will of the Father.

Father, help me to learn from my mistakes. I thank You for the times You say "no" because I know it is the best answer.

Steve Hershey is a teacher and speaker at White Oak Church of the Brethren. Steve and his wife, Brenda, have opened their home to young adults

AUGUST 4

Children

"And whoso shall receive one such little child in my name receiveth me." Matthew 18:6 (King James Version)

Fifty years ago, we received a wedding card from my husband's ag teacher with a blessing that ended in these words: "May all your troubles be Little Ones." We had no idea that during the next fifty years, our home would be filled with many children and teenagers. We had no degree in psychology, yet God chose to send us children, some with huge needs that boggled our minds: abandoned, victims of drug addiction, prostitution and sexual abuse.

One of the greatest challenges was being mom and dad to children whose mothers were at New Life for Girls, a Christian rehabilitation facility. In two years' time, about one hundred children were under our care. Each child was a precious gift from our heavenly Father. Some were so easy to love and some brought me daily to my knees begging God to fill me with His love and compassion.

Our own five daughters can scarcely remember a time that there weren't at least one or two extra children at our table. It wasn't something we planned, it just seemed there was always a needy one brought to our door and somehow we knew that this was God's plan for us as a family.

My compassion for children began after my mother died when I was seven years old. God birthed in me a love for children who are hurting and separated from their own mothers.

These days there are less children spending time in our home, but I am finding there is a special place in my prayer closet to hold children with special needs before the Throne and believe for God's purposes to be fulfilled in them. There is no greater joy.

Father God, thank You for giving me the privilege of caring for some of these that You love. May I be faithful to be there for each one that You choose to lay on my heart.

Ruth Ann Hollinger is a wife, mother of five girls and grandmother of eighteen. She and her husband are grateful to be a part of Petra Christian Fellowship.

AUGUST 5

Visited by Love

"... may you have the power to understand ... how wide, how long, how high, and how deep his love really is." Ephesians 3:18 (New Living Translation)

I dealt with a lot of pain, depression and self-loathing during my high school years. My problems stemmed from a traumatic childhood incident, a near-rape one New Year's Eve while partying with my co-workers and being forced to accept my mother's new boyfriend. At the time, I handled my problems by drinking alcohol.

Although I wasn't living a Christian life, I did love God. One night I had an amazing experience where God showed His love towards me. An extremely bright light filled my bedroom. I became very fearful and yelled out, "I can't open my eyes!" Just then, I heard a loving voice, "I'm taking care of you."

Suddenly, I could open my eyes and the room became dark again. While contemplating what had happened, I realized that my "visitor" was Jesus. Then, I noticed a very ugly monster-like figure looking in the window at me then disappearing. The message I took from the ugly "visitor" was that the enemy was making it clear that he was just as real as Jesus. It was reassuring to know that Jesus' Presence could fill my bedroom, while the enemy had to stay outside and remain in the background.

At age twenty-three, I turned my life over to God. It was from Him that I received strength to get through my own difficult divorce and complete healing from my years of anguish.

Father, thanks for reminding me of Your great love exactly when I needed to hear it. I'll praise You daily for my happiness.

Happily married to Duane, **Rochelle Allgyer** and her family attend the Worship Center.

AUGUST 6

Safe Traveling

"He got up, rebuked the wind and said to the waves, 'Quiet! Be still!' Then the wind died down, and it was completely calm." Mark 4:39

On Thursday morning, August 18, 2011, I awakened to pouring rain. The weather forecast for that day was scattered thunderstorms. My only mode of transportation was a motorcycle. I finally made it to work, kept a check on the weather throughout the day and prayed for clear skies on my way home. I had a volleyball match later that evening and the weather was supposed to turn nasty right after the game. My place of work and the site of the volleyball game are located more than an hour's drive from my home.

I trusted the Lord to keep me safe. I knew, in my heart, that He wouldn't let me down.

On my way home that evening, the clouds were ominous and I could hear the thunder rolling in the background. As I was getting closer to home, the lightning streaked across the sky. All I could do was watch in amazement at the wonderful light display God was putting on. I didn't duck in fear as the lightning was streaking across the sky. It started to drizzle a little but there was no pouring rain.

I reached my home relatively dry and thanked God for the safe ride home. Later, I learned there were hail storms and pouring rain all around my route home, but God saw to it that I got home unscathed.

Thank You, Lord, for safe passage wherever I go. You are the Master of the sea, wind and rain. I trust that You will always keep me safe.

Carol Denson is a member of On Eagles Wings, the music ministry team of the Christian Motorcycle Association.

AUGUST 7

My Portion

"Let me inherit a double portion of your spirit." 2 Kings 2:9

I had sensed my first call to the ministry at age ten. Sitting in church one Sunday morning I felt a nudge that "someday you will do this." But now I was sixteen, sitting in the back row of a camp meeting service with my friends and trying to ignore a speaker who was inviting those who felt a call to professional ministry to come forward. I didn't want to embarrass myself in front of my friends. And the invitation implied a commitment that I wasn't sure I was ready to make. But God kept nudging and I grew more miserable until I finally went forward.

My pastor, who had been acting as a mentor to me, saw me coming down the aisle and met me at the altar. He knelt with me and asked, "Do you remember the story of Elijah who when he was taken up into heaven. Elisha asked for a double portion of his spirit?"

"Yes, I remember."

"Well, for whatever it's worth, I'm praying tonight that you will have a double portion of my spirit in your own ministry." From that night forward I pursued my calling as one set apart for ministry.

My mentor's life did not turn out very well, and that troubled me for a while. Then I realized that it was not his spirit that had been bestowed upon me, but God's Spirit. What my portion is compared to him or anyone else doesn't matter as long as I receive all of the gifts and invitations God's Spirit has for me. He is enough for me … for whatever He calls me to. And He is enough for you as well. He is enough for all those set apart for His glory.

Beloved Father, thank You for the gift of Your Spirit, who guides us and comforts us and makes us ready for the glories that await us. You are enough for me.

Dr. Tony Blair is president of Evangelical Theological Seminary, Myerstown.

AUGUST 8

Clean House

"So clean house! Make a clean sweep of malice and pretense, envy and hurtful talk." 1 Peter 2:1 (The Message)

I have had a busy schedule lately and was relishing spending more time with the Lord this morning. As I read 1 Peter 2:1 the word *pretense* stood out to me. I like to know the exact meaning of words and went to look it up. Pretense: putting on a false appearance in order to hide what is real … deception, also make-believe.

I immediately remembered an incident that happened many years ago during my teenage years. I used make-believe to influence someone in their opinion and response to me. So how could I "clean house"?

I confessed and renounced pretense as sin. Asked God to forgive me and forgave myself. When this process was completed my eyes were opened as to how pretense had influenced me all these years. I said that things didn't matter when they did matter. I didn't express true feelings that were necessary to get to the root of issues between myself and others. I received pretense from others because I had injected pretense into the relationship. (Whatever we sow we reap.) I am sure that pretense has influenced me in ways I don't yet understand. I believe I can walk free from pretense now. I have no illusion that I won't be tempted to accept pretense sometime again. But I can choose not to accept it because of God's love and power and the blood of Jesus.

God says in His word, "be holy for I am Holy." Holy means separated from sin to God. Somehow God chooses to use me even when I am incomplete.

Father, I am so grateful for your loving-kindness in exposing the need to clean house. Help me to resist pretense by the power of Your Spirit, who is Christ in me.

Kathleen Hollinger is a prayer leader at ACTS Covenant Fellowship.

AUGUST 9

You Are Precious to God

"Forgetting what is behind and straining toward what is ahead." Philippians 3:13

A client was both creative and vulnerable one day as she entered our session. She showed me photos of herself as a child, then she pulled out a little metal box. Inside were her razor blades. These razors had sliced through her lovely skin on numerous occasions. Cutting has been one of my client's favored modes of coping. She's been caught up in its addictive cycle for too long.

As we looked at each of her "little girl" pictures, she told me how they reminded her of her young niece. How she couldn't imagine taking a razor to that little girl. That she finally was beginning to understand that when she cut, she was not helping herself but hurting the "little girl" inside her. My client cried, which was a huge step for her. To her tears are "illegal." She passionately said, "I don't know how to do it, but I know these (the razors) have to go!"

We prayed for the client to have the grace and strength to get rid of her "tools of destruction." Then we walked outside and chucked those razors into the dumpster. When I heard that metal ping against metal, my heart rejoiced. My client renounced those destructive tools and willingly proclaimed that she would use "tools for life" on her body. We now have a date and a time with which we can war against the temptation and desire to return to old habits. She presses onward in life's battlefield with a victory marked on her heart.

We all must mimic my client's resolve to press on toward the goal to win the prize for which God has called us heavenward in Christ Jesus … His glorification.

Lord, thank You that you hear us when we cry. Be glorified through our vulnerability and Your victories in our lives.

Shannon Shertzer is a professional counselor at New Hope Community Life Ministry in Quarryville. Shannon is married to Jere. They live in Lititz and are members at Ephrata Community Church.

AUGUST 10

Take the Short Route

"Those who had been scattered preached the word wherever they went. Philip went down to a city in Samaria and proclaimed the Messiah there." Acts 8:4-5 (New Living Translation)

About a decade ago while listening to an urban theologian speak on the wonders of God in the city, I was called to minister within that environment. This was miraculous given that I had grown up in a country club neighborhood and spent most of my life judging the city, its people, institutions and structures. Years later, my wife and I found ourselves raising our kids in a neighborhood troubled by drugs, violence and poverty in all forms. Yet, God's beauty shines bright in the darkness.

In biblical times, the Jewish people wanted nothing to do with the land or people in Samaria, who were racially and religiously impure. Jews would often choose to walk miles around Samaria in order to avoid this land when traveling north and south.

Despite Jewish hatred of the Samaritans, one Jewish man, Philip, had the courage to preach the Good News of Jesus Christ to them. The people in Samaria heard the message and received their birthright as children of God. It is an amazing story when you understand the historical, cultural and religious divide that separated Jews and Samaritans for eight hundred years. In Acts 8, the Jews and the Samaritans stood side by side as brothers and sisters in Christ.

As you look at your own community, are there places that you avoid because of the people who live, shop or work there? Do they speak a different language? Is there skin a different color? Is there lifestyle offensive to your value system?

Be challenged to take the shorter route and travel directly through your Samaria when the opportunity arises. As you pass through, ask God to show you what He sees in that place.

God, let us hear Your call to the places and people that we avoid so that we might see Your Son. Move us to a new level of compassion and desire to demonstrate Your living gospel there.

Matthew Hershey is pastor of Cornerstone Christian Fellowship, Lebanon.

AUGUST 11

Restoration of Hope

"I will repay you for the years the locusts have eaten." Joel 2:25

This passage was written to an ancient Israeli agrarian society. Their entire existence rested upon how well their crops produced. If their crops failed, they couldn't simply cash their paycheck from down at the factory and buy groceries; they starved to death.

It reminds me when I was a young teenager working as a hired man on a neighbor's farm. One year we were having a particularly stellar growing season. We had planted all the crops very early that spring, we experienced excellent rain during that spring and early summer and it looked like we were heading toward a record harvest. Then one hot sticky afternoon on the last day of June, thunderstorms began to build. The sky turned a nasty copper color, and a wicked thunderstorm roared in. High winds blew and torrential rains poured down as we rushed to shut the barn doors and batten down everything. Suddenly, the rain turned to hail and it hailed harder than I've ever seen. We stood by and helplessly watched as hail, driven by the wicked winds, shredded and ruined field after field of beautiful crops. I had never experienced a more helpless feeling.

This is exactly how the people of ancient Israel must have felt as they watched the locusts heartlessly devouring their crops.

But God, the restorer and redeemer, is telling these people that He will repay them for the years that the locusts have destroyed their crops. They will experience abundance. He will restore their hope unto them.

What about you? Have the locusts devoured years of your life? Do you believe that things have been unfairly and unjustly taken from you? Have you begun to give up hope of ever seeing these things restored back to you? Trust God, maintain hope, and respond in faith.

God, I thank You that You are a redeemer and restorer of hope. I choose to trust You and Your ways.

Deryl Hurst serves as the senior pastor of DOVE Westgate Church in Ephrata.

AUGUST 12

God Has a Plan

"'For I know the plans I have for you,' declares the Lord, 'plans to prosper you and not to harm you, plans to give you hope and a future.'" Jeremiah 29:11

I drove through the tan-colored California hills on a warm July day, my thoughts in turmoil. My husband Bill had called me at work to tell me he'd been accepted to a Ph.D. program in North Dakota.

"What do you think?" he'd asked excitedly. "We'd have to leave in five weeks."

North Dakota! It was so distant, I had dismissed the idea as soon as he'd sent his application. Acceptance in an Arizona program was more likely—and closer to home. But no acceptance letter came.

Now I had to decide. We'd agreed a Ph.D. for Bill was a good step toward a secure future. But so far away! "North Dakota, Lord?" I said to the blue sky above the freeway. I didn't expect an answer.

Suddenly, a profound feeling of peace enveloped me. Amazed, I knew it was my heavenly Father saying, "Go." The decision was made. "Okay, Lord, we'll go," I said. The next day, I reserved a rental truck for August 12, five weeks hence.

Ten days later, I found the lump. The biopsy showed malignancy. "But we're leaving for North Dakota in three weeks!" I told the surgeon, who swung into action. Within days I was recovering well from major surgery, even with my diabetes. In every circumstance, I saw God's hand. I went home with a week to go, enough time to slowly pack up our small household.

On August 12, we pulled the rental truck away from the curb while friends waved good bye. I understood then that the peace I'd felt was not only my loving Father telling me to go to North Dakota—it was His promise I would go. It was His plan for me.

Father, thank You for Your loving plan for me. When my circumstances seem bad, help me to trust in You.

Robin Archibald and her husband, Bill, attend Grace Baptist Church of Millersville.

AUGUST 13

What Is Required

"He has shown you, O mortal, what is good. And what does the Lord require of you? To act justly and to love mercy and to walk humbly with your God." Micah 6:8

Oh, how does a mother react? My lovely daughter is growing up into such a helpful young lady. A helpful but sometimes forgetful, young lady.

I love that she wants to make cookies for the whole family with her Easy Bake Oven. But it is not a treat to have to clean up all her dishes.

It is great she wants to make lunches for the other kids, but leaving out peanut butter, bread, and spots of jelly on the counter can make for less enjoyable moments.

The point is, I love her heart and am glad she wants to serve. But preparing food is not what I require of her. One thing I do require of my children is that they clean up after themselves. (Boy, does that sound harsh.)

God has one requirement of us: to follow wholly after Him in honor of Jesus' loving sacrifice. I am sure He enjoys all the extras we want to do for Him, but not at the expense of what comes first—loving Him. Maybe it is time to put away the bread before it gets stale and sit at his feet.

Lord, sometimes I want to do so much for You I forget who I am doing it for. Please help me to just put You before anything else today, including serving others.

Tracy Slonaker, director of Christian education at Harvest Fellowship of Colebrookedale, enjoys being Jeremy's wife and mother of Hannah, Christian and Audrey.

AUGUST 14

Sandpiper or Pelican?

"For God did not give us a spirit of timidity, but a spirit of power, of love and self-discipline." 2 Timothy 1:7

Recently I was sitting on the beach, enjoying and observing God's creation. Nature inspires me and often teaches me life lessons as I allow the Holy Spirit to speak to me. That particular day I was observing many tiny sandpipers running alongside the water's edge. I watched them hurriedly run back and forth as the rhythmic waves ebbed and flowed. The sandpipers were diligent in their efforts to stay out of the water. I also observed large pelicans fearlessly diving into the water from a great height and at a high rate of speed. Wow, what a sight to see.

All the birds were functioning in their element; however, I couldn't help but analyze their distinctive differences. One species so timidly going after what it wanted versus the other one boldly chasing its pursuits.

Which one is my style? Do I fearlessly dive into life and new experiences or am I diligently running to safety and familiarity? Am I diving into and embracing emotions, feelings, responsibilities, gifts and the calling God has for me or am I escaping to safety like the sandpiper; running from uncertainty, trying to keep my feet from getting wet? Am I willing to lean into and embrace growth and development, being stretched way beyond my comfort zone? What am I running from today? Will I choose to live my life as a sandpiper or a pelican?

Lord, I want to live each day to the fullest, knowing that You work everything for my good. Help me to not walk in fear or timidity but to embrace each circumstance with faith, courage and Your amazing love.

Mim Hurst lives in Lititz and is a wife and a mother of three young adult sons. She serves in leadership along with her husband, Deryl, at DOVE Westgate Church in Ephrata.

AUGUST 15

Witnessing

"When the Holy Spirit comes on you, you will be able to be my witnesses in Jerusalem, all over Judea and Samaria, even to the ends of the world."Acts 1:8 (The Message)

Apostle Peter tells us we are chosen by God "to do his work and speak out for him to tell others of the night and day difference he made for you" (1 Peter 2:9).

connecting with our community

This is what witnessing is all about—sharing the difference Jesus makes in your life. You are not to argue your case or try to prove you are right. You're not an attorney. You're a witness. You report what happens in your life. Share your story. Stories attract attention. Your story is unique. You have no exact duplicate. Only you can share it.

Your testimony often has more authority than a sermon. The unchurched may see pastors as professional salesmen, but the unchurched see you as one who has voluntarily chosen to follow Jesus. This gives you credibility.

Your story is exactly that—your story. People have to accept it or write you off. If your character is consistent, they cannot write you off that easily. We remember people longer than principles or doctrines. The Holy Spirit will take your testimony and use it to convict them of their need for Jesus. There will be times in the unbelievers' life when the Spirit brings you and your story to their remembrance.

Many people today don't accept the authority of the Bible, but they will listen to your God moments. Paul told his experiences frequently. (See Acts 22-26.) Luke reports in Acts 8:4, the believers went everywhere sharing Jesus. I'm sure they shared how Jesus changed their lives.

Share what life was like before you met Jesus, then how you met him and what happened when you met him. Share what difference, he is making in your life today. God will use your story to bring others to himself.

Lord, help me to follow the Holy Spirit so I don't miss the opportunities to share my story.

Dave Eshleman served as pastor and church planter for fifty years.

AUGUST 16

Will He Do It?

"God also bound himself with an oath, so that those who received the promise could be perfectly sure that he would never change his mind." Hebrews 6:17 (New Living Translation)

When confronted with the question on the limitations of God, all of us would say there are none. God is able and powerful enough to do anything He chooses to do. There is nothing that can stand in His way and there is no power that is above or greater than He. Not even death. He defeated that as well as every other power. The problem we grapple with is not "can He do it" but "will He do it?"

Let me draw your attention to what the writer of Hebrews says in chapter 6:13-20, "Since there was no one greater to swear by, God took an oath in his own name, saying: 'I will certainly bless you, and I will multiply your descendants beyond number.' Then Abraham waited patiently, and he received what God had promised. Now when people take an oath, they call on someone greater than themselves to hold them to it. And without any question that oath is binding. God also bound himself with an oath, so that those who received the promise could be perfectly sure that he would never change his mind. So God has given both his promise and his oath. These two things are unchangeable because it is impossible for God to lie. Therefore, we who have fled to him for refuge can have great confidence as we hold to the hope that lies before us. This hope is a strong and trustworthy anchor for our souls. It leads us through the curtain into God's inner sanctuary."

Let these words strengthen your faith in that what the Lord has promised, He not only stands by with a promise, but with an oath that He will do as He said. And that my friend cancels all doubts and fears so that when we are in the storms of life, it is an anchor for our souls.

Because of You, Jesus, we are the victory side! We declare our victory: Emmanuel.

Ron Myer is international director of DOVE Christian Fellowship International.

AUGUST 17

Coincidence or Calling

"Therefore, my brothers, be all the more eager to make your calling and election sure...." 2 Peter 1:10

CM fidgeted in his seat. The YWAM Discipleship Training School in Chennai, India, had been going on for several weeks. Many good biblical teachings had been given, but CM still felt unsatisfied. Before the week's speaker began the class on Monday morning, CM muttered a prayer: "Lord, I want You to show me if You are calling me into the ministry. I want Your will to be very clear. If you are setting me apart for Your work, then have Mike Bordon reach out and touch me today. In Jesus' name. Amen."

Class started and Mike began teaching. Nothing happened. Then, after the tea break, as Mike spoke, he walked up the center aisle, and suddenly reached out his hand and squeezed CM's shoulder. "Wow," CM thought, "is that you Lord?"

On Wednesday, CM prayed, "Lord, I'm still doubting. Was that You, or just a coincidence?" Again that day, Mike reached out and squeezed CM's shoulder during the teaching. CM was so sure of God's will.

But as the day progressed, and then as Thursday came and went, CM began to doubt again. "Lord, in YWAM I won't get a salary. What if it's not Your will? I'd be making a mistake."

By Friday morning CM sat in class, knotted up on the inside. He had slept fitfully. "Forgive me for doubting Lord, but let me ask You one more time. If You are calling me into Your ministry, then have Mike Bordon touch me again today. In Christ's name. Amen."

Mike taught, the class ended, and he left the classroom, intently talking with another student. CM was the only one left in the classroom and his heart sank. Just then, Mike walked back into the room, strode over to CM, reached out and squeezed CM's shoulder.

Today, many years later, CM and his wife, Ratna, continue to lead Discipleship Training Schools for YWAM in Chennai, India. CM was set apart by a squeeze of the shoulder.

Lord, You work through us in ways we are not always aware of. Help us to be sensitive to the Holy Spirit.

Mike Bordon served with YWAM in India from 1982 to 2011 and now directs YWAM in Lebanon.

AUGUST 18

Seeking

"The earth is the Lord's and everything in it, the world and all who live in it ... Who may ascend the hill of the Lord? Who may stand in his holy place? He who has clean hands and a pure heart, who does not lift up his soul to an idol or swear by what is false. He will receive blessing from the Lord and vindication from God his Savior. Such is the generation of those who seek him, who seek your face, oh God of Jacob. Selah." Psalm 24:1-6

Green Piece

I'm trekking for some green;
Searching for that favored spot
On verdant carpet thick,
Shielded from the scorch of sun;
Suited for quiet reflection.

Sometimes I'm wandering like a refugee
Till I find the place that's right for me—
Outside earshot of other human beings;
Beyond cacophony of man-made noise—
Techno music and machines.

When I find my niche, I unwind
In meditative existence
Where my mind roams freely,
Winnows the wheat from the chaff
And gathers in a harvest.

In this tabernacle I commune with my king,
Dining at this banquet prepared for me.
Though enemies watch with envious eye,
They cannot penetrate my cover
Nor disturb my sanctuary.

I leave the table feasted full,
Radiant with unearthly glory;
Prepared for earthly life.
I bid good-bye my temporary abode,
As I become His dwelling place and home.

Father, help us to seek Your face so that we may know you better. Purify our hearts from all that fogs our understanding of you. Abiding in You is the greatest blessing of all, because in Your presence is fullness of joy.

Arnolda Brenneman is a member of the Lord's House of Prayer in Lancaster. She and her husband, Jan, function as pastors to artists through In His Shadow Ministries.

AUGUST 19

Lepers and Leopards

"And stretching out His hand, He touched him, saying, 'I am willing; be cleansed.' And immediately his leprosy was cleansed." Matthew 8:3 (New American Standard)

My daughter told me she had recently run into an acquaintance from her past and that he had changed for the better. Remembering her bitter experience and how she had been disappointed, I quickly said, "A leopard doesn't change his spots." I was cynical that he could ever change.

Immediately, the Holy Spirit nudged my heart with the words, "No, but it was I who cleansed the leper's spots." I recalled the stories in the Bible where Jesus healed the lepers. They were unable to heal themselves, but their lives were completely changed by His touch, just as my life had been transformed when He touched my heart and forgave my sins.

Who was I to judge this young man so severely? At his age I was still unsaved, unable to change on my own. Jesus died to do what we cannot. He can change our hearts, erase our blemishes and bring us spotless before Him.

Convinced, I prayed and asked the Lord to forgive my sinful attitude and to help me see with Christ-like eyes. I began to pray often for his salvation. I don't know how he's doing today or where he stands with the Lord, but I do know that the Lord loves him and died for him, so I will continue to pray.

Thank You, Jesus, that Your love for us is so great that You willingly died and rose again so that we could be forgiven and cleansed of all unrighteousness. Thank You for washing our spots away with Your precious blood. Amen.

Bonnie M. Evans is a member of Lancaster Christian Writer's group and Long Green Baptist Church in Maryland.

AUGUST 20

God's Transforming Love

"Don't copy the behavior of this world, but let God transform you into a new person." Romans 12:2
"May you experience the Love of Christ, though it is too great to understand fully!" Ephesians 3:19 (New Living Translation)

When I was nineteen years old and got my own apartment, I started conforming to the world and got trapped by my own desire for love and marriage. I was somewhat naive and became rebellious in my relationships with guys.

I had a four-year-long relationship that I thought would lead to marriage, but it wasn't meant to be. Shortly after, I moved to Ocean City, New Jersey, for my job as a flight attendant.

On August 9, 1992, I had a life-changing, head-on car accident. It was through this car accident that God transformed my heart. In the months leading up to the accident, I was crying out to God to help me stop my sinful sexual habits that I had felt were necessary to get a husband. I started having realization from God that my own self-serving ways were not bringing the kind of lasting love my heart was longing for.

Through several miracles during my car accident and thirteen-month recovery, God profoundly and interpersonally showed me that He alone can give me the love that fills every longing and need.

I had to move back to my parents' home in Pennsylvania and I started attending Hempfield Brethren in Christ Church. In 1993 I was baptized and became a member. About fifthteen months later I met Bryan, the man who would eventually be my husband. We married in 1999 and had a very challenging first two years of marriage. Bryan and I are thankful how far our loving Jesus has brought our relationship. We praise the Lord that we are both committed to working together and being continually molded by Jesus.

Precious Savior, thank You that Your love never ends, and for teaching me that I can't expect any human to provide the love that only You can fill!

Kristine and Bryan Forry serve as church deacons and Kristine works at Tabor Community Services as a credit counselor.

AUGUST 21

Set Apart by Love to Love

"And we know that God causes all things to work together for good to those who love God, to those who are called according to His purpose." Romans 8:28 (New American Standard Version)

On a particularly stressful day at work I was struggling with the reality of working in a very difficult environment. I wanted to crawl into a hole and have a good cry for myself. Unfortunately, my attitude wasn't the best, because I was resentful of this trial. Then, God graciously reminded me that people all over the world are suffering. As a Christian, at least, my tears had purpose. Then the remarkable and humbling question emerged: Who am I that I should have purposeful tears? After all, I am a sinner saved by the love and grace of God. But I am also one of God's beloved children, and over the years I have learned to believe that He wants what is best for me.

Most of my tears have occurred while I was in God's refining fire. His purpose has always been to conform me to the image of His Son. One of the severest trials was His plan for my husband and me to remain childless, which has crushed my heart with pain. However, I have come to believe that I resemble my beloved Savior more because I too tearfully prayed, "Not my will, but Yours be done."

Today, August 21, 2011, the Lord gave me a taste of the victory that He has been working into my life. For the first time in many years I attended a baby shower. As we prayed together as sisters, I thanked our Father for the grace to attend this event. Also, by faith, I thank Him for my purposeful tears.

Abba Father, thank You for never giving up on me, since I resisted Your gracious work so many times. What a privilege it is to be transformed into the image of Jesus, my Savior.

Susan Marie Davis and husband, Karl, are graduates of Lancaster Bible College and members of Calvary Church, Lancaster.

AUGUST 22

It Is Well with My Soul

"Rejoice in the Lord always: and again I say, Rejoice."
Philippians 4:4 (American King James Version)

Horatio Spafford wrote the well-known hymn "It is Well with my Soul" after tragedy struck his family. His only son died, and his business was destroyed by fire. Then his four daughters died in a ship collision while crossing the Atlantic. While at sea several weeks later, Spafford was inspired to write this hymn.

I first became familiar with the hymn at a Christian women's conference where it was sung each session. The conference topic highlighted the biblical imperative to rejoice always in all circumstances. The missionary speaker shared several personal traumas, summing up each one with God's faithfulness and His peace. The hymn lyrics declare the confidence in God that all believers possess, no matter the pain or grief under which they struggle.

"When peace, like a river, attendeth my way,
When sorrows like sea billows roll;
Whatever my lot, Thou has taught me to say,
It is well, it is well, with my soul."

I was emotionally and spiritually broken, unhappy in every aspect of my life. Rejoicing was not my normal response to hardship, rather gloom and doom overshadowed me. Would it ever be well with my soul, I agonized? Oh, how I longed for it to be so. With every stanza of the song, I prayed that God would make the sentiment of the hymn a reality in my life.

God is faithful. He ordained events in my life that required my crying out to Him. He held my hand when my feet were slipping. Gradually, I began to heal and praise Him regardless of my circumstances. It was several years before that conference prayer became an actuality, but now I claim the truth of the lyrics. Yes, "It Is Well with My Soul" and God has made it so!

Lord, I thank You that it is indeed well with my soul.

Sally K. Owens lives with her husband, Don, in Lancaster, where they participate in two home fellowship groups. They share many children and oodles of amazing grandchildren.

AUGUST 23

Water Bottles

"The one who drinks of this water shall never thirst…." John 4:14

It's funny how our society has come to embrace carrying water bottles and thermoses of water with us wherever we go. I wonder sometimes how I grew up getting through a church service or a car trip without a bottle of water. Particularly when I am in other nations, I like to know that I have the "security" of bottled water with me.

Jesus was not only a water bottle carrier, He was pure Living Water. He was always prepared to be the drink needed. Christ in us is that same hope of a glorious drink of Living Water.

We drink deep from the well of salvation not only because we are thirsty, but because we never know when someone will need the overflow of that drink (Isaiah 12:3).

I have pondered about some of the instances where Jesus asked of me to give my water bottle ration to someone else. Perhaps they might also represent the plans and types of situations He has for the Body of Christ to give out Living Water: Selah.

Maternity Ward: Gulu, Uganda, girl recovering from C-section without food or water.

Restaurant: Manila, Philippines, a waitress wants to be baptized

Slum: Marikina, Philippines, a teenager needs her feet washed for new sandals and a new commissioning.

Mountaintop: Meango, Uganda, planting and watering wildflower seeds with a child.

Displacement: Mbale, Uganda, one crying out for a drink after deliverance.

Narrow passage: Swaziland, given to guard in the mountains as a favor to cross into new territory.

Desert: Lima, Peru, shared with thirsty teammate

Are any of these situations modern-day parables that might apply to your life as a Living Water bottle?

God, You are endlessly creative when it comes to using us as vessels to pour new life into the thirsty. May our water bottles always overflow and introduce others to the Well of endless Living Water.

Nancy Clegg is a thirsty friend of the Living Water source.

AUGUST 24

Velcroed to God

"My soul clings to you; your right hand upholds me." Psalm 63:8

Before leaving to study abroad in Spain during my junior year of college, my spiritual mentor, Jenny, prayed with me that I would cling to God—like Velcro. She also prayed for God to provide me with at least one close Christian sister.

And so I arrived in Spain with the piece of Velcro Jenny had given me as a reminder to cling to Christ and the hope that I would find a Christian friend.

The very first day of classes, my host mother walked me to the university, and wanting to make sure I was not alone, she marched me right over to a girl sitting on the stone steps outside the entrance. After quick introductions my host mother left us to ourselves and we exchanged the basic get-to-know-you questions. I learned her name was Mary, that she was from England, and that she was studying in Spain for a semester. The next logical question was: Why are you studying Spanish? Mary's answer: "I'm studying languages so one day I can work with Wycliffe to translate the Bible."

I told Mary I thought she was the answer to my prayer—and she was. Mary became an amazing friend who encouraged and blessed me beyond measure. She also introduced me to her host family's church where we both participated in the Spanish version of Intervarsity Christian Fellowship and developed more God-given friendships. When Mary left halfway through the year, God brought another wonderful sister, Pauline from Texas, into my life.

I kept the piece of Velcro on my desk that whole year. It served daily to remind me to put my life in His hand and how His hand had blessed me with more than I could have imagined in the friends He sent.

Help me, Lord, to cling to You like Velcro. Thank You for Your hand that holds me and the beautiful relationships we have in Christ.

Brinton Culp, Lives Changed By Christ Church, prefers Velcro on the shoes of her two preschool boys.

AUGUST 25

Mercy Triumphs over Judgment

"Judgment without mercy will be shown to anyone who has not been merciful. Mercy triumphs over judgment." James 2:13

One day I was reflecting on a situation that had happened a few years ago. We had been out of work, and in debt with many threats of foreclosure by the mortgage company. We were praying much about the situation. I remembered how the Lord arranged some miraculous events that enabled us to buy another house and provide new work for my husband, which combined to bring us out of debt. That was such a miraculous chain of events.

As I thought about these events, I asked the Lord, "Why didn't the mortgage company foreclose on us back then?" I sensed the Lord replying immediately by saying, "You showed mercy to your son when you paid for his second semester tuition at college when he didn't deserve it."

As I recalled James 2:13, God really got my attention. He showed me how giving mercy to our son allowed God to give us triumph in our situation with the bank.

We praise You, Lord, for the triumph of mercy. Lead us to those who need mercy to triumph in their lives today.

Betty Cowley is a member of Ephrata Community Church, a member of HarvestNet and vice president of Papa's New Generals Corporation (an outreach to Papua, New Guinea).

AUGUST 26

Letting Go of the Past

"Brethren, I do not count myself to have apprehended; but one thing I do, forgetting those things which are behind and reaching forward to those things which are ahead, I press toward the goal for the prize of the upward call of God in Christ Jesus." Philippians 3:14

I have had many struggles in my life. I walked alone through most of them because I had turned my back on God. Two years ago when I was at the lowest point in my life, I finally turned to God.

He has been transforming me since that time. He has put amazing people in my path and led me to a wonderful church where I am loved and accepted. But I was so infused with the pain of the past that I had great difficulty living in the present.

However, God rescued me from the pain of the past in an unusual way on the day that I purchased a new vehicle. When I returned to my apartment that afternoon, I read a *God Stories* entry in last year's book in which the writer told about unloading trash at a landfill and used that time to throw away all the mental and emotional debris she had been struggling with for years. Each time she unloaded a bag of trash she named a toxic emotion such as regret, anger and bitterness that she was giving to God to cast away forever.

I decided to put that concept into practice in my life. I wrote down thirty-three fears I was letting go of and thirty-four toxic emotions that I was leaving behind. I folded the papers and shoved them into a spot in the vehicle I was getting rid of.

I found this process to be very healing. I continue to work on breaking long-ingrained thought and behavior patterns associated with my past, but I have hope, which had been absent in my life for far too long.

I know that God, in His perfect timing, arranged to have that story in the book on that day for me. I marvel at what God did for me.

Praise to You, God, for transforming me into who I have always been in You. Thank You for using my pain to bless others.

Shelley Dolak is a nurse, a member of Oasis Fellowship and a volunteer at Peter's Porch, a monthly community outreach in Akron.

AUGUST 27

When You Come to the End

"In all thy ways acknowledge him, and he shall direct thy paths." Proverbs 3:6 (King James Version)

A hymn often floods my soul when I awaken each day, but one morning, from where in my mind's computer I will never know, came a jingle I had learned in my teenage years.

I chuckled as so clearly the musical tidbit "When you come to the end of the lollypop," by Max Bygraves, brought to my memory a longing for another lick and yet needing to stop because it was the end of the lollypop.

Until recently, I had never thought of my life being like a lollypop, but in many respects it has been. My mind goes back over my life in the writing of memories as I lick the candy stick of life. What a privilege it had been to share the Christian witness with a surgeon husband who always had one foot in the work of a hospital and one foot in the building of Christ's church.

During our fifty years of service in Africa, we experienced times of drooling, however, when some of the sweetness was lost. I longed for another "lick of the lollypop" when my life seemed thwarted by the illness and death of my husband.

At ninety I'm holding the stick. The jingle states, "When you come to the end of a lollypop, you stop!"

But life isn't isn't like the jingle. As I step into my nineties, I am passing from the "youth group" as it is called at Landis Homes into a new era. And when that era is finished, I will pass into life eternal.

How sweet is that?

Father, Your Spirit within me leaves me not holding an empty stick, but the unchangeable promise of life everlasting with You.

Lois Eshleman is a retired missionary living at Landis Homes, where her present ministry is prayer.

AUGUST 28

Don't Buy the Lies

"When he lies, he speaks his native language, for he is a liar and the father of lies." John 8:44

Satan will do his best to keep your mouth shut about Jesus. He will whisper lies to you so you come up with the following excuses:

1. I really don't know them well enough.
2. They are too busy. Now is not the time. Just build relationships a little longer.
3. They need to see Jesus in my life before I can talk to them.
4. If I share the gospel, they will reject me and reject Jesus.
5. My life is not consistent with my message anyway. They won't believe me.

Compare this with Paul's words in 2 Corinthians 5:11: "That's why we work urgently with everyone we meet to get them ready to face God because sooner or later we'll all have to face God, regardless of our conditions. We will appear before Christ and take what's coming to us as a result of our actions, either good or bad. That keeps us vigilant. It's no light thing to know that we'll all one day stand in the place of judgment."

Jesus' brother Jude didn't buy these lies. He writes that we must snatch our friends from the fire and save them. Jude 1:23 (The Message) reads: "Go after those who take the wrong way. Be tender with sinners, but not soft on sin. The sin itself stinks to high heaven."

A vivacious second-grade teacher was gloriously saved. She came into my study and said, "I don't understand what is wrong with me. In the teachers' lounge I can talk about anything but when it comes to sharing Jesus, I clam up."

The devil is right there every time to tell us they don't want to hear our witness. Don't buy his lies!

Lord Jesus, make me bold. Give me the courage I need to follow Your Spirit in sharing Jesus with my friends and neighbors.

Dave Eshleman served as pastor and church planter for fifty years.

AUGUST 29

Hearing God a Second Time

"Then God said, 'Take your son, your only son … Isaac … sacrifice him … as a burnt offering.'" Genesis 22:2

Early the next morning after God had instructed Abraham to sacrifice his only son, Abraham set out to obey what he clearly heard from God. Arriving at the place of sacrifice, he tied his son on a makeshift alter and then "reached out his hand and took his knife to slay his son." While the knife was still raised in the air, at just the right moment, an angel yelled, "Abraham! Abraham!" Abraham immediately stopped and wisely answered, "Here I am" as he heard the voice of God a second time.

Having been a counselor for many years, I often heard the statement: "God told me to ____." (You can fill in the blank.) How do you argue with those words? How are we to reply when we hear such a phrase? Is our input at that point simply not valid? After all, how do you compete with the voice of God?

If Abraham would not have listened to God a second time and insisted on what he initially heard, then there would be no Isaac. If hearing God means one is crossing a boundary clearly set in the Scriptures, it's not only suspect, it's dangerous. If someone "hears God" and it is going to bring a direct hurt or harm to another, I would question what they heard. If spiritual advisors and counselors are advising something completely different, this person just may have missed God's voice. And finally, has this person heard God correctly 100 percent of the time? I know I haven't.

Lest we think we've heard God's final word on a matter, let's stay open in spirit and heart to hear differently from Him, His word or His messenger today and every day.

God, give us ears to hear, minds to receive and hearts to discern.

Steve Prokopchak is married to Mary for thirty-five years and a member of the Dove Christian Fellowship International Apostolic Council, giving oversight to DOVE churches in various regions of the world.

AUGUST 30

Consider It Done

"Trust in the Lord with all of your heart and lean not on your own understanding. In all of your ways, acknowledge Him, and He will direct your path." Proverbs 3:5, 6

As the Lord has been drawing me, I am determined to diligently seek Him both through His word and in worship. I find that it is easy to speak a verse in the Bible, yet another thing to see it come to pass. While waiting for a breakthrough, the Lord has encouraged me to take time every day to write down what He is saying. The following is an example of one:

"Know that I am looking for those who will not be afraid to go forward in these difficult days. Those who will not look back, but will keep looking straight ahead and go forward. For though it may seem that the answer tarries, it will not.

"You have only to look to me, the Alpha and Omega, the beginning and the end. I have perfected the things that concern you. Now look to me, and see the reflection of yourself and your inheritance, for it is being poured out to you. Open your spiritual eyes, and see it, receive it.

It is all by faith. Believe and receive my child, it is here for the taking: All that you have need and more. You have asked and now you will receive. Open your heart and let me impart what you will need to fulfill My will. I call you to be in agreement with me. Consider it done my child, consider it done. Now rest in me and you will see the glory of the Lord. All my love I give to You, Abba Father."

Lord, draw us to Yourself. Empower us to trust You with all of our hearts. Open our hearts to receive Your unconditional love and guide us to the place where we can receive all that You have for us.

Sandra J. Bernhardt Smith is the founder of Joy Celebration Ministries, Lancaster. She is also an itinerant pastor and speaker connected to Global Awakening Network.

AUGUST 31

The Runaway Volkswagen Bug

"Lean not on your own understanding, acknowledge him and he will make your paths straight." Proverbs 3:5,6

I had decided to go to graduate school. My wife, Rose, and I sold all we had and bought a 1964 used Ford van. We packed our things and were ready to head to California when a friend asked if he could go along. He wanted to go to the same graduate school, and he asked if we could pull his green Volkswagen Beetle to California. I said, "No way," as my van could hardly make it by itself let alone pull a car over the Rockies. But he persisted, and we gave in.

We had decided to visit all the national parks along the way. We were near Mt. Rushmore on a four-lane undivided highway when a Volkswagen bug passed us. It was our Volkswagen! I remember watching it pass through traffic as if it knew where it was going, eventually heading toward a mobile home park. My friend yelled, "Go get it!" It appeared the Volkswagen was going to crash into a mobile home when it hit a ditch, broke its axles and stopped.

We set up our tents at a nearby campground and thought, now what? Our friend said that he remembered passing a Christian wax museum a few miles back—maybe they can help. At the museum a gentleman greeted us saying, "Welcome and praise the Lord." We explained our situation. He asked if the car was a green Volkswagen. We answered affirmatively, and he told us he had been praying for a green Volkswagen. I said, "Sold!"

What looked like a disaster turned into a miracle and a blessing. The man's pastor gave us his car to tour Mt. Rushmore, fed us and asked what school we were going to. After telling him, he informed us that someone from his church was a senior at this school. He called this student on our behalf. The student had us pre-enrolled and found us a place to live in an area where we knew no one.

What could have been a disaster, instead thanks to You, Lord, became a blessing.

Thanks, God, for turning potential disasters into miracles.

Steve Shank is a strategic coach for Eastern Mennonite Missions.

Photo by Mark Van Scyoc

September

SEPTEMBER 1

Are You on a Low-Sodium Diet?

"We are the salt of the earth." Matthew 5:13

I opened a can of green beans for dinner one night and started to pick at them. (I am Italian and we Italians pick at everything that is in front of us.) As I started to chew, I choked. The taste caught me off guard and I had trouble swallowing the beans because they were the low-sodium variety. The can looked like all the other cans that I previously purchased except for the words "low sodium."

I hadn't previously noticed those extra words on the can until I tasted the beans. I made a face just like the one that my son makes when he eats my meatloaf. I added some salt and kept on picking.

A few weeks later, I was walking downtown past a gentleman who looked lost. I kept on walking but asked myself, "Should I go back and see if I can help him?" I did. He thanked me for my help and went on his way.

I am glad I went back, but for some reason I thought of that can of low-sodium green beans and how they made me almost choke. In Matthew 5:13, Jesus said that we are to be the salt of the earth. Salt is only good if it is touching something. If it just sits in its glass container, it is just an accessory for the dinner table. It needs to touch something else to be of use. We need to touch other people's lives if we are to be salt of the earth.

The next time you pass by someone who might need help, ask yourself … are you on a low-sodium diet?

Lord, help us to see the opportunities that come our way to help others, so we can shake our "salt" in large quantities.

Lisa M. Garvey serves with Hosanna Christian Fellowship in Lititz with the women's group and the prayer ministries.

SEPTEMBER 2

From Sidelines to Playing Field

"I have much more to say to you.... The Spirit of Truth will guide you into all truth." John 16:12-13

In the midst of career-changing decisions and life-changing situations, I called out to the Lord. As a loving Father, He replied: "You want to and will leave a legacy. Keep building. Your predecessors did the best they could with their situations. Many could have done better but so can you. If you were in their place, you may have done exactly as they did or even fared worse. Nothing they did can hold you back from what I've called you to do.

"Although everything changes, I do not change. My love for you is constant. My ability to supply your needs hasn't changed. Don't have more faith in the enemy's ability to stop you than you have faith in Me to help you through the contest.

"I am calling you to a higher level of integrity where others see more of Me. I am in you, but everything of Me doesn't yet show on the outside. There's time. We're still in practice. But I would like to move you along before the next game.

"You must not be afraid. That doesn't mean you won't feel fear, only that you won't be fear. It is doing, not thinking, that moves the kingdom forward. Don't live a life of thinking and not doing. Doing the thing that feels fearful is the way you will not be afraid. Increase your trust level. I will be with you, especially in the times you feel afraid. After doing things with Me by your side, you will gain confidence and feel the fear less and less—because the fear is a lie. You will know the truth and the truth will set you free!"

Lord, help me. I want to be ready for the game and don't want to be kept in practice because of my past failures. Help me be healed, washed and ready. Please don't let me sit on the sidelines. I want to be Your player at the highest level.

Bill Goodberlet is a member of the convening council for York Coalition for Transformation and an elder at Emmanuel Christian Fellowship.

SEPTEMBER 3

Our Cross

"Then Jesus said to his disciples, 'If any of you wants to be my follower, you must turn from your selfish ways, take up your cross, and follow me.'" Matthew 16:24 (New Living Translation)

On my way to the office one morning, I was listening to a tape on fulfilling our destiny. Theoretically, we all want to do that. I say theoretically because sometimes the cost to fulfill our destiny is greater than we are willing to pay.

Jesus had a cross to carry. It was cut for Him and Him alone. No one else could have bore that cross for it to have the effect on humanity that it did. The writer of Hebrews 12:2 says it this way when he encourages us to run with endurance the race set before each of us: "We do this by keeping our eyes on Jesus, the champion who initiates and perfects our faith. Because of the joy awaiting him, he endured the cross, disregarding its shame. Now he is seated in the place of honor beside God's throne."

Jesus was able to go through all that He went through because He could see beyond it. We all have a cross to carry or a destiny to fulfill. Funny thing about crosses is that everyone else's looks easier than mine. If I had the abilities the other person has, it would be a whole lot easier … or so our thoughts go. But the truth is that the Lord takes us down paths that we may not want to go but are necessary to get us to our destination. This is only possible when His will becomes our will.

What is your cross? I don't know. Jesus needs to tell you that. But I can encourage you to embrace it and when you do, you will fulfill your destiny. It will not be a theoretical decision as much as a practical one with application.

Lord, I embrace the cross You have chosen for me. Not my will but Yours be done.

Ron Myer serves as director of DOVE-USA.

SEPTEMBER 4

Giving All

"When he heard this, he was shocked and went away grieving, for he had many possessions." Mark 10:22 (New Revised Standard Version)

I was settling in for a much anticipated Sunday afternoon nap when one of our residents asked if I would come and talk to a couple of her friends. I went to the garage to find a hollow-eyed young man sitting in a worn chair. He started off by saying, "I am so lost. Can you help me?" He began to talk about his drug addictions, his family and the probation he was serving that would land him in jail if his parole officer found out what he was doing. After we were finished talking, he said, "I have taken enough of your time. Can you talk to my friend?"

A nineteen-year-old boy slid into the makeshift psychiatrist's couch and said, "I know I will need to give up my drugs someday, but I'm not ready yet." Within two weeks, I received the news that he was in the hospital in intensive care from a drug overdose.

When Jesus walked the earth, there was only one requirement to become his disciple: to leave all and follow him. Too often, our obedience to Jesus is conditional. Maybe our condition is "not yet." Maybe like Ananias and Sapphira, we say "not all of it." Maybe we prefer to serve Christ "not all of the time." We tend to be "cafeteria Christians" going through the Bible and through life, picking and choosing the parts that fit our schedule and our personal tastes. In the Gospels, Jesus made it clear that putting Him in second place in our lives is not an option.

Father it is Yours. All of it. Take my resources, my time, my all. Use it as You see fit.

Steve Hershey is a teacher and speaker at White Oak Church of the Brethren. Steve and his wife, Brenda, have opened their home to young adults.

SEPTEMBER 5

Amazing Reunion

"What god is so great as our God? You are the God who performs miracles...." Psalm 77:14

The Lord performed an unexpected miracle for me. The thought came to me and wouldn't leave: "How about teaching your Sunday School class again?" Making it happen could only have come from the Lord!

You see, fifty years ago the Lord led our family to a small church in Harrisburg. I was assigned to a class of ten African-American girls barely into their teens. We have four children of our own, but these girls soon became our second family. We had a wonderful ten years at this church and had those girls the entire time. Most of them accepted the Lord and now attend various churches.

We had little contact after we came back to our home church in Lititz, however many prayers followed. Now fifty years later and at age eighty-five, I became excited about teaching again. I relied fully on the Lord as I made arrangements with the church, set the date, sent out thirteen invitations, which included "bring your Bibles ... and you must behave." I received thirteen responses. The next week I worked on the topic the Lord gave me: "Where are you on your spiritual journey?"

I met thirteen of my "teenagers, now turned grandmas" at Herr Street Mennonite Church Sunday morning, June 12, 2011. I used Joseph's Journey for my theme, and the girls mentioned some of their struggles and how they felt the Lord's presence through it all. We rehashed and laughed over memories. When the bell rang for dismissal, they said they were not leaving. We continued our session throughout the service, followed by a Fellowship meal. I think I heard angels singing that morning. It was so glorious. What a blessing from my Lord!

God, thank You for this amazing experience and for watching over "my girls" all these years. You truly are a God of miracles and wonders. Praise Your name.

Grace Graybill and her husband, Paul, live at Fairmount Homes and are members of Crossroads Community Church near Lititz.

SEPTEMBER 6

Why Don't I Share My Faith?

"You have forsaken your first love." Revelation 2:4

Some surveys claim that only about 10 percent to 13 percent of Christians are actively sharing their faith. Why is this true? There are many reasons:

1. We have lost our first love. (See Revelation 2:4.) Pray for the zeal and the spirit of Peter and John: "We can't keep quiet about what we have seen and heard" Acts 4:20 (The Message).

2. We don't relate to unchurched people. We don't have unchurched friends. The longer you are a Christian, the more likely it is that you have only a very few relationships with those outside Christian circles. Jesus, our example, gave much of His time to those who were not His disciples. We need to intentionally go into the world. (See Matthew 18:12-14.)
3. We are uncomfortable bringing people to our church. Do you hesitate to invite people to Jesus because you know if they receive Him they need a family to welcome and nurture them? Is your church family a welcoming place? If you are not enthusiastic about your church you will be greatly hindered in your witness. Bringing a Christian into new life without a family is like a woman giving birth to her baby in the hospital, but as she leaves the hospital she lets the baby in the street.
4. Satan wants us to be quiet. He will whisper lies to you such as "They don't want to hear what I have to say," "They are too busy" or "You can't talk."

We need to say, "Get behind me Satan!" and claim God's Holy Spirit's power. We must take Jesus to the workplace, to the schoolroom and our communities.

Lord Jesus, forgive me for making excuses. Help me to be obedient to Your Holy Spirit as I seek to share Jesus with my friends and neighbors.

Dave Eshleman served as pastor and church planter for fifty years.

SEPTEMBER 7

Kings and Priests

"To him who loves us and has freed us from our sins by his blood, and has made us to be a kingdom and priests to serve his God and Father—to him be glory and power forever and ever!" Amen. Revelation 1:5-6

On a recent return trip from a medical mission to Iraq, we spent a day in the Strasbourg region of France. Our team visited a restored castle overlooking the beautiful valley in the Alsace countryside. Walking through the rooms filled with grand furniture and paraphernalia fit for a king made me think of times in bygone eras when royalty governed over the people. Soon after, I watched the royal wedding of William and Kate as they made their grand entrance down the center aisle of Westminster Abbey in all of the pomp and circumstance.

Thoughts of royalty intrigue us as we think of all of the privileges and responsibilities. We think of the few that are born into this lifestyle and sometimes even envy this grand position. God tells us throughout His Word, however, that He has made us to be kings and priests in His Kingdom. We, as born-again believers, are given privileges and responsibilities to reign with Him. Yes, even in this present life on earth. We all too often refuse to acknowledge His calling to walk along with Him doing His "bidding" here on earth. We often miss those moments when He calls us to partner with Him to move mountains and to see His kingdom come to earth. In these last days, let's resolve to live as kings and priests in God's kingdom.

Father, give us a new awareness that we have been made to be kings and priests in Your kingdom. Show us the privileges and responsibilities that we are called to as sons and daughters in Your royal family.

Dr. Scott Jackson serves as the coordinator of DMI Medical Missions. He works as a family physician at Crossroad Medical Center and also serves as an elder at Oasis Fellowship in Akron.

SEPTEMBER 8

Human Hearts

"The heart is deceitful above all things and desperately wicked." Jeremiah 17:9

On a dreadful night in April 1994, neighbors whose children had played together for years took machetes and savagely murdered their friends and neighbors who were a part of the wrong tribe in Rwanda. The devastation continued for three horrendous months and resulted in more than 800,000 slaughtered.

Some of the murderers were religious people who had attended church every Sunday. How could churchgoing people be so cruel and not have the love of Jesus in their hearts? The Scriptures tell us that the heart is deceitful above all things and desperately wicked.

Seventeen years later, things have changed in Rwanda. Family members of those who were slaughtered through the genocide are now going into the prisons to minister the forgiveness of Christ to those who had murdered their loved ones. The murderers are coming to Christ and receiving the Lord's forgiveness. The nation is becoming a model nation for the rest of Africa. It is by far the cleanest African nation I have ever visited. God has restored a sense of dignity to His people in this beautiful nation. Redemption at its greatest!

The government of Rwanda has erected a genocide memorial in the capital of Kigali, so that all Rwandese and visitors will never forget the 1994 atrocity and the tendency of the human heart.

There are lessons we can learn from Rwanda:

- Our hearts without a relationship with God are desperately wicked, no matter how religious our actions.
- God is faithful and redemptive. No matter what happens in our lives, through Christ we can see horrible situations turned around for good if we trust Him and walk in humility before the Lord.

God, search our hearts for any unforgiveness that could produce devastation in the lives of others. Cleanse us. Redeem us.

Larry Kreider loves being a husband, father and grandfather and serves the church as international director of DOVE International.

SEPTEMBER 9

Grandmother's Prayers

"I prayed for this child, and the Lord has granted me what I asked of him." 1 Samuel 1:27

Faithful were the prayers of my grandmother sown many years ago. Augusta (Pfeiffer) Bastouil, my maternal grandmother, was twenty-nine years old when she sailed from Germany to America, arriving at Ellis Island six weeks later. Oma brought a very important person with her: my mother, Marguerite Anna Lisa, eight years old. The year was 1926.

My mother and father were married in 1943. Dad was born Catholic, Mom born Lutheran and Oma was "born again." I regularly attended Sunday school and services at the Presbyterian Church. Oma worshipped and prayed fervently every day, setting a fine example in our home. It became clear through the prayers and faith of my grandmother that someday I would find my Savior.

With tears of joy, my grandmother reassured me that she would soon be going home to be with the Lord. I only understood I was losing my Oma. She was seven-two years old and I was eighteen.

How blessed I was to have my grandmother in my life. We often prayed together and considered this a special time. You could always find Oma in her room quietly praying, reading her German Bible or perhaps sewing. Her room was her sanctuary and the most peaceful place in our home. One would only spend a few minutes there to find peace and love from her kindness. She became my soft place to fall.

Years later, after the anguish and heartache of divorce at age twenty-nine, I gave my life to Jesus. Our faithful Lord answered my grandmother's prayers. Two generations later, my daughter and I are blessed to walk with the Lord.

Thank You, Lord, for the blessing of having a grandmother who prayed for me and for answering her prayer.

Barbara Ann Morgan, member of the Worship Center, was born and raised in Manhattan and moved to Lancaster County in 1994. She is the proud mother of Deborah Ann (Morgan) Glass of Lancaster.

SEPTEMBER 10

An Attention Getter

"Be still and know that I am God." Psalm 46:10

My husband was watching television from his favorite chair, and I was nearby in the kitchen. Trying to get his attention, I called his name three times but there was no response. On the fourth try I used a little strategy and yelled, "Power tools." Wouldn't you know it—he turned his head and looked at me and asked, "Did you want me?"

Some of us may have developed the bad habit of tuning others out when they talk. I am guilty, too. Sometimes, we hear only what we want to hear.

How about when God is trying to get our attention? Do we tune Him out by being too busy in our everyday schedule? It is easy to do in this hurried society. We are on the run so much and so busy, that we aren't quiet long enough to hear what He has to say.

It is vital that we make time for God. Let Him minister to us through quiet time and prayer time. Reading His word is like spending time with someone and getting to know them. You only get to know others if you spend time with them.

The next time you are trying to get someone's attention and they aren't listening, strategize and say something they would love to hear and see if they respond.

God, You are listening. Help me to make You a priority in my busy schedule and to sit still long enough to listen and hear You. Help me not to get distracted from You.

Lisa M. Garvey is a member of Hosanna! A Fellowship of Christians in Lititz. She is involved in women's ministry and prayer ministry.

SEPTEMBER 11

Still Engaged

"For our struggle is not against flesh and blood, but against the rulers ... authorities ... powers of this dark world...." Ephesians 6:12

The abrupt aggression of September 11, 2001, reechoed: "Some things do not change."

Two years before 9/11, my husband retired from twenty-three years of air force service. As a B-52 pilot, Bob served nine years of nuclear alert. Having moved thirteen times, we survived both remote northern-tier bases (the nearest shopping experience was a Sears catalogue) and the Deep South, where our Yankee accents revealed our childhood roots.

In hindsight, we'd do it all again. But, after the military, we also looked forward to a more relaxing and stable life in Lancaster County (away from deployments and dangers). Bob still flew one of Fred Boeing's jets and still wore a uniform. We were enjoying "retirement."

Then our serene civilian life shattered.

Our daughter finally reached me by phone: "Is Daddy alright?" Bob had landed the night before in Las Vegas. I wouldn't see him again for five days until the airlines resumed flights. This was familiar territory for us: during a crisis, service members are "away." But here was a "new normal." My husband used to fly bombers, now his nonmilitary aircraft could crash as a bomb. He remains under this "umbrella" of warfare, as we all do.

External circumstances may change, but the Christian life does not. One is always on "active duty" even during lulling retirement. One never escapes the call to deny self. In the military, to courageously die in combat while serving in lieu of one's countrymen is the understood obligation. For Christians, Christ's example inspires His followers to die to themselves to selflessly serve others. Our degree of "engagement" is not meant to change—until our marriage is consummated at that great heavenly feast.

Lord, remind us that while some of us fight men's battles in uniform, we all are fighting in a spiritual battle. Help us to be alert to both complacency and skirmishes, and to willingly engage head-on, but always in Your strength.

Tamalyn Jo Heim dances through the minefields with her husband, Bob, of thirty-four years.

SEPTEMBER 12

Waiting on God

"Do not be anxious about anything, but in every situation, by prayer and petition, with thanksgiving, present your requests to God." Philippians 4:6

I tend to give God deadlines.

Why? I'm human and live in a world where people are used to immediate results. After all, I think God should be faster than a tweet, text or Google. To be honest, sometimes He is. But, it is more common for His answers to come either when He is ready or when He thinks I need it most.

My good intentions are always to allow God to use my circumstances. I give the right to Him freely, believing He will do what is best for me. Generally, I wait patiently for His answer—for a week or two. When no answer comes, I become anxious and worried. Did God hear me? Foolishly, I think God must be waiting for my help. Then, too often, I stop waiting patiently for an answer and try my best to solve my own problems, choosing all of the avenues God surely hasn't thought of yet.

For reasons completely beyond my understanding, my efforts do not help. Then my anxiousness turns to panic. Crying, I question God's love for me. Unbecomingly, I throw a mini-temper tantrum, hoping that this will convince Him how urgent my need is.

Finally, with my emotions spent, I listen quietly. Then I hear His voice saying, "Do you trust me?"

I reply, "Forgive me, Lord. I always have." This time, I lay my problems down at His feet and walk away.

I thank You, God, for allowing me the freedom to make mistakes. For it is in my failure that I learn to lean on and trust fully in You.

Karen Helm is records coordinator at Messiah College.

SEPTEMBER 13

Perfect Storm

"But seeing the wind, he became frightened, and beginning to sink, he cried out 'Lord, save me!' Immediately Jesus stretched out His hand and took hold of him....'You of little faith, why did you doubt?'" Matthew 14:30, 31 (New American Standard Version)

In 2009 I found myself out of work. With my wife's part-time income and my unemployment compensation, we managed a household with two college students and elderly parents with mental and physical difficulties.

After two years, finding employment seems improbable. Being middle-aged, I ask myself what I am going to do with my life. My experience appears to have become unmarketable. My unemployment compensation and savings are depleted. With a now poor credit rating, obtaining a loan for retraining is unlikely.

I say this to point out that God has a way of getting our attention through life's storms. This "perfect storm" He has used forces me to focus on Him, because I am easily distracted with stuff and life's demands. I understand Peter, who became preoccupied with the wind and the huge encompassing waves. Sometimes, when considering my age, debts, nonexistent savings, no insurance, and dealing with two recent deaths in our family, I get anxious and, taking my eyes off of Christ, cry, "Lord, save me!" Yet, when I immerse myself in Scripture, plead with God in prayer, and reaffirm my trust in Him, I experience His peace.

I cannot say that I continually focus on Christ. Yet, on any given day, whether at peace or afraid, I know that God is in control, that He holds the ultimate outcome, and He is always good. Someday, when I behold Jesus, I will probably ask myself the question He asked of Peter, "Why did you doubt?"

Lord, You are sovereign over all things and Your love is everlasting. Strengthen my timid heart and cause my dull eyes to see Your blessings through the storm. Thank You for Your grace and faithfulness. Glorify Yourself through my weakness.

Steve Henson is a member of Grace Baptist Church, Millersville, where he is the AWANA commander.

SEPTEMBER 14

Hear His Whisperings

"Be still and know that I am God" Psalm 46:10

Silence Speaks
Hush ... are you listening?
Cease the busyness, the cackling,
The horde of bandits
Vying for attention.
Come away,
Be still,
Listen to the whispers;
Discover sounds you never heard...
Or not for a long while.
In the quietness,
Listen to the music of the soul;
Then go beyond
To hear the lyrics of heaven.
This is the place where wise men go—
And wise women.
Intended for receptors were we all,
And I dare to say,
We would not fumble easily
If we would come early
To this place of solitude,
Listening in the quietude;
Finding unmistakable gratitude
At the core from where life flows.

Help us, Father, to be silent; to be still, and to listen for Your whisperings.

Arnolda Brenneman is a member of the Lord's House of Prayer in Lancaster. She is multi-gifted as an artist in worship dance, poetry, prose, song and the visual arts. She and her husband, Jan, make and use worship flags and function as pastors to artists through In His Shadow Ministries.

SEPTEMBER 15

Refuge of Healing

"God is our refuge and strength, an ever present help in trouble." Psalm 46:1

In the one hundred fifty chapters of the book of Psalms, the word *refuge* is explicitly mentioned forty-three times in thirty-four different chapters (New International Version). Defined as a place of shelter, protection or safety, the concept of refuge is used many more times in the Psalms. Refuge is also a key theme throughout the entire Bible.

"My soul finds rest in God alone; my salvation comes from Him (Psalm 62:1). The psalmist David found a refuge in God for the human soul. According to the central theme of the Christian life, this refuge is ultimately expressed in God sending His Son Jesus to provide salvation for the human soul. "Therefore, since we have a great high priest who has gone through the heavens, Jesus the Son of God, let us hold firmly to the faith we profess. Let us then approach the throne of grace with confidence, so that we may receive mercy and find grace to help us in our time of need" (Hebrews 4:14, 16).

I am amazed every day by the contrast of God's power and love, justice and mercy, complexity and simplicity. He loves me so much; He demonstrates His power in my powerlessness to love. In my inability to act justly, He provides mercy that triumphs over my absolute best attempts at justice. When I forget the simplicity and purity of devotion to Christ as my refuge, His shield surrounds me to protect me from the most complex strategies of the enemy trying to take me out. When I become afraid and seek false refuges for comfort or fulfillment (too much food or things craved until they become an idol), Father stands with arms wide open, once again inviting my trust and healing the wounds created by my unfaithfulness. His perfect, unfailing love casts out all fear.

Lord, renew the simplicity of my heart's devotion to You today. I repent of the things I have made refuge in place of You. I desire You, and You alone as refuge. I renounce any ungodly security in the things of this world and thank You for Your peace and rest that will lead me in every circumstance of life, today and forever.

Dr. Edward Hersh provides counseling and healing prayer ministry. He has authored a book called *Escaping the Pain of Offense: Empowered to Forgive from the Heart.*

SEPTEMBER 16

We Called Him "Trouble"

"Show me your strong love in wonderful ways …" Psalm 17:7 (New Living Bible)

My husband surprised me with a stuffed animal. That night I took the white beanie bear with a blue jacket to bed with me to show my husband my appreciation, and then I had an idea. The next morning I tucked it under Greg's pillow where he would surely find it. Then I would find it in my coffee cup the next morning. On and on this little bear would show up in suitcases when we traveled, in one another's car, in our shoes, my purse and other unlikely places. We named the bear "Trouble." Once in a while when we went away and forgot Trouble, it was like forgetting a best friend. We had to retrieve it!

After my husband passed away, I sat Trouble on my desk next to my computer. Now I look at the bear in a different light. I hear Greg's laughter and see my heavenly Father's love through its beady-brown eyes.

Though I would never name the Lord "Trouble," I see godly comfort in that little bear as it looks at me. The Lord says to me, "I am your help in the midst of trouble; I am a husband to you as a widow; I am your laughter in the midst of your sorrow; and, I am with you always, even in your time of loneliness."

I talk back to it saying, "Thank you for all the good times you have given me. Thank you for the sweet memories of my husband, and thank you that even a little bear can be used as communication to my heavenly Father."

"Oh thank the Lord for He is so good! His loving-kindness is forever" (Psalm 118:1).

Dear Father God, sometimes it is the small things in life that become real and comforting to Your children.

Jan Dorward lives in Ephrata where she attends DOVE Westgate Church. She loves to write, travel and share her knowledge as a Messianic Jew.

SEPTEMBER 17

Loving God

"Love the Lord your God with all your heart and with all your soul and with all your mind and with all your strength." Mark 12:30

Have you ever thought about what it looks like to love God with all your heart, soul, mind and strength? We know we should love God more, but the real question is—how?

Loving God is about a heartfelt passionate response to what our hearts know, believe and love about God. The heart to seek God can only be birthed in us by God Himself. Like all desires, it is not something that can be forced, but rather it grows within us as we become exposed to His nature. He actually creates an appetite in us for Himself by lavishing us with the reality of His goodness.

All too often we allow our experiences, instead of the truth, to dictate how we see God and how we respond to Him. We must begin to grab hold of the revelation that God's love for us is beyond comprehension and imagination—He is for us, not against us and He is good all the time. His very essence and nature is that of goodness.

This reality will begin to burn deeply into our hearts if we simply take the time to behold Him. Paul describes this place of beholding as that place where "we all, with unveiled face, beholding as in a mirror the glory of the Lord, are being transformed into the same image from glory to glory, just as by the Spirit of the Lord."

Only when we perceive the face of the One in whose image we were made, do we come to know who we are and the One for whom we were made. And because of who He is, to behold Him and remain unchanged is impossible. As He overwhelms us with His presence, we find it easier and easier to love God with all our heart, soul, mind and strength.

Lord God, I declare Your goodness today. Thank You that I can truly know You with all of who I am. I invite Your transforming presence to make me more like You.

Kara Graver is the director of prayer ministry at Petra Christian Fellowship in New Holland.

SEPTEMBER 18

Simple Ordinary Opportunities

"The ways of right living people glow with light, the longer they live, the brighter they shine." Proverbs 4:18 (The Message Bible)

One Saturday my father felt the urge to visit his ninety-year-old sister in a Brittingham area nursing home. She was moving from the nursing home to her son and daughter-in-law's home in New York. Our family had undergone much change, but I noticed these changes helped knit my scattered family closely together, giving my parents the status of head of the family that had originally been held by my Christian grandparents.

In all of this, I saw God working, but I didn't expect that God would answer one of my prayers that day. My father invited my great-nephew Jacob to travel to visit Aunt Dot and to experience family history. The day trip involved hours of travel, visits to the cemetery, viewing previous homes, church and local landmarks like popular attractions. The simple and ordinary beginnings of generations of family love, history and, most importantly, Jacob's Christian roots. Jacob, who is almost thirteen years old, agreed to the trip but, like his peers, his favorite things to do involve modern technology. I join other family members in feeling concern about the balance of social activities and the technological influence on the younger generation. My prayers continually petition the Lord to have Christian family values and love passed on through the generations. That day, Jacob experienced a day of good memories while accompanying us on the family trip.

God's promises are true. At times it is difficult to experience the generational changes, but I continually see the goodness of God passed so eloquently from one person to the next and from generation to generation.

Dear Lord, thank You for Your promises, truth and generous love that You give freely and abundantly.

Cindy Healey attends Calvary Assembly with her mother and is a freelance Christian writer.

SEPTEMBER 19

Getting Ready for the Day

"Therefore put on the full armor of God, so that when the day of evil comes, you may be able to stand your ground, and after you have done everything, to stand. Stand firm then, with the belt of truth buckled around your waist, with the breastplate of righteousness in place, and with your feet fitted with the readiness that comes from the gospel of peace. In addition to all this, take up the shield of faith, with which you can extinguish all the flaming arrows of the evil one. Take the helmet of salvation and the sword of the Spirit, which is the word of God." Ephesians 6:13-17

Several years ago, as I was driving my children to school, each day we would pass an antique shop which displayed a full suit of armor outside its front door. For two small boys, this was exciting. It was a great opportunity to talk about the verses in Ephesians 6 about putting on the armor of God for the day ahead to protect yourself from whatever you might face.

A friend, Peggy, suggested that it is easier to remember each part of the armor by naming them head to toe. So as often as possible I would pray with the boys before leaving for school and pray that they would put on the helmet of salvation, the breastplate of righteousness, the belt of truth, the shoes of the gospel of peace and that they would hold the sword of the spirit and the shield of faith, something we can all still do today.

As I face today's challenges, Lord, help me meet them with the strength of Your might. Remind me that I am in a spiritual battle and that victory is in You.

Beth Holden is a wife, mother and grandmother. She is a former nursing instructor. She and her husband, Bill, worship at Lancaster Alliance Church.

SEPTEMBER 20

House Versus a Home

"Then he said to them, 'Watch out! Be on your guard against all kinds of greed; a man's life does not consist in the abundance of his possessions.'" Luke 12:15

Recently I have witnessed several house fires. I stood on the street and watched with one of my students as her house burned down to the ground. Several months later, down the road from our house, another family lost their house due to an electrical fire.

As I walk by that house and watch them try to rebuild, I see most of the house is made of wood. I think about how much we pay on mortgages just for a house made of lumber and how quickly our house can come tumbling down to the ground. We put so much money and value on our houses, but in most cases it's just made of a bunch of wood.

I vowed then that I would not put so much importance on my house itself, but on the people who live inside it and those who just come to visit for a little. Yes, I will continue to try to keep it clean and do my best to fix leaking ceilings and keep it nicely painted. But a house can go in an instant. The people we live with will be with us forever into eternity if they know Jesus. A house is made of wood or brick, but the people inside the house is what makes it a home. I want my house to be a home. A home where Jesus can feel comfortable entering every room, and the presence of the Holy Spirit can roam free.

Lord, help me not to put so much emphasis on things and stuff. But help me to reach out to those around me, such as family, friends and neighbors. Focus my attention on building stronger, lasting relationships and friendships instead of a more expensive house. Help me to use my home as a refuge and shelter to those hurting around me.

Jennifer Paules Kanode is an English as-a-second-anguage instructor and part-time disc jockey on FM 90.3 WJTL. More importantly she is a full-time wife and mother.

SEPTEMBER 21

Three Questions

"Finally, my friends, keep your minds on whatever is true, pure, right, holy, friendly, and proper. Don't ever stop thinking about what is truly worthwhile and worthy of praise." Philippians 4:8 (Contemporary English Version)

Three questions have changed my life: Is it kind? Is it necessary? Is it true?

If we ask ourselves these three questions every time we open our mouths, we would find that we won't have to dig ourselves out of holes as often. (I've personally had these questions help in my own life, although I still do need a shovel every now and again.)

These questions have become our family mantra. If someone is saying something unkind, all we have to say is: Is it kind, necessary or true?

That usually stops the offending party and helps them reflect on their words before going any further. These questions have helped us as parents to guide our children but also have helped us as individuals. These questions help us make sure what we say is true, pure, right, holy, friendly and proper.

So as you go about your day and interact with people ask yourself: Is what I am speaking kind, necessary and true?

If yes, than God can be glorified through your life.

Dear heavenly Father, help us to make sure our words are kind, necessary and true and that our lives honor and glorify You in all we do and say. Thank You, Father, for all You will do in our lives as we surrender our will to Yours.

Lynnea Hameloth says she has learned a lot from her beloved church family at DOVE E-town.

SEPTEMBER 22

God's Messengers

"Be cheerful no matter what, pray all the time; thank God no matter what happens. This is the way God wants you who belong to Christ Jesus to live." 1 Thessalonians 5:16-18

Our God is so loving that He will use anything at any time to speak to us, if we remain open to the Holy Spirit's whispers in our lives.

One delightful afternoon in the fall of 2009, I was busy running errands with my precious neighbors. In the parking lot of Martin's grocery store, we were all stopped in our tracks as other shoppers pointed out a praying mantis on the store's logo above our heads. We all paused in our busy day to look up at the logo and absorb the clear call to prayer that was delivered by a simple insect.

In the early morning hours two days later another praying mantis appeared on the screen of my bedroom window, greeting me as I sleepily got out of bed. Sometimes the Father in His mercy and grace sends His children multiple messages until they "get it" and are willing to allow the Father to incorporate His concept into their daily lives. This little praying mantis stayed on that screen all day long and into the night until yours truly received its message into her head and heart. It was such a clear word that we are daily challenged to remain in a prayerful attitude whether we are going through times of darkness and trial or seasons of light and blessings.

Thank You, Lord, for allowing that little praying mantis to stay on my window screen until this daughter truly "got" Your message for her that day in the fall of 2009.

Susan Kulka is a wife, mother and grandmother. She and her husband, Michael, attend the Worship Center.

SEPTEMBER 23

Gift of Friendship

"… a sweet friendship refreshes the soul." Proverbs 27:9 (The Message)

I only met this friend a year ago, and now I have to say good-bye. She and her family moved to Lancaster County last spring and we got connected because of our sons going to a local preschool together. It had been so nice to have a friend living in the same neighborhood. We carpooled together, babysat each other's kids, had playdates; we even watched each other's children so the other couple could have a date night. She's one of those friends who would do anything for you. And it was always a privilege to return the favor. She brought encouragement and refreshment, being a true woman of God.

She and her husband have had it on their hearts to do church planting, and now the time came for them to step into that new role. I have been so excited for them; however, when it means moving ten hours away, it makes it sad to say good-bye to them. I know that we're living in a day where technology keeps us feeling closer, such as Facebook, email, texting and similar ways, and I thank God for those options. But the idea of her moving made me realize how much I had taken her for granted. It's a reminder of how friendships are such a sweet gift from God. I want to remember to be thankful for the many people that God has put around me to support, encourage and believe in me. We so need each other to walk alongside of us in this journey of life. God brings friends into our lives, and they may only be nearby for a short time. This is a reminder that my dear friends are true gifts from heaven.

Lord, let my life be one that refreshes and encourages my friends. I am so thankful for the body of Christ, for they are an extension of Your hands and feet.

Cindy Zeyak is a blessed wife and mother of two boys and lives in Manheim Township. She and her family are a part of Worship Center.

SEPTEMBER 24

Comfort Your Child

"And I will pray to the Father, and he shall give you another Comforter, that he may be with you forever, even the Spirit of truth: whom the world cannot receive; for it beholdeth him not, neither knoweth him: ye know him; for he abideth with you, and shall be in you." John 14:16-17 (American Standard Version)

I remember the angst of taking care of my first baby. There were the days when every cry sounded like failure to me. I learned a lot in those early days.

My goal was to wake up at least a half hour before Hannah awoke so I could start the day freshly showered. But, my early riser made that time about 6:30 in the morning, which was not a time I found enjoyable to begin my day.

One day I awakened at 7:15 and saw that Hannah was not awake. I decided to chance a quick shower, knowing she would likely awaken during that time. I turned on my "supermom hearing" and jumped in. Just as my head was completely lathered in shampoo, I thought I heard something. Not wanting to get out in this condition, I just prayed, "Lord, I have given her to You and she is Yours. Please comfort Your child."

A voice inside me immediately said, "She is safe in her crib." The child God chose to comfort that morning was me. I finished my shower and went to greet my smiling baby, safe in her crib.

God knows what we need better than we do. This is good, because although I have gained more experience since those early baby years, I am not a supermom. God takes care of His children—all of them—as promised in His Word.

Lord, comfort Your child today. Make me aware of Your Holy Spirit that I might go about with a spirit of confidence.

Tracy Slonaker, director of Christian education at Harvest Fellowship of Colebrookedale, enjoys being Jeremy's wife and mother of Hannah, Christian and Audrey.

SEPTEMBER 25

Getting through the Firsts

"But seek first His Kingdom and His righteousness and all these things will be given to you as well." Matthew 6:33

On September 25, 2010, I lost a beloved sister to cancer. A friend has been sensitive to mark what she calls the "firsts without my sister." My sister has been dearly missed on several "firsts" such as the first Thanksgiving, the first Christmas, the first Easter, her birthday and my birthday. I now understand why people who have walked this journey before me say that getting past the "firsts" is the hardest.

There really has only been one way for me to get through these "firsts." That way has been to put "first things first" and seek the things of the kingdom of God and His righteousness. Seeking the kingdom first has meant searching with all my heart for God's comfort, His peace, His presence, His Word and desiring to have a deeper eternal perspective.

I am so grateful to the Lord that my sister and I belong to Him, and that she is now experiencing everlasting joy with Him. As I have sought the things of the kingdom, our precious Lord has transformed my mourning into gladness, gladness that this loss is truly temporary, and eternity with Him, for both of us, is forever.

Lord, thank You for helping me put first things first and trusting You with the walking through a journey of "firsts."

Patti Wilcox serves at Good Works, Inc., a ministry that repairs homes and restores hope for low-income homeowners in Chester County.

SEPTEMBER 26

Faithful Regardless of Circumstances

"Therefore, I will look unto the Lord; I will wait for the God of my salvation; my God will hear me." Micah 7:7

The Lord has been faithful, even when things appear to be not as they should be. I have discovered that whenever I get discouraged, I need only to look to the Lord, take Him at His Word and wait for His salvation.

Here are some biblically related promises that encourage me: "I am the Lord thy God, is there anything too hard for me? Wait on me says the Lord your God, and watch and see what I will do for you; for you have been faithful even when the times have been hard, you have stayed by me and turned to me for help, comfort and strength. I am going to show you how to pray. I will show you the things that are hidden, so that you will be able to combat them in the spirit realm. Take me at my Word, speak what I give you to speak, for as you declare a thing, it will be done. For even as times get tougher in the world, you will see my glory upon you and what I give you to do. Turn to me continuously, and I will continue to give you songs of praise that will break through the barriers that have been holding you back. Get ready to fight with the weapons that are not carnal, but mighty in pulling down the strongholds. The battle is mine, the victory is yours, in the mighty name of Jesus Christ my Son."

I pray that the eyes of our hearts and understanding be enlightened that we may know that God hears and wants to give us what He has promised in His written word. May we continue to look to the author and finisher of our faith, so that as we run the race, we will not grow weary in well doing. May we reap the harvest of souls in our places of influence and carry the gospel of peace everywhere we go.

Sandra J. Bernhardt Smith is the founder of Joy Celebration Ministries, Lancaster, and an itinerant pastor and speaker connected to Global Awakening Network.

SEPTEMBER 27

Dependent

"He said to her 'Daughter, your faith has healed you. Go in peace and be freed from your suffering.'" Matthew 5:34

I have read this scripture many times during my Christian walk and I believed in my head that God healed people. But I was convinced that God healed when he wanted and who he wanted ... and that certainly He did not heal in an emergency situation.

In May 2010 I went on a mission trip to Arizona with my church. We were located forty-five minutes from the nearest town and did not have transportation most of the time to leave the Indian Reservation where we were working. To phone home, we had to climb up a mountain. A group of us climbed up one evening and after phoning home, we began our descent down the mountain. I slipped and fell about a foot down the side of the mountain. Immediately I knew my back was hurt and had trouble breathing. The people who were with me immediately went to God in prayer. I cried out to the Lord in my spirit saying "Father God, it is getting dark and we need to get out of this mountain. I need you to heal me now."

Plus I was the team cook, so I needed to get up early the next morning to cook for our team. With some help from the guys, I was able to get up and walk down the mountain.

All through the night I prayed, "Lord I believe you will do this. Please allow me to get up and do what you brought me here to do."

I am pleased to say I got up the next morning to cook our team's breakfast and praised the Lord the whole time. I now believe that God heals in a way that I never did before.

Father God, teach us all to believe in You always and in all ways to be dependent on You.

Kendra Kramer is a youth director at St. Jacob's Kimmerling's Church in Lebanon.

SEPTEMBER 28

Bend Down

“But Jesus bent down and started to write on the ground with his finger.” John 8:6

The atmosphere was tense. The crowd was angry and wanted blood. They saw this woman as a sinner and in need of punishment. They were ready to hurl a torrent of stones her way. But the only one who could stone her instead bent down and began to write in the sand.

Theologians and writers have long wondered and pondered what exactly Jesus wrote in the ground. Some think he wrote the sins of those who were ready to stone the woman. Some believe he was writing the names of those gathered there that day. Some believe that Jesus was buying time in order to process his response to the question.

But I think we often miss the bigger point of the verse above. The bigger point I believe is the fact that Jesus bent down. Why did Jesus bend down? The woman was more than likely bending down, trying to protect herself from the possibility of oncoming stones. Jesus, I believe bent down, because he was next to her but more than that he wanted her to know that he was there. Maybe he bent down to protect her. He bent down because he loved her, forgave her and wanted the best for her.

If we think about it, we are that woman. Jesus bent down for us. Jesus loves, forgives, protects and calls us to live a new reality, a set apart reality. As followers of Jesus we are set apart, in order to bend down and love the people that God brings into our midst. We are to love them, protect them, be an advocate for them and not to judge them. Just like Jesus was an advocate for that woman so long ago.

Jesus, You bent down for us. May we bend down and love those You bring our way each day.

Ryan Braught is the husband of Kim, Father of Kaiden and Trinity, church planter of Veritas and a follower of Jesus.

SEPTEMBER 29

Never Too Young, Never Too Old

"For no matter how many promises God has made they are "Yes" in Christ." 2 Corinthians 1:20

I am amazed by the unique and creative ways God encourages us and shows us that He has His hand on our lives. Discouragement has a way of stealing life from us, eroding our faith and interfering with God's plans and promises for our lives.

One of the ways I was encouraged recently was how God spoke through our two-year-old granddaughter at a very timely moment. Her mother was passionately praying for a cousin, Gene, who was seriously injured in a motorcycle accident weeks earlier. During the prayer time our granddaughter brought a Bible to her mother. This toddler pointed to 2 Corinthians chapter one, fervently calling out Gene's name. Unbeknownst to her, 2 Corinthians 1:19 was the very passage that Gene's church leaders declared over his lifeless body on the day of the accident.

While Gene is still unable to walk or talk, this incident helped us hold on to God's promises for Gene's healing. God used this child as a mighty minister to deliver a significant message of encouragement to our entire family and others. Throughout time God has used individuals of all ages to accomplish His purposes. This girl has a special call of God on her life, but so does each and every child ever born. Let's dream of what good could happen if adults recognized the strengths of young children and called them forth into their destiny. Let's dream of what good could happen if adults affirmed each other in the area of their strengths and call each other into areas of purpose in life.

Lord, thank You for the way You reveal Yourself even to the youngest of children. Give me eyes to see You at work in the lives of others and to encourage them by sharing what I see.

Lloyd Hoover serves as a bishop in Lancaster Mennonite Conference, on the executive team of the Regional Church of Lancaster County, executive director of Transition to Community and other transformational and healing ministries.

SEPTEMBER 30

You Can't Hide a Van in a Driveway

"Jonah arose to flee to Tarshish from the presence of the Lord." Jonah 1:3

No matter how small a vehicle is, you are not going to be able to hide it from your spouse in your driveway. Several years ago, my husband bought a 1986 Volkeswagon van, called a Vanagon. He tried to "hide" it in our driveway. He parked all of his work trucks around it, hoping I wouldn't notice it. I went outside the next morning to get the newspaper. As I turned, I stopped in my tracks. I saw the van. Surely, he was borrowing it from someone; he wouldn't buy a vehicle and not tell me.

I went back into the house and asked about the Vanagon. He shamefully admitted he purchased it off of his friend for a price that was a steal ... I wished someone would. My decibels were raised a few octaves as I asked, "What were you thinking? You tried to hide it in our own driveway?" At that moment, the Vanagon's name changed to "Vagabond." According to Webster's Third Edition, a vagabond wanders, sometimes strolling and worthless.

Mr. Webster was right. Sometimes it would only stroll and didn't have enough power to go up a low-grade hill. I'd say it's worthless when you have to push it. This van had two amenities … armrests and windshield wipers. No cup holders, no automatic windows, nada. I'm sure by now my husband wanted to run and hide like Jonah.

Jonah did run from God. God asked him to go to Nineveh. Jonah found a ship, paid passage and went down into the lowest part of the ship. He was trying to run and hide from God.

In a way, sometimes we do that when God asks us to do something. We put it off or ignore it. We might run from God altogether. God wants our obedience and our availabilities, so we can do His work. Not only will you be blessing others, but you will be blessed by doing it.

Lord, help us to be more available in our lives for Your work to bless others.

Lisa M. Garvey goes to Hosanna Christian Fellowship in Lititz.

October

OCTOBER 1

Asking the Right Questions

"Adonai (Lord), you have probed me, and you know me. You know when I sit and when I stand up, you discern my inclinations from afar, you scrutinize my daily activities … For you fashioned my inmost being, you knit me together in my mother's womb. I thank you because I am awesomely made, wonderfully; your works are wonders—I know this very well. My bones were not hidden from you when I was being made in secret, intricately woven in the depths of the earth. Your eyes could see me as an embryo, but in your book all my days were already written; my days had been shaped before any of them existed." Psalm 139:1-3, 13-16 (The Complete Jewish Bible)

For quite some time, I have been asking God the wrong questions: "When are you going to bring about the dreams I have for my life?" "What is wrong with me?" "What are other people doing correctly that I'm doing incorrectly, therefore keeping me from seeing my dreams fulfilled?"

Recently our patient Father has planted new questions in my head: "God, what do you want with my life? What are your plans for me?" As I focus on waiting to hear His answers to these questions, I spend less time worrying, less time wishing I had someone else's life, and more time seeking God's direction.

Asking the wrong questions causes us to doubt the plans and character of God.

Our view of things is very limited compared to God who sees everything. He can even see into the human heart. Our view is based on what we physically see and what we know from the past. Only God can see the future. And, only He knows exactly how everything should happen … including our dreams.

Jesus, help me trust Your best plan instead of my best idea. Thank You for caring about the dreams and details of our lives.

Mandi Wissler attends New Covenant Christian Church and is on staff at Lancaster Bible College.

Photo by Yulia Bagwell

OCTOBER 2

Let There Be Light

"For it is the God who commanded light to shine out of darkness, who has shown in our hearts to give the light of the knowledge of the glory of God in the face of Jesus Christ." 2 Corinthians 4:6 (New King James Version)

A song echoed in my mind as I awoke this morning. It was one of those mornings when the Lord comes to me with a waking thought, verse or song that causes me to ponder throughout the day. I have become accustomed to taking these precious moments seriously and often write down the truths that are for my instruction specifically.

I began to search the hymnbook for the song and found it was written in 1832 by Henrich C. Zeuner. The first verse caught my attention as I sat down at the piano and began to worship as my fingers touched the keys:

Let there be light, Lord God of hosts!
Let there be wisdom on the earth!
Let broad humanity have birth!
Let there be deeds instead of boasts.

This song is a call to take notice of the Creator, who is high above any of my puny thoughts and knowledge. The world makes its daily appeals to my pride, my worth or lack of it. This will only lead me down a road to depression and focus on self. God would have me see Him for who He really is. It is He who gives me birth, salvation and purpose in Him.

Today I choose to boast in Christ and His wisdom. I choose to allow Him to direct me to the deeds that will honor Him most. I choose to point the world around me to Him today.

O God, truly You are the Lord of Hosts and the Light of the world. Fill me with the love of Christ. In Jesus' name.

Naomi Sensenig is a mother and grandmother, serves alongside husband, LaMarr, at Lancaster Evangelical Free Church and at Abundant Living Ministries in Lititz.

OCTOBER 3

Chained Elephants

"Set me free from my prison, that I may praise your name. Then the righteous will gather about me because of your goodness to me." Psalm 142:7

Recently, I was listening to a speaker at a conference discussing breaking the chains of our pasts that keep us from experiencing God's freedom in specific areas of our lives. Suddenly the image of a circus elephant came into my mind. Something about elephants always attracts and intrigues me. Elephants are huge and mighty animals. They can pull trees out of the ground with their trunks. Yet they also seem to be sensitive and intelligent beings.

As a child I would feel sad when I noticed the chains at their legs restraining the elephants. However, if one thinks about it, those chains are not strong enough to resist the strength of a full-grown elephant. Why don't they just break free and leave?

It is because when a baby elephant is taken into captivity, its leg is chained. The baby soon learns it is too weak to break that chain. As the elephant grows up, it continues to believe the chain holds it back. The elephant is in bondage to its false beliefs about the strength of that small chain. He believes a lie.

What lies do I believe? What fears or past hurts chain me in place instead of doing the things God leads me to do? Do I let my past rejections keep me from reaching out to others? Do I withdraw from situations where I have been hurt, believing I will be hurt again? Whenever I believe a lie from the enemy, I limit the power of God in my life. I must choose to believe the truth that greater is He that is in me, than he that is in the world.

Lord, show us the tiny chains or lies that we believe about ourselves. Help us to trust and believe Your Word so we can be set free from our prisons and praise Your name.

Karen Boyd is a contributing editor for *God Stories 7* and attends ACTS Covenant Fellowship.

OCTOBER 4

He Touched My Heart

"Blessed are the meek, for they will inherit the earth." Matthew 5:5

The handsome boy's eyes were enormous with eyelashes "that could touch the floor." Jayan was sixteen years old and lived in poverty beyond belief.

It was my first mission trip to Brazil, visiting my sister church, Comunidade Crista DOVE. One day we did a prayer walk through the streets of Fortelaza, intentionally stopping at Jayan's house. We prayed for his alcoholic father, young mother and brother. The small, block, adobe-type row home had no windows and on this ninety- degree day—it was winter in July—the room must have been well over one-hundred degrees. Jayan's family camped under a tarp outside their home to stay cool.

In the two weeks I was there, this shy, timid boy started to slowly open up. First a stunted smile, then a few words in English and finally, by the time I left, a hug and a high five.

I will never forget his beautiful, sweet face, hearing his heart cry out to God for his father and the desire to improve his living conditions. I thank God for his future hope that can only be in Christ Jesus.

Dear heavenly Father, there is a whole world of dire needs out there. I thank You that our hope, provisions and faith comes from You and You alone. How can we be a servant to You by ministering to those less fortunate than us?

Jan Dorward is a Messianic Jew attending DOVE Westgate Church, Ephrata. She is grateful for all the opportunities the Lord has laid before her—including writing, editing and presenting Messianic Passover teachings.

OCTOBER 5

Getting on with My Life

"Behold! I am with thee…." Matthew 28:15 (King James Version)

I was born with a rare eye disease that limited my vision throughout my childhood. I lost my vision entirely when I was twenty-three years old and had a bicycle accident. My dark world made me feel very much alone.

The Lancaster Blind Association encouraged me to apply for a guide dog. Both Artie and I received extensive instructions and tests to prepare us for independence. One day, I was told that I needed to go to New York City with Artie.

"No way!" I said. But I had no choice. The trip to New York was mandatory. A van transported us to New York City and dropped us off in a designated area.

"Just trust your dog. They were trained in the city and know what to do," I was told.

I was so scared. Artie and I walked for blocks, weaving in and out among the crowds. We even waited at a construction site. Artie led me down four flights of steps to the subway station. My heart nearly stopped remembering that my teacher had said, "Martha, this is a very wide platform. At the end is a bumpy strip. Never go beyond that strip or you'll drop eight feet to the tracks below."

When the train arrived, I gave the command. Artie hesitated, took a big step and led me inside the train. After riding around the city, we got off and went into a restaurant before heading back to the van. I was exhausted, but I survived New York City.

Since then, I've survived many scary times. Yes, I get discouraged at times. Some days it is hard to go into a dark world. But I run to my Jesus and He whispers to me, "My dear child, keep on. This life will not be long until you are home with Me."

I know God plans my life, and He makes no mistakes.

Lord, with Your help I want to encourage others.

Martha Hoover lives independently, has a full-time job, uses Braille cookbooks, types, sews and crochets.

OCTOBER 6

How God Sees Me

"For God made Christ, who never sinned, to be the offering for our sins, so that we could be made right with God through Christ."
2 Corinthians 5:21 (New Living Translation)

Our granddaughter, Sarah, was a beautiful and delightful little girl who preferred to wear jeans and a T-shirt. She didn't mind getting dirty while playing with her two older brothers. Her fine blonde hair was often tousled around her sweaty cheeks.

Sarah was excited to be chosen to be the flower girl in an upcoming wedding. Since I wasn't attending the wedding, I asked Sarah's parents to stop on the way home from the wedding so we could see her in her flower girl's dress.

Her parents told me to close my eyes until Sarah entered the room. When I opened my eyes, it was like looking at an angel. She was dressed in a pale yellow dress, white socks and shoes. Her hair was curled and tied up in a ribbon. She wore a choker necklace of daisies.

As I gasped at her beauty, I sensed God saying to me, "That is what I see when I look at you. You see your mistakes, failures and everything that is wrong with you, but I see the righteousness of Jesus Christ."

Lord, thank You for the righteousness I have in Christ. Because He died for the forgiveness of my sins, I am in right standing with You.

Joanne Miller worships at Ephrata Church of the Nazarene and has ten beautiful grandchildren.

OCTOBER 7

In the Garden

"Under His wings … refuge." Psalm 91:4

In 2009 I went on retreat at a Jesuit Center, where I was determined to listen attentively for the still small voice of the Holy Spirit. I journaled, prayed, sang and read. Free from the distractions of busy home life, I walked among the lovely gardens, ponds, statuary and landscaped grounds, including wooded areas. Praying out loud, I felt I was walking and talking with the Lord as Adam and Eve did in the Garden of Eden.

One day, as I sat on a bench to pray, the sky darkened and a breeze picked up. In the field before me, I saw a fluttering of plant leaves under the pattering of raindrop sprinkles. "No," I said within myself, "I am not leaving this place and interrupting this sacred time. If the Lord wants, He can put an umbrella over me and keep me dry, but I don't care if I get soaking wet; I am not leaving here until this time is completed."

So I stayed. The spattering on the leaves increased to a downpour. The trees in the wooded area to my right were assaulted with driving rain; the bench on my left gathered a puddle, and all was wet behind me. Yet all remained dry in a circle around me. Amazing! I hadn't even asked the Lord to give me an umbrella, but He knew my thoughts. As the rain poured down, I poured out my heart to the Lord. Ah, peace, conflict resolution, comfort, rest. Meanwhile, the rains ceased, clouds rolled away and the sun took over the day.

Though we can't always have a retreat, the Lord is pleased with our determination to set apart time with Him and will even put us in a "bubble" to meet us in our hour of need and bring us into the sunshine.

Abba, meet us in quiet places and in our daily routines, for You are available and accessible and will even change the atmosphere for us.

Arnolda Brenneman, Lord's House of Prayer, is a writer, poet, portraitist and functions pastorally among artists.

OCTOBER 8

Ever-Enlightened Perspective

"And the disciples were filled with joy and with the Holy Spirit."
Acts 13:52

While on a daily bike ride, I encountered God's presence in an unexpected way. While lasting a short duration, it has had an impact that continues to embrace and free me with its subtlety and clarity.

On this particular day, I had been wrestling with personal discernment matters. As I began my ascent up a hill that challenged both legs and lungs, I kept my head down applying myself to a steady climb. When I felt a whisper instructing me to look up, I did and there was a bird soaring within the reaches of my field of view. Calling to mind the scripture of the dove at Jesus' baptism, sighting this bird drew me closer into the moment and God's presence in it. With an inner ear of attention to listening to God while my eye continued to track the movement of the bird across the sky I spoke aloud my heart's concern, "Lord, how I so easily wander from the safety of You, Your presence and the present."

Just at that moment a second bird appeared. It floated a short distance from the other bird, again speaking truth to me, "I am with you." In reading Anthony D. Mello, SJ's writings recently, I found this statement describing the paradox of our relationship to God and God to us. Delighted and mindful of the deep joy of this moment I felt like a disciple with a seat in the Master's classroom.

The moment timed perfectly with the final rotations of my peddles to crest the top of the hill.

Suddenly, the second bird, as quickly as it came onto the scene, vanished. I thought, "there I go wandering from that joy of Presence again and the Holy Spirit remains," but then I felt gently corrected, "Ah, but that remaining bird is you continuing life's journey and the decision to keep going through its seasons of both hardship and ease. When you can't see Me, be still, know that My Presence has not left you." As the first bird continued on its way, my road too turned to much easier downhill riding with God's embrace now palpable. With my "lens" adjusted regarding the vanished bird, I now imagined it to be just below the visible one, so I was actually riding piggyback!

Yes, Lord, even when we cannot see You, You are there. You are my joy. Thank You for teaching Your disciple a fresh perspective along life's way.

Susan K. Shiner is a wife, mother of four sons and serves as a Songs for the Journey minister to the dying and a volunteer for Love in the Name of Christ.

OCTOBER 9

Set Apart to Love, Trust and Serve God

"For you were once darkness, but now you are light in the Lord. Walk as children of light." Ephesians 5:8 (New King James Version)

As I was acquainting myself with a computer game, a message appeared stating that each new level would get harder. My immediate reaction was, "Who says that I am ready for harder?" Oftentimes that is my initial reaction when something unexpected and unwelcome happens. However, as one who is set apart for God's plan and glory, I do not have the luxury of camping on that attitude. I can no longer live as I did before I knew Christ, following my own wisdom and will. Currently, I am dealing with two trials that are testing me to the core of my being.

In April of 2010 my beloved husband of thirty years was diagnosed with Parkinson's Disease. My once healthy husband now has a degenerative neurological disease. It hasn't been easy submitting to the Lord's wisdom and will. However, Christ is Lord of our lives and marriage, and because we love Him, we are trusting Him to develop His character more fully within us through this suffering. No doubt we will be more useful in Christ's service since we will cling to Him for strength and guidance. As set apart ones, we accept this as our responsibility and privilege.

In addition to this, I have recently become unexpectedly unemployed. Apparently our heavenly Father believes that we are ready to deal with this as well. Since His faithfulness to Karl and me over the years has been astounding, we desire to respond to Him with humble, childlike faith. Tonight I found a note in my Bible based on Hebrews 11:11 and 19. Yes, we will consider our God both faithful and able to bring us safely home!

Abba Father, thank You for my salvation and for Your precious promises which enable me to live for Christ Jesus, my Lord.

Susan Marie Davis and her husband, Karl, are graduates of Lancaster Bible College and members of Calvary Church in Lancaster.

OCTOBER 10

Called to Be Little Christs

"The disciples were called Christians first at Antioch." Acts 11:26

We sat on the porch and talked. She was homeless and looking for a place to live. We talked about her family and her job. We talked about her pet rabbit that died. We talked about her neighbors where she grew up. She told me that the neighbors to their right were psychos and their son kicked in her door when she would not open the door to him. He is in jail now. The neighbors to the left looked normal, but both had ongoing marital affairs, and both of their children are now drug addicts.

Then she said, "Oh yes, we had Christians living to the back of us. I did not see them much. They didn't let me come into their house because they didn't like my clothing. When I started to smoke, they told me they would call the cops if I set foot on their property."

Our comfort zone is with those most similar to us. We tend to avoid those who are racially, socially or spiritually different than ourselves. Our natural inclination is to barricade ourselves against the outside world.

We are called Christians. The term means "little Christs." How good a job do we do at reflecting the Christ we serve? Mahatma Gandhi is quoted as saying,"I like your Christ; I do not like your Christians. Your Christians are so unlike your Christ."

Jesus was scorned by the religious leaders because of the company he kept. When He was criticized in the book of Luke, Jesus answered that it is not the healthy but the sick that need a doctor. Although doctors take safety precautions when treating contagious diseases, they do not quarantine themselves. Their primary business is among the sick.

Father, on this day, help me to reflect Your light to a world that lives in darkness.

Steve Hershey is a teacher and speaker at White Oak Church of the Brethren. Steve and his wife, Brenda, have opened their home to young adults.

OCTOBER 11

Mountains and Valleys

"Come up to me on the mountain." Exodus 24:12

I had a difficult decision to make and was trying to discern God's will in it. Should I leave my current job and accept another position? The new position would carry some heavy responsibilities, put limits on my freedom, and force me to give up some security. But it would also provide opportunities to do the things I love to do, things I was set apart to do.

I consulted with others, who encouraged me to do it. But I was still a bit wary and prayed for guidance. Then one day I heard an invitation, deep in my heart, to run up a small mountain near my home. I like to run mountain trails, so I went. I climbed and climbed until I was out of breath and my legs were hurting, but I ran some more and finally came to where a rocky outcrop provided a long-distance view of the valley to the north. And there and then I felt the blessing and affirmation of my Beloved, whispering in my ear. "See that valley. That's where your new job is. This is what I've been preparing you for."

The next day I accepted the job.

Why did He call me up to the mountain to tell me that? As I read the Scriptures, I am aware that He very often uses mountains to reveal Himself. It might be because of the change of perspective that occurs as we go higher in elevation … we see more and we see differently than we can down below in the valley. And the same is true when we live in the Spirit. Those set apart for God are invited to see what cannot be seen through the eyes of the flesh. We are given glimpses of the kingdom of God at work in the world.

Beloved Father, thank You for eyes to see and ears to hear. Give us spiritual sight to see You and the path You would have us take.

Dr. Tony Blair is president of Evangelical Theological Seminary, Myerstown.

OCTOBER 12

What Does the Tag on Your Soul Say?

"May your unfailing love come to me, oh Lord." Psalm 119:41

Have you ever tried to share a product that no one seemed to notice or want? A product that even you did not believe in? No matter how good that product may be, without zeal and confidence, you may have problems convincing others they will like what you have to share.

I didn't have a product, but I had a lot of compassion and kindness to offer. I was also in need of love and understanding, which I tried to earn by being what others needed me to be. I did not believe that I could find what I wanted by being my true self, because that self was despicable. I had been told so during my formative years. I had a failed marriage. Therefore I believed that I was a total failure. In believing this, I opened myself up for just the opposite of what I sought. I became someone who invited people to use me in order that I may feel needed and loved. I became the prime victim for mental, physical, and emotional abuse.

One day a Christian friend whom I had just met asked me, "Sandy, how can you love others when you don't love yourself?"

I considered her question and reflected on what I had always believed. Subconsciously I felt I was worth no more than I received. Consequently, I accepted what I received from others, because something was better than nothing.

Slowly my friend helped me to look for the tag that was printed on my soul. It read, "This child of mine was made with tender, loving, care. God." At that moment, I felt the glow of His love, and the embrace of His arms. I was worth something because I was lovingly created by the Master Creator. His unconditional love set me apart to serve my Maker.

What does the tag on your soul say?

Lord, help us to realize that all tags are created equal.

Sandy Arnold is a scribe for the Rossmere Mennonite Church, Lancaster.

OCTOBER 13

Manifest Presence of God

"If Your presence does not go with us, do not lead us up from here. Is it not by Your going with us, so that we ... may be distinguished from all the other people who are upon the face of the earth?"
Exodus 33:15, 16 (New American Standard Bible)

What distinguishes Christianity from all other peoples of the world is the manifest presence of God in our midst. In the above passage Moses prevails upon God for a continuation of His manifest presence. His desperation is evident. Scripture makes it clear that God is everywhere present. Yet, for His people, He manifests His presence to guide, comfort and empower us. Even today, in a time when the American church can do amazing things without God, we must choose to pursue His presence. Redemptive history is essentially a record, not of amazing people, but of a God who personally comes and dwells among us.

Scripture speaks of times when the heavens are like brass toward us. Then there are examples of places like Bethel where Jacob discovered an open heaven where there was constant activity between earth and heaven. The Bible speaks of the heavens opening as God pours out blessings upon us like rain that refreshes and gives life. Even today, while we have resources and technology to do many things, we still must depend on God's presence for our Kingdom work. We can no longer say, "Silver and gold have I none," but neither can we say, "Rise up and walk." We desperately need to cry out to God to send His refreshing and empowering presence.

When Jesus told Nathaniel that he was a man without guile, He promised that because of this, Nathaniel would see the heavens open over him. This would make him a "mobile open heaven" which would take the presence of God wherever he went.

God, I desperately need Your manifest presence. Forgive me for any arrogance and open the heavens over us.

Barry Wissler pastors Ephrata Community Church and leads HarvestNet, a family of churches and ministries.

OCTOBER 14

A Spiritual Journey

"I'll shower blessings on the pilgrims who come here, and give supper to those who arrive hungry…." Psalm 132:15 (The Message)

I was one of twelve pilgrims who recently traveled to Scotland to see and hear how God has been present and at work throughout the centuries. Coming from hot summer weather in the United States and Canada, it was a quick adjustment to the cold wind and rains near the coast at the YWAM Centre in Seamill. Immediately our hosts shared hot soup, showed us our places to rest and offered us a spacious meeting room.

A few days later, the group headed to Edinburgh and was greeted by hosts of Emmaus House, a guesthouse in a major historical city. A beautiful table decorated with fresh flowers welcomed us to break bread together by enjoying fresh homemade pizza and salads. How delightful. How refreshing to be greeted with compassion, friendliness, and a well-prepared meal. Heated rooms, hot coffee, tea and chocolate were offered. Shelves of books and walls of artwork provided the feel of a home away from home. What a delightful welcome! The host's philosophy of "eating together around the table is the perfect opportunity to meet visitors" was evident to the weary travelers.

Emmaus House invites guests to the prayer chapel located in their backyard for morning and evening prayers and Bible reading. Prayer brings real refreshment to the inner being just as natural food revives the body. God's heart of compassion was expressed by praying for the sick and dying and for the caregivers watching over them.

As we journeyed on this pilgrimage, we frequently pondered the following insights:

- What were today's gifts? (thanksgiving)
- What were today's challenges? (petition and forgiveness)
- What are my hopes for tomorrow? (trust and grace)

May our ears, eyes and heart be open to divine instruction as we continue a journey of faith.

Father, as I have opportunity, help me shower blessings on pilgrims I meet. May I share food with those who are hungry and give warmth to those who have traveled in the cold.

Nancy Leatherman is chair of the Lancaster North Women's Connection, Lancaster. She is the mother of two and finds opportunities to help others.

OCTOBER 15

Why Don't I Share My Faith?

"When I first came to you I didn't use lofty words and brilliant ideas to tell you God's message. For I decided to concentrate only on Jesus Christ and his death on the cross. I came to you in weakness—timid and trembling. And my message and my preaching were very plain. I did not use wise and persuasive speeches, but the Holy Spirit was powerful among you. I did this so that you might trust the power of God rather than human wisdom." 1 Corinthians 2:1-5 (New Living Translation)

1. Intellectualism robs us of our zeal. Often the more education we have, the more reasons we come up with not to share our faith.
2. Obnoxious approaches by others have turned us off. Just because someone uses an inappropriate approach does not mean we should stop sharing our faith. "We reject all shameful and underhanded methods. We do not try to trick anyone, and we do not distort the word of God. We tell the truth before God, and all who are honest know that." 2 Corinthians 4:2 (New Living Translation).
3. We don't really believe our good neighbors are lost. Many Christians today don't believe a loving God would send anyone to eternal judgment. I find it helpful to remember that we send ourselves there when we reject the truth. Romans 1:18 in the New Living Translation reads: "God shows his anger from heaven against all sinful, wicked people who push the truth away from themselves."
4. We don't know how to relate to people. We are afraid. Perhaps we use the excuse that we are introverts. God will use the witness of everyone. Jesus had to tell us who He was so we need to explain that our good deeds are because Jesus has been so good to us.

Lord, whenever I am tempted to make excuses for not sharing my faith, help me to hear Your voice and say what You want me to say. Empower my words and actions to bring people to You.

Dave Eshleman served as pastor and church planter for fifty years.

OCTOBER 16

A New Heart

"And I will give you a new heart, and a new spirit I will put within you. And I will remove the heart of stone from your flesh and give you a heart of flesh." Ezekiel 36:26 (English Standard Version)

One fall I was having a minor surgery to remove a small but painful lump from my leg. Before I could have the procedure, I had some tests which revealed what I have known for thirty years—I have an irregular heartbeat. Of course the doctors wouldn't believe me when I explained this until after thousands of dollars of intrusive and inconclusive tests. It was hard not to succumb to worry, while having a stress test, EKG's and wearing 24-hour heart monitors.

During this time a dear older woman came to rebuke me for something I had said to her a couple of months before. After I gave her a compliment, she had told me that I was a sweetheart, and I argued with her, saying that was not true. I know my heart and it is not sweet. This time, my friend pointed out the fact that God in me was sweet. While I wanted to argue again, I was wise enough to accept her words and consider what God was telling me.

Here is the truth. While I continue to have the death of sin in my heart, God is giving me a new heart, and it is a sweet heart. Instead of focusing on what was, I need to speak what is and what will be. And someday I will meet Him face-to-face and through the work of His son, my Savior, will present to Him a pure heart. On that day, I will have a regular heartbeat.

Lord, as I face the realities of my own sin, help me to recognize the new life in and around me. Help me to believe Your word as my truth, rather than my own thoughts. Help me to truly be a sweetheart.

Karen Boyd is a contributing editor of God Stories and attends ACTS Covenant Church.

OCTOBER 17

Come Dance with Me

"The steps of a good man are ordered by the Lord." Psalm 37:23 (New King James Version)

In a recent dream, I was handing God an old, tattered jewelry box that I knew represented my life. He didn't take it, but handed it back and instructed me to open it. Upon opening, we both could see that the little spinning ballerina was missing. God looked at me and asked me where the ballerina was.

Intuitively, I seemed to know that it was in my pocket, although I had no memory of putting it there. Without a moment's hesitation, I reached in and pulled it out. Immediately, I noticed how bright, beautiful and shiny she was. The beautiful porcelain figurine had a white ballet outfit on that was accented in red. I was stopped in my tracks as I stared at her beauty.

Almost as if I was startled out of a trance, I heard Him say, "Put her where she belongs." The moment I did, the ballerina twirled and the music started up in a way that seemed like it was picking up right where it left off, as though it never stopped. As soon as she started up, the old, tattered jewelry box instantly became bright and beautiful, matching the beauty of the twirling ballerina.

Without even a moment of lapsed time, I found myself gracefully dancing with Him like a bride dances with her groom, twirling and swirling! Amazed by the gracefulness with which I was moving, I looked down at my feet. The moment that I took my eyes off of Him, I became clumsy and stumbled, as though I had two left feet.

It was then that He warmly said if I keep my eyes on Him, life for me would be like a spectacular series of graceful steps!

Thank You, Lord, that You are in control and that my life is not my own. Help me to focus and follow You always.

Wendy S. Domkoski is restored by understanding her identity in Christ and attends Harvest Chapel, Abbottstown.

OCTOBER 18

Cold Water

"So, because you are lukewarm, and neither cold nor hot, I will spew you out of my mouth." Revelation 3:16 (Revised Standard Version)

"Ordinary tap water?" asked the astonished French waiter.

"Yes. Ordinary water."

He shrugged and walked away brushing against the white cloths on the outdoor cafe tables.

"I have never in my life been so thirsty," I said to my husband. "My throat feels like it's parched."

Bob nodded and turned from watching the European passersby, but he waited for another soft drink.

Not that the small glass of tepid water the waiter set in front of me would quench my thirst. Lukewarm water, how I disliked it, almost as much as lukewarm soft drinks.

"I can't wait to get back to America for a glass of good cold water."

In fact, it was about the only reason I wanted to go home. I loved France and other European countries and people. In just a matter of days, they had won my heart.

They took me in; they gave me bread, but they offered me no cold water. With small refrigerators and tiny freezers, maybe they had none to give?

Laodicea had none. Their closest water supply was six miles away from the city limits. Water had to be piped in across the desert. No wonder it was lukewarm when it reached the wells of Laodicea.

The analogy of the lukewarm church in a lukewarm city was not lost on the readers of John's Revelation.

Their good works were like a small glass of lukewarm water, which could never quench the real thirst of needy people.

Thank You, Lord, for living water that satisfies our real thirst. And thank You for cold water given in Your Name.

Kathy Scott is a writer. Her new life in Jesus Christ began at Calvary Church fifty-two years ago, where she continues to grow in faith and knowledge.

OCTOBER 19

All about Perspective

"As for God, His way is perfect; The word of the Lord is proven; He is a shield to all who trust in Him." Psalm 18:30 (New King James Version)

In 2010 our family went on a mission trip to India. Whirlwind preparations were needed—immunizations, school releases, schedule arrangements and so forth. Don had been to India multiple times, so he had lots of hands-on experience. I was trying to prepare my two teens by showing pictures and reading up on the country. Visual preparation is particularly important for my son with autism in order to relieve his anxiety and give him some black-and-white concrete things to anticipate. Shortly before we were to leave, I remembered that the plane trip would take twenty hours, and he had never even been in a plane.

I got the idea to go to our community airport, hoping to get him onto a large plane so he could see, smell, touch and get the overall feel of what it would be like. When we arrived, the airport security offered to let us go inside the planes. As we walked across the tarmac there was only one plane on the runway, a small six-seater passenger plane. We crawled through the entry and climbed over a seat in order to sit down. It was very tight and our shoulders touched. Jordon's long legs barely had space, and his head touched the ceiling.

As we returned to the car, I felt extremely disappointed and kept wondering, "What was that all about, Lord? That is not the picture I wanted to plant in his mind. Did I miss hearing You?"

Suddenly I burst out laughing. "I get it! Thank You, Lord." Because of this awkward and small "point of reference," the jet we would be flying on would seem huge, with aisles and armrests, food and even a restroom. What a wise God we serve!

Thank You, Lord, that we can trust Your judgment—You do all things well.

Cindy Riker loves her family, supports Teaching the Word and co-leads at Change of Pace.

OCTOBER 20

Broken Stained Glass

"For God, who said, 'Let light shine out of darkness,' made his light shine in our hearts to give us the light of the knowledge of God's glory displayed in the face of Christ." 2 Corinthians 4:6

I look back at my life amazed at what God has brought me through. Being chipped by life, a broken vessel, God has put me back together to use me for His glory. He has healed my heart of life's disappointments, which has made me want to serve Him all the more. I am forever indebted to His faithfulness in my life.

Are we not all broken vessels, chipped away, smashed by life and stained by sin? God is more than able to forgive our sin, restore our broken lives and heal us through the shed blood of Jesus Christ. We are all different shapes with different purposes, but all used in some way to ultimately serve our God.

It reminds me of stained glass windows in a church. A stained glass window is simply broken pieces of stained glass put back together in an arrangement that displays a picture or design that when light shines on it, it becomes even more dazzling. Together, we are all broken pieces that God, in His amazing ability, arranges in such a way that reflects images of His glory.

I recently watched a video of a master craftsman of stained glass. Most likely, little do they realize that they depict an image of Almighty God. Father God is the Master Craftsman, who, in His artistic ability, desires to take the broken pieces of our lives and mold and make them into images of beauty. Truly amazing.

Father God, when the light of our Savior, Jesus Christ, Your one and only Son, shines on our broken, stained lives, individually and corporately as the church body, may we light up in a beautiful display for your glory! Amen.

Diana Sheehan, DOVE-Westgate, is blessed to be married to Robert and loves being a stay-at-home mom to three wonderful children.

OCTOBER 21

Transformed as We Worship

"But we all, with unveiled face, beholding as in a mirror the glory of the Lord, are being transformed into the same image from glory to glory, just as by the Spirit of the Lord." 2 Corinthians 3:18 (New King James)

"You can't teach an old dog new tricks." While this adage is used to describe canine and human stubbornness, it's not always true. For instance, if I can get our nine-year-old dog to look me in the eye, I can get her to behave. Granted, she may turn her head away to delay obedience as long as possible, but when I'm persistent and we lock eyes, she gives in.

The same is true for us. When we behold the Lord—when we fix our eyes on Him—we are changed. We see His glory and goodness, we see our self-glory and selfishness and we repent to become more like Him. Or we receive His relentless love, we love Him back and we purpose to love others more. In incremental steps throughout our whole lives, we are being transformed as we worship.

Worship is foundational to transformation because when we encounter our amazing God, He changes us. Whether we're worshiping with music, with scripture, in nature, through work, or at play—when we revere Him and respond to His prodding, we are transformed.

And transformed people want to help others to know, worship and obey this amazing God! A man who's being transformed helps his neighbor stain his deck. A woman who's going from glory to glory mentors a young single mom. A worshipping teenager hangs out with a misfit schoolmate. And one by one, a whole region is impacted by the glory of God.

Father, the transformation of our region begins and ends with You. Help us to worship You wholeheartedly. Transform us personally. Use us to love others and share the Good News of Jesus so You receive glory.

Lisa Hosler serves with Susquehanna Valley Pregnancy Services, the Regional Church of Lancaster County and worships with her husband, Ron, at Calvary Church.

OCTOBER 22

Go Home

"God told Abram: 'Leave your country, your family, and your father's home for a land that I will show you.'" Genesis 12:1 (The Message)

Being involved in ministry is wonderful and life-fulfilling. I was a part of Celebrate Recovery for almost ten years and loved it. Recently the Lord told me to "go home." That was it. No instruction, no direction. When I told my ministry leaders, they questioned my interpretation of the words "go home."

After some time of discussing it, the Lord kept giving me the same verse as I wrote above. He didn't tell Abraham anything, it was out of faith that Abraham moved forward. We tried to transition me out of the ministry, but I loved my position, and it made sense for me to be there. We dragged our feet while awaiting more instructions from the Lord.

In the meantime, my leadership training continued, and our next training was on our profile. My chart was unlike any of the others—and that caused concern to the facilitator. We spoke afterwards and he explained that my chart showed that if I wasn't yet burned out, I would be shortly. I shared with him what the Lord said to me, and he agreed that it was time for me to "go home."

I stepped down from my leadership role and went home to be with my children. It has been amazing to be home with them, and our relationship with each other has grown. There is more peace and joy than before. I'm learning who my children are, their desires and their personalities. I am now able to give back to them, spend time with them, lead them and guide them as the Lord directs.

Thank You, God, for Your direction, Your care and love for us. Help us see that our ministries start in the home.

Eileen Christiansen is a full-time employee with status of stay-at-home mom.

OCTOBER 23

Triggers

"Resist the devil and he will flee from you, draw near to God and He will draw near to you." James 4:7, 8 (New American Standard Version)

Our pastor was relating an experience of a harrowing bike ride down a steep hill and how later bike rides triggered that experience in his mind. God used the telling of that incident to help me understand how certain activities triggered my compulsion to overeat, react in anger or allow pride to rise up in my heart and not give God the glory.

This illustration was the means God used to help me to gain victory over these compulsions. Through giving the Holy Spirit permission to put a "check" in my spirit whenever a wrong attitude rears its ugly head, He has given me the power to resist these ungodly reactions. There are still times these behaviors surprise me by suddenly rising and catching me off guard. So I've asked God for wisdom to understand the source and in His amazing long-suffering and patience, He has!

Living with quick repentance and restoration has brought great peace and joy into my life. Now and then I get into a foul mood and my wrong attitude lingers longer that it should. Then the Holy Spirit gets my attention which causes me to be sorry that I've allowed sin to abide in my heart and mind too long.

The wonder of His amazing grace is this: As soon as I acknowledge the sin and repent, I'm again flooded with His joy and peace. A hymn that has been a longtime prayer of mine includes the words: "Let the beauty of Jesus be seen in me, all His wonderful passion and purity. O Thou Savior, divine, all my nature refine, 'Til the beauty of Jesus be seen in me."

Lord, thank You so much for sending Your Holy Spirit, my heavenly Helper, to me to put a check in my spirit and thus alert me to my "triggers."

Sandra Kirkpatrick is a special needs tutor and member of DOVE Westgate.

OCTOBER 24

Embracing the Land

"… then if my people will humble themselves and pray and search for me, and turn from their wicked ways, I will hear them from heaven and forgive their sins and heal their land." 2 Chronicles 7:14 (The Living Bible)

In Germany there is a small group of about thirty people who meet to seek God for the direction their nation should take concerning issues of life. They come from all walks of life: businessmen, financial managers, educators, apostolic church leaders, landowners and so forth. They wait on the Lord to hear His heart and His voice, and then they pray for the nation according to His will. These are the spiritual fathers and mothers of Germany. They have taken seriously the mandate to exercise dominion over their nation in the name of Jesus.

Fathers identify the gifts and callings of their children and they protect and provide for them. Mothers nurture and teach children so they will be prepared to walk in their destinies. Together, they keep the family on the path of health and well-being, passing on a lasting inheritance and a legacy.

Spiritual fathers and mothers do likewise. They recognize the gifts God has placed in the land, and they rise up to call forth those blessings for the benefit of all the people who live there. They also recognize when an enemy comes to steal, kill or destroy, and they stand in the gate to keep the enemy from entering. Spiritual parents of the land release heaven to manifest on earth.

These people walk in God-given authority that directs the affairs of their nation. In the last federal election, they heard the Lord direct them to declare that the next chancellor would be a woman from the former Communist East Germany. Angela Merkel, a pastor's daughter, was elected.

So, when we question how many does it take to change a nation? We discover, fewer than you think.

Lord, help us to change nations, one prayer at a time.

Rusty and Janet Richards serve in strategic intercession in France and Lancaster County as Pray Big!, a partner ministry of HarvestNet.

OCTOBER 25

Jumping into the Unknown

"Consecrate yourselves, for tomorrow the Lord will do amazing things among you." Joshua 3:5

As a college senior, I sensed God calling me to lay down my vocational goals for ministry. Frankly a change of plans seemed foolish. It meant saying "no" to dreams and things dear to me and jumping off into the unknown. I wrestled with God for many months before finally yielding to go God's way. Shortly afterward I received an invitation, which resulted in a pastoral assignment.

After twenty-nine years of ministry with that same wonderful congregation, I sensed God calling my wife and me to bring our ministry with them to an end. In college, I had wrestled with the decision to obey for six months, but this time I wrestled only three weeks. We announced our departure date with no idea about what would be next. Jumping off into the unknown carried a lot more "risk" than it had in college, but years of walking with Jesus enabled us to trust Him more, and He gave us genuine peace.

My last Sunday was approaching, but I had no job lined up. Others worried "for" us or suspected we had plans we weren't revealing, yet Mary Lou and I knew God would provide. One day I learned of a local congregation that needed an interim pastor and offered a short prayer regarding that possibility. Within an hour, I ran into the man responsible to find a pastor for that church. "Joe," he asked, "have you ever thought about doing an interim?" I went on to pastor that congregation. Once again God had amazing things in store.

Like you, I have been set apart to serve God. I wish I could say I always trust God, but I don't. But slowly, oh so slowly, I am learning to lean on God, learning to trust Him to pull through and learning that He always has amazing things in mind for us.

Thank You, Jesus, that often when we think we are making a big sacrifice to follow You, we end up accomplishing much more and being more fulfilled than had we followed our own plans. Continue to draw us into Your future.

Joe Sherer is intentional interim pastor at Willow Street Mennonite Church and board chair for Eastern Mennonite Missions. He and Mary Lou have three daughters.

OCTOBER 26

I'm Free

"Delight yourself in the Lord and he will give you the desires of your heart. Commit your way to the Lord; trust in him and he will do this." Psalm 37:4-5

I worked diligently for a company for more than twelve years. In fact, I often worked above and beyond the call of duty, but one day I was called into the office and told I was getting too slow. I was fired.

I was angry, fed up. I cried out bitterly to the Lord.

The Lord didn't leave me hanging for long. God clearly revealed to me that He wanted me out of that job because there was other work for me to do. I found myself very busy: helping a friend who had knee surgery, making meals for my daughter who hadn't been feeling well, creating a new, closer relationship with my daughter and my grandchildren and doing what I do best—playing board games and putting together puzzles with the elderly at the Denver Nursing Home. I am free to do whatever God calls me to do.

And, did the Lord provide for me? My former employer paid me three weeks of vacation and I qualified for unemployment. I was able to pay off all my bills with the 401-K I had been contributing to. And I am at the age where I am able to collect my full social security check.

God not only released me from the pressures that were put upon me at work, but being fired turned out to be a blessing instead of a tragedy. God has restored me, and I am free. I feel so much of God's joy and freedom in my life. Getting fired was the best thing that could have ever happened to me.

Sweet Lord, help us to allow You to work in us so You can bless us with our heart's desires.

Kathleen Masters is an encourager who attends DOVE Westgate Church, Ephrata, and is involved with its café outreach.

OCTOBER 27

My All in All

"And my God shall supply all your needs according to his riches in glory by Christ Jesus." Philippians 4:19 (New King James Version)

We may never fully understand the depths of the above verse until we find ourselves in circumstances where God alone is the One we depend on. In my earlier years as a Christian, there was a time when I had very limited contact with other born-again believers. My heart longed to be able to fellowship with those who would understand this newly found life and love I had for Jesus Christ—the One who gave His own life for me.

In the midst of walking through this time, I came across a poem titled, "God Is Enough." It brought out the concept that no matter what situation we find ourselves—we can truly find God in a way that He is enough to supply our needs. It ministered to my heart's cry, and as I cried out to the Lord in prayer, drawing closer to Him, I truly found God to be enough. I learned that there are times in my life that nothing can satisfy the deep inner longings of my heart like spending time alone with Jesus—the Lover of my soul—my All in All!

It was both a bitter and a sweet time to walk through. Bitter because in the flesh, it hurt. Yet, sweet to my spirit, for as we learn to cry out to the Lord and trust Him to see us through whatever we may be facing, we can "taste and see that the Lord is good" (Psalm 34:8a).

Even though now I have fellowship with other born-again believers, I still love those alone times with God when I can pour out my heart to Him, whether it's a burden or in praise and thanksgiving.

Lord God, let me never lose sight of my need of You and of knowing that You will meet my deepest need. I love You and praise You.

Miriam Fisher has a ministry of exhortation. She attends Charity Christian Fellowship in Leola.

OCTOBER 28

Pancake Breakfast

"The Lord is … not willing that any should perish but that all should come to repentance." 2 Peter 3:19

Recently our small church had a free pancake breakfast for the community. As we prepared, we read and prayed this verse: "The Lord is not willing that any should perish but that all should come to repentance." We asked the Lord how we could reach into the community. As our committee prayed and discussed, Deb came up with the idea of a pancake breakfast. This seemed a good fit for our church. As we prayed and prepared some more, a question arose, "How many should we expect?" Pastor Derek said the number could be six hundred, which stretched our faith, or as few as sixty. We asked the Lord to guide us and to multiply the food.

The day came and people began to come at 6:50 a.m. Neighbors, friends, those who saw the sign in passing, grownups who had previously come as children to Bible school, churched and unchurched. We had more than enough food. In fact we had so much food that the next Sunday we had a sausage and pancake brunch after church.

The contacts we made that day are, I believe, invaluable. We may never know the value of that morning when we gathered on the lawn at Chestnut Hill Church to eat together. Some asked for prayer, some mentioned they should come back to church, neighbors were pleased at the invitation, for some it was catch-up time as they had come to Bible school as children, a few shared that they had drifted away but now know Jesus as Lord.

As I write this it's only a week later. As we pray and reflect, we ask, "Lord show us the next step. There are many who do not have a personal relationship with You. How can we be pertinent in people's lives as they explore following You?"

Lord, help us not to be stuck thinking that we did our evangelism because we had a successful pancake breakfast. Help us to know Your will. Help us to move forward in obedience to Your plan. Show us what that is. Thank You, Lord.

Yvonne Zeiset is a financial counselor (consumer credit and default mortgage) with Tabor Community Services in Lancaster. She is also a prayer intercessor.

OCTOBER 29

Free Hermit Crab?

"For the grace of God has appeared, that offers salvation to all people." Titus 2:11

The sign in the shop window read, Free Hermit Crab, so at the urging of my six-year old son, I went in to claim my gift.

"Yes," said the shopkeeper, "the hermit crab is free, but you have to buy a cage for $14.99."

I looked to my left and saw another smaller cage. "Can I buy this one for $9.99 instead?" I asked.

"Sure," he answered, "but then you must pay $5.99 for the crab."

"Oh," I said, "I will buy the larger cage."

I went to the counter to pay while my son picked out a crab.

"Do you have hermit crab food?" the shopkeeper asked me.

"No," I answered. "I guess I will buy some of that, too."

"How about a sponge?" he asked.

"No," I said, "why do I need a sponge?"

"So the hermit crab doesn't dry out and die," he replied.

"Okay," I said, begrudgingly agreeing to buy the sponge.

"Now you need to choose an extra shell," he told me, "because the crab will want to move into a larger shell once he grows."

"This is getting to be an expensive pet," I commented, but the shopkeeper didn't seem to hear me.

"This is a book about hermit crab care. You will need to read it," he explained as he rung it up at the register.

Then he opened up the book and pointed out, "Hermit crabs are social animals. Do you want to buy another one?"

"Sure, why not?" I answered.

So, I paid forty dollars for the free hermit crab and left the store, completely amazed.

God, how grateful I am that Your gift of salvation is completely free. I believe in You, and I do not have to do anything more to have that gift. There is no catch. Thank You, God, for Your mercy and grace.

Bob Schwartz is a husband and father of two young boys. He attends a simple home church in Maytown.

OCTOBER 30

Eliminating Walls

"He [Jesus] left Judea to return to Galilee. He had to go through Samaria on the way. Eventually he came to the Samaritan village of Sychar.... Jesus, tired from the walk, sat wearily beside the well about noontime. Soon a Samaritan woman came to draw water and Jesus said to her, 'Please give me a drink.'" John 4:3-7 (New Living Translation)

Was Jesus provincial? He was the opposite. He was focused on the world. He came to take down the walls. "He has broken down the wall of hostility that used to separate us. By his death he ended the whole system of Jewish law that excluded the Gentiles. His purpose was to make peace between Jews and Gentiles by creating in himself one new person …" (Ephesians 2:14-16).

"God so loved the world that he gave his only Son, so that everyone who believes in him will not perish but have eternal life ..." (John 3:16).

We tend to build walls—walls between husband and wife, parents and children, extended family walls, walls with our neighbors, walls with Christians in other congregations, walls with people of other cultures. Jesus came to do away with walls.

He touched the lepers. He spoke with women and treated prostitutes with respect. He ate with the tax collectors who were looked upon as traitors. He healed Roman citizens. He associated with the poor and the rich, the religious and those who claimed no religion or a different religion. There were no walls with Jesus.

He chose Simon the Zealot whose passion was to eliminate the Romans. Jesus chose Levi the tax collector who cooperated with the Romans. With His great love and wisdom, He was able to help them to forget their differences so they could work together.

Do all you can to eliminate walls.

Lord, Your love extends to all people. Enable me to express Your love. Push me out of my comfort zone empowering me to relate to those whom I have been avoiding.

Dave Eshleman served as pastor and church planter for fifty years.

OCTOBER 31

Shining Brightly

"You are the light of the world. A city on a hill that cannot be hidden. Neither do people light a lamp and put it under a bowl. Instead they put it on its stand, and it gives light to everyone in the house. In the same way, let your light shine before men, that they may see your good deeds and praise your Father in heaven." Matthew 5:14-16

Each year on Halloween, my townhouse neighborhood buzzed with children running door to door collecting candy. I always made plans to be someplace else.

One year it occurred to me that maybe I should stay home, even though Halloween wasn't a holiday I really wanted to celebrate. I always had looked for ways to connect with my neighbors, and this was one time they wanted to come to my door. Why not be there to greet them?

I filled my basket with candy, turned on my light and waited for the children to come. Come they did! Many were dressed adorably with parents close behind.

Between the little visitors I prayed for the children that had just been through my door. At the end of my evening I had a deep sense of satisfaction I had been a blessing to my neighbors.

Since that time my church has developed a Harvest Festival tradition on the same night as Halloween. It has been meaningful and fun to see the doors of the church building open to reach our neighbors in this way, too.

Father, open our eyes to see new ways to touch others around us with Your love.

Sarah Sauder enjoys being a mom, works as a graphic designer and attends DOVE Westgate Church with her family.

November

NOVEMBER 1

Darkness and Light

"I can do all things through Christ which strengtheneth me." Philippians 4:13 (King James Version)

When I create a painting, I am concerned about the focal point and where the light comes from. I need to use some dark colors so the light can be seen. My goal is to create beauty, balance and harmony.

And so it is in real life. If I don't experience the darkness, can I see my need for Jesus who is the Light? In order to create balance and harmony in my life, my focus is on Jesus who can make something beautiful.

His ways are not always what I would choose. I have experienced loss and disappointments and have done well at wallowing in my grief. But guess what? That brings no relief. I continue to surrender what I think is good to the God who is always good. God has blessed us with two sons with mental disabilities. And oh how they teach us. One thing is sure, they love us unconditionally. I believe that because of them, I can empathize with other parents who hurt for their children. I care more for those who are different instead of living in my own little self-centered world.

It is hard to see our sons continue to be children in adult bodies. But I have chosen to believe God's promise that His grace is sufficient.

As an artist, I have the liberty to discard a painting that doesn't meet my expectations. I'm thankful that God doesn't give up on me and discard me. He is a God of grace and mercy. Our sons are teaching me to be a servant. The verse that comes to mind constantly is "Inasmuch as you have done it unto the least of these, you have done it unto me."

Dear Lord, thank You for the strength You give when I am weak. Help me to remember that whatever I do for others in their need, I do for You.

Gladys Zeiset is a member of Bethany Grace Fellowship. She volunteers at the "heART" of Friendship Gallery, which sells art done by persons with disabilities and by professional artists.

Photo by Mark Van Scyoc

NOVEMBER 2

Sanctification

"But you were washed, you were sanctified, you were justified in the name of the Lord Jesus Christ and by the Spirit of our God."
1 Corinthians 6:11

According to the dictionary, the word *sanctify* means to set apart to a sacred purpose or to religious use or to consecrate. The word *justify* means to declare innocent or guiltless. Sanctification and justification aren't topics we hear too much about from today's pulpits. In the days of my youth (a very long time ago), I heard many sermons on these topics, many which pierced my heart. My heart's desire was to be set apart and be holy, innocent before God.

Unfortunately, even after I was saved and dedicated my life to the Lord Jesus Christ, I struggled with the whole concept of sanctification and justification mentioned in the Bible. As a child and into my teens, I had been abused physically and emotionally by several people in my life who should have been my protectors. Although I knew in my head that I had been made clean through the blood of Jesus Christ, my heart seemed to tell me that I just wasn't good enough. I held anger and unforgiveness toward these men in my heart. No matter how much I tried to serve God, it never seemed like I could do enough. Just like many people today, I thought I had to earn God's acceptance and forgiveness.

It took me many years to finally realize that it wasn't anything I could do to earn God's favor; it was all God's doing through the work of Jesus Christ and the power of the Holy Spirit. At the same time, I discovered that to be truly free from my past, I had to forgive the people who harmed me and robbed me of my innocence. I can now stand before God sanctified and innocent before Him through the shed blood of Jesus Christ and the infilling of the Holy Spirit.

Thank You, God, that I am sanctified and justified through the shed blood of Jesus Christ.

Grace Arnold is a member of DOVE Westgate Church where she serves in many capacities, not because she has to earn God's favor but because of His love to her.

NOVEMBER 3

Include International People

"I saw a large crowd with more people than could be counted. They were from every race, tribe, nation, and language, and they stood before the throne and before the Lamb." Revelation 7:9 (Contemporary English Version)

In my fifty years of pastoral ministry I was blessed with many wonderful relationships with people from many nations. I miss the cultural diversity when there's only one nation, culture, sex or race present in a group. Heaven is pictured as an international community all focused on Jesus.

Make special effort to build relationships with people of different races and nationalities in your life and in the life of your congregation. Your Bible studies will be enriched. Your concept of God will be enlarged. Your diet may even be enriched. One thing sure is your worship will become a foretaste of heaven.

Jesus made no mistake when he created diversity. Let's embrace, encourage and promote it. I am greatly grieved and embarrassed that Sunday morning is the most segregated hour of our week. We need to intentionally break down those walls that divide us.

Jesus is our model. In John 4:4 and 9, he went through Samaria even though the Jews had no dealing with the Samaritans. He chose to go this route to break down the barriers between the Jews and Samaritans. Jews usually avoided Samaria by crossing the Jordan and traveling on the east side to get to Galilee. Jesus was intentional. We too must be intentional to overcome these barriers. Welcome international people into your life and church. Churches that make this effort are being revitalized. Include international people and empower them. Many of them will teach us new levels of faithfulness to our Lord.

Jesus, forgive me for being so provincial. Help me go out of my way to develop friendships with those of different cultures and nationalities.

Dave Eshleman served as pastor and church planter for fifty years.

NOVEMBER 4

Open for Business

"Always be prepared to give an answer to everyone who asks you to give the reason for the hope that you have. But do this with gentleness and respect." 1 Peter 3:15

It was becoming a long day and I had been on the road for most of it. My stomach was calling for attention when I saw the sign for a small pizza shop that I had patronized several times before. I pulled my truck up into the small parking lot, got out and headed for the pizzeria. I was stopped in my tracks by a Closed sign on the door. I stood, confused as to why the shop would be closed at 1:00 in the afternoon. I was heading back to my truck when the proprietor came out onto the porch.

"Are you open?" I asked.

He said, "Yes we are."

I asked him, "Did you know that you have a closed sign on your door?" He turned around in surprise and said, "Oh. That may be why business was so slow this morning."

As I left with my pizza, I was wondering if that is the reason that many of us have so little impact on our world. We have the most amazing message any man or woman could share, but we wear a "closed" sign on our faces.

We are not told "to witness," but we are told to "be witnesses." John describes witnessing as "that … which we have heard, which we have seen with our eyes, which we have looked at and our hands have touched" (1 John 1:1).

Have we observed the workings of God, or are we too immersed in our own lives? Do we have an "open" sign, and a willingness to share that witness with those around us?

Father, take away the "closed" sign that I so easily show the world, and draw to me a broken world seeking for answers that only You can provide.

Steve Hershey is a teacher and speaker at White Oak Church of the Brethren. Steve and his wife, Brenda, have opened their home to young adults.

NOVEMBER 5

The God of Redemption

"He provided redemption for his people; he ordained his covenant forever—holy and awesome is his name." Psalm 111:9

Today as I pondered in my devotional how, as broken vessels, God chooses to use us, a revelation came to me. God uses our brokenness for His glory. He uses our mistakes, failures, disappointments and humanness to reveal that He is a God of redemption.

One biblical reference to this would be the example of Moses' life. Moses killed a man and would be considered a murderer in our modern mind set. God redeemed Moses' life and used him to deliver the Israelites.

Another example would be that of the affair of David and Bathsheba. God could have used any of David's sons but chose Solomon. Solomon became David's successor and the wisest and wealthiest man who ever lived.

A New Testament example is Peter. He denied Jesus three times and was redeemed to being one of the key players to which the church of today was built.

The greatest example of redemption is how God took Adam and Eve's sin in the Garden of Eden and chose to send Jesus as the second Adam to redeem what man had lost to Satan. Amazing.

In my quiet time, I was questioning God as to why He would want to use little Diana. I feel so small sometimes and so overwhelmed with life in general. How such an awesome God would, could or even want to use me? It blows me away at the thought of this. God wants a relationship with me. With you. He wants to use us in our failures and our humanness for His glory in order to reveal Himself to the world.

Thank You, Lord, that there is no situation that You're not able to redeem for Your glory. You are able to do exceedingly, abundantly more than we can ask or think. You're amazing, God!

Diana Sheehan is blessed to be married to Robert and loves being a stay-at-home mom to three children. They are members of DOVE Westgate Church.

NOVEMBER 6

God out of the Box

"For now we see only a reflection as in a mirror; then we shall see face to face. Now I know in part; then I shall know fully, even as I am fully known." 1 Corinthians 13:12

Picture this: You are in a giant box. It is tightly sealed and holds nothing more than you and complete darkness. Yes, it reminds me of the *Twilight Zone*, but this is where you are, wandering around in the darkness, unaware of what lies outside of the box.

All of a sudden a nail pierces the lid of the box that you call home. You open your eyes to see the empty box fill with light. How beautiful the light!

You are not alone. There are others in the box that you had not even noticed before. Their eyes are closed, and you cannot understand why they would choose to stay in their blindness and miss this brilliance.

Now you feel yourself being pulled upward toward the source of the light. You are brought through the tiny nail hole, not sure how you could have made it until you see that your body has been left behind with those who choose not to see.

The light you bathed in while inside the box could not compare to the source of the light outside the box. While in the box, you could only see a part of the light, as the box blocked much of it. You are so transfixed by the source that the light itself becomes a new emotion like joy in your being. You can barely move for the powerful presence of it.

Here you are, now, where you are sure you have always belonged, so grateful to be here. The Source of the light shows itself fully, and the box burns away.

But even as incomplete as the light through the nail hole had been, you are thankful for it. That was what brought you home.

Thank You, Lord, that as the Source of Light, You have made a way for me to get out of the box and see You fully.

Tracy Slonaker, director of Christian education at Harvest Fellowship of Colebrookdale, longs for the Light.

NOVEMBER 7

Called by God

"Paul, an apostle—sent not from men nor by man, but by Jesus Christ and God the Father, who raised him from the dead.... Am I now trying to win the approval of men, or of God? Or am I trying to please men? If I were still trying to please men, I would not be a servant of Christ." Galatians 1:1, 10

Nineteen years ago, I almost quit as the senior pastor of our church. My immaturity as a leader and my inability to communicate clearly the things that I felt God was showing me led to my frustration. After serving as a senior pastor for twelve years, I was ready to "throw in the towel." I felt misunderstood, and I was not sure if it was worth all the hassle. I was frustrated, exhausted and overworked. In a misguided attempt to try to please everyone, I was listening to dozens of voices that seemed to be giving conflicting advice and direction. I felt unable to get back on track. I was tired and was encouraged to take a sabbatical.

It was during the sabbatical, spending time with God in the mountains, that I remembered the original call from God to lead this church. The call had not changed! God never told me to quit! I went back to my original call from God and led our church through a transition to decentralize into eight churches and then start a family of churches scattered all over the world. Today, by the grace of God, I am extremely fulfilled in my call and role of leadership.

We all need to learn to know how to hear the voice of God for ourselves. We need to know we are called by God and not by man. Only God is able to see us through the tough times of life.

Father God, forgive us for seeking the approval of others rather than You. We want to please You and be Your servants.

Larry Kreider loves being a husband, father and grandfather and serves the church as international director of DOVE International.

NOVEMBER 8

Was That You Lord?

"Now to each one the manifestation of the Spirit is given for the common good." 1 Corinthians 12:7

Several years ago during a devotional time I received a vision concerning a friend. This particular person was experiencing some struggles. My vision portrayed a picture of her struggles and some direction on how she could overcome them.

When the revelation ended, I questioned whether it was from the Lord or from my own imagination. So, I prayed, "Lord, if this is truly from You, then You need to show me what to do with this. Should I go to her and share this 'word' or simply keep it to myself and pray for her?" I sensed in my spirit that I was not to make a move to do anything about it except to ponder it and let God work out what, if anything, should be done. With that, I laid the whole thing aside and went on with my day.

Later that day as I was sitting in the living room pondering and reading over what I had written that morning, one of my granddaughters, who was at my house that day, came into the living room and said, "Grandma, someone is at the door."

Imagine my surprise when I saw this friend for whom I had the vision earlier that day. She came in profusely apologizing and said, "I just don't understand why I am here, but I was on my way home from work, and the Lord said I am to stop in to see you. I started to go home, but I knew that I had to come here. So I turned around and came here."

My spirit leaped within me and I replied, "Well, I know why you are here!" I was amazed and thrilled at how I knew at that moment that God had indeed spoken to me, and that He truly did work out how my friend was to receive His instruction. My friend received the word and we were both blessed at how our heavenly Father guided in this situation.

Lord, I thank You for Your faithfulness in working out the details of our lives and I ask that You would cause our faith to increase as we hear Your voice.

Sarah Zeiset and her husband, Carl, live near Mastersonville and are members of Ephrata Community Church where they lead a home group. The Zeisets have four children and sixteen grandchildren who are the joy of their lives.

NOVEMBER 9

What's in Your House?

"But as for me and my household, we will serve the Lord."
Joshua 24:15b

Most of us have seen that commercial that asks, "What's in your wallet?" It is true, you can tell a lot about a person by what is in their wallets. If they have a lot of family pictures, they probably value the importance of family. If they have a lot of credit cards, quite possibly they like to spend a lot of money. You might also be able to tell where they buy their groceries if they have a bonus card to a certain store. These are just some generalizations.

While driving down the street the other day, it occurred to me that you can also tell some things about a person by what they have inside and around their house. If they have a big screen TV, watching television might be a favorite pasttime of theirs. If there are a lot of toys strewn about the floor or lying outside in the yard, they probably have several young children. You can even tell what kind of food and beverages they might drink by looking at their recyclables outside their door. These are things we can assume just by observing and not even knowing the person.

So when people see your house, what are some things they might be able to tell about you? Would they be able to see that something about your house is different? And more importantly, would God be pleased by what He found inside your house?

Dear heavenly Father, may what is in my house please You. Take away anything that does not honor or glorify you.

Jennifer Paules Kanode is an English-as-a-second-language instructor and part-time disc jockey on FM 90.3 WJTL. But more importantly, she is a full-time wife and mother.

NOVEMBER 10

Immortality

"For this perishable body must put on imperishability, and this mortal body must put on immortality." 1 Corinthians 15:53 (New Revised Standard Version)

Jess and the boys had just been added to our eclectic family. I decided to take Cayden, then in Kindergarten, with me in the farm truck as I made my circuit of farm stores.

As we drove, we talked, and Cayden began increasingly to try to impress his new grandpa. "Hey Grandpa, did you know I can drive a mini-bike?" I answered, "Really?" Since I did not seem too impressed, he moved on. "Did you know I can drive a four-wheeler?" I responded with an "uh huh." I still did not seem to get the point of how amazing he was, so in desperation, he said, "Did you know I can drive a pickup truck?" I nodded my head.

He was quiet for a long time. Finally he said, "Did you know that I have sneakers that make me run so fast that sometimes I have to slow down for cars?" I smiled. He was quiet for a little and then looked up at me and said, "Grandpa. Is it true that when you tell lies your nose turns blue?"

The dream athletic shoe may be the one that makes us have to slow down for cars, but we are promised that we will someday "mount up with wings as eagles … run, and not be weary … walk, and not faint" (Isaiah 30:41).

When we are children, it seems like we are immortal. As we age, we realize we are indeed immortal, but immortality does not mean we never die, instead we cast off this body like a worn-out tent, and put on a perfect body that will never age.

Father, when the body aches and spirit is weak, remind me that this is only temporary. Not only is there a home reserved for me, but a spiritual body as well.

Steve Hershey is a teacher and speaker at White Oak Church of the Brethren. Steve and his wife, Brenda, have opened their home to young adults.

NOVEMBER 11

Bought with a Price

"Or do you not know that your body is a temple of the Holy Spirit within you, whom you have from God? You are not your own, for you were bought with a price. So glorify God in your body."
1 Corinthians 6:19-20

Years ago, after a homeschool field trip to Washington, D.C., my husband, children and I agreed to stop at Arlington National Cemetery before heading home. It was a beautiful morning, with sparkling sunshine, crystal-blue skies, and the deep greens of the huge expanse of grass … and hundreds of thousands of stark white grave markers. The beauty before our eyes contrasted sharply with the message of those arched marble headstones marked only with a name, service branch and history and birth and death dates.

While we watched the precise steps in the changing of the guard at the tomb of the Unknown Soldier, we heard the clip-clop of horse hooves as a funeral procession passed. In the distance we heard the bugler play taps and the salute of guns. There are several funerals conducted at the site every day. Standing there, it was hard to ignore the bloody history of our nation.

Our present lives in the United States were fought for and won by millions of men and woman who, like those buried at Arlington, offered to pay the ultimate price so that I and my family can enjoy the freedom and opportunities that many others covet. But even more than that, my eternal life was also paid for with blood.

I was humbled as I realized that I do not deserve any of the blessings I experience. I did nothing to be born here at this time and this country. I did nothing to earn salvation through Christ. It is all a gift from God. The only thing I can do is to honor the Lord for all of my days.

Lord, help me to walk worthy of the price that has been paid for me.

Karen Boyd is a contributing editor of God Stories and a online teacher of homeschooled high school students.

NOVEMBER 12

Time for Everything

"There is a time for everything and a season for every activity under heaven." Ecclesiastes 3:1

In the beginning of 2010, my mother began preparing herself and us for the time she would leave for her heavenly home. She mentioned that she didn't believe she would live to the end of the year. She began giving instructions to my two brothers and me about how her personal possessions were to be handled when she was gone. She had given a lot of thought to the arrangements for her funeral and communicated her desires. Mom was a very upbeat person. She loved life and she loved people. She wasn't being morbid, just making preparations.

In June we celebrated her ninety-fourth birthday. She loved seeing her family and being "queen for the day."

Early in November, she was admitted to the hospital. She called in her family and her pastor, believing she would pass on to heaven before the next day. She didn't die that night. God kept her here a while longer. She continued to fulfill her purpose as she told many people that she was going to see Jesus. She witnessed to the doctors and the nurses saying, "I'll see you in heaven." She encouraged us to follow Jesus and serve Him.

Finally on November 12, 2010 she breathed her last breath and was received into God's open arms. I can imagine Him saying, "Well done my good and faithful servant."

God had given my mother ninety-four years of life. She knew Him as her friend and wanted others to know Him that way too. Today we reap the benefits of her prayers, her interest in our lives and her godly example … in all seasons!

Thank You, Lord, for your steadfast love in all seasons of life.

Jean Horning and her husband, Jim, serve at Carpenter Community Church. They have a passion to see people healed and set free as they are embraced by the family of God.

NOVEMBER 13

Refuge in Trial

"O my people, trust in him at all times ... for God is our refuge." Psalm 62:8

Coming home from a family vacation, our pickup truck broke down. Before leaving, we all prayed for safety and that the three vehicles in our group would run properly. Twenty minutes into our drive home, our truck just stopped running. Didn't God hear our prayers? After more prayers, some frustrating moments and a five-hour delay, we all arrived home safely—including our truck.

The amazing thing was, after it was over, I couldn't remember the trouble as much as the divine steps God prepared in advance for us as we went through it.

The place of the breakdown wasn't a dangerous site, but at a large yard where we could exit safely and wait for the tow truck to arrive. Someone in our group had one hundred free towing miles, which took us closer to home at a twenty-four-hour garage. The tow truck driver was glad for Saturday business because his work was slow. (Sometimes our trials are someone else's blessings.)

The wait at the garage ended up shorter than we were first told. Would you believe there was an Applebee's Restaurant right beside the garage where we could all retreat for an enjoyable lunch during our wait?

Although too many problems and blessings went down that day, one thing I do know, Satan's intentions were for us to complain, be upset and doubt God's favor and protection. But God's intentions were to show us many blessings if we trusted Him throughout the ordeal. He is our refuge. Did God answer our prayers? You bet He did!

Which is greater: mountaintop experiences or going through the valleys victoriously? We need to learn to give thanks and trust God through both experiences.

Lord, help us to trust You and give thanks in all things today, because You are our refuge.

Jeanette Weaver is still learning to trust God in all things and loves being a wife to Don, mother of two, G-ma of six and serves at DOVE Westgate Church, Ephrata.

NOVEMBER 14

Opinions Versus Convictions

"My teaching is not my own. It comes from him who sent me."
John 7:16

Have you ever gotten tired of hearing the opinions of others concerning you, your family, your church or your son or daughter's latest tattoo or haircut? How come everyone has given themselves the job of making sure you are aware of what it is they like or do not like about you? Everyone seems quick to spout off personal opinions and advice.

Are we to conform to the advice of others or do we ignore their opinions?

Jesus was at a feast one day as recorded in John 7. He sent His disciples ahead and then traveled there in secret. People were talking about him at the feast. As Jesus began to teach them, he said something that really stood out to me the other day in my devotional time. In verse 16, Jesus revealed that His teaching was from the Father, it was not His own. Then, Jesus said if we choose to do God's will, we will find out if His teaching is from God (conviction) or simply from Himself (opinion). Jesus continues, "… He who speaks on his own does so to gain honor for himself (opinion), but he who works for the honor of the one who sent him is a man of truth; there is nothing false about him (conviction)."

An opinion according to this verse is to preserve one's own thoughts and ideas in order to gain honor for oneself. It is made up of this world's wisdom. It is spoken at times to protect the one sharing the opinion. A conviction, however, is spoken to protect the integrity of another, to honor what another has spoken as truth. An opinion can be offered in true humility and be very helpful, but a conviction is spoken from the spirit because of a greater truth one feels compelled to uphold.

Trying to sort out everyone's advice is easier if we compare it with the scriptural definition of opinions versus the convictions of truth.

Father, give us Your discernment today for the many opinions that will come our way.

Steve Prokopchak is married to Mary for thirty-five years and is a member of the Dove Christian Fellowship International Apostolic Council.

NOVEMBER 15

Harvest Time Is Now

"Now is the time of God's favor, now is the day of salvation."
1 Corinthians 6:2

"Do not say, 'Four months more and then the harvest'? I tell you, open your eyes and look at the fields! They are ripe for harvest. Even now the reaper draws his wages, even now he harvests the crop for eternal life, so that the sower and the reaper may be glad together." John 4:35-36.

Now is the time to pray for workers. Jesus commands His disciples: "The harvest is plentiful, but the workers are few. Ask the Lord of the harvest, therefore, to send out workers into his harvest field. Go! I am sending you out like lambs, among wolves" (Luke 10:2-3).

Ed Steltzer writes, "We've jazzed up the music, spiced up the sermons, and spruced up the building, but the wheat still isn't harvesting itself." How true! Jesus says we are to pray for more workers. The problem is not the harvest. The harvest is everywhere. We bump into the harvest every time we go to the supermarket, service station, dental office, post office or a football game. The harvest is work peers or classmates. Be conscious of the harvest every time you see the U-haul truck in your neighborhood, every time a new house is being built. God loved the people of the world so much He sent Jesus to give eternal life. We are called to give our lives for them as well.

Ask the Lord to give you His passion 24/7. Pray throughout the day for the Holy Spirit to guide your heart and mind so you can point people to Jesus. Eventually many will be brought into the wonderful harvest of eternal life. How blessed you and I are today to have the privilege of introducing people to the Good News of eternal life through Jesus Christ our creator and savior.

Lord, help me to remember that today is the day of salvation, now is the time to offer the Good News to those we meet. Give me a passion for the harvest.

Dave Eshleman served as pastor and church planter for fifty years.

NOVEMBER 16

Make a Legal U-Turn

"Trust in the Lord with all your heart … in all your ways acknowledge Him and He will direct your path." Proverbs 3:5

"When possible make a legal U-turn." Those instructions came from the disembodied voice of Matilda, my GPS. I had never traveled to this city before and I was nervous about being on time for my speaking engagement. I glanced at my watch and wondered if the arrival time listed on the GPS was correct, because it seemed that Matilda was taking me through the most confusing route imaginable to get to my destination. As I wound my way through the unfamiliar city, I thought about my dependence on Matilda and my response to her. When her voice said, "Prepare to turn right," I never questioned the wisdom, I just followed the directions and did something that I rarely do in this complicated world. I trusted without question.

After my trip was over, I paused to think about that. I would like to say that I fully trust God that way: every turn, every step, even every "U-turn" when I hear His voice whisper in my ear. But the truth is, even though I know the power and presence of God in my life, I often turn off that voice, wondering if my own way is just as good. It never is.

When God says that He will direct our paths, He can be trusted to keep us on the right road as long as we let Him lead the way. Acknowledging Him is not as easy as just listening to His directions. It means that we must fully trust without doubting or trying to find a better route in our own power. As certain as I am of satellite guidance, I know with greater certainty that God's plans for me are more secure and more trustworthy.

Heavenly Father, help us to completely trust Your plan and promises. Keep us dependant on You and You alone for today's journey. Guide us safely in the paths that we should go. Help us to follow with total trust and obedience.

Karen Knight is a former actress with Sight & Sound Theaters. She is an inspirational speaker, dramatist and concert artist for Heartsongs Ministries, Inc., Lancaster.

NOVEMBER 17

So Different ... So Blessed

"It is more blessed to give than to receive." Acts 20:35

When my husband and I dated (many years ago) we believed we were SO similar. What John liked, I enthusiastically supported, and what I enjoyed, he participated in wholeheartedly. It wasn't until after the wedding that we discovered our vast differences. The very traits that had originally attracted us to each other began to drive us apart.

One day, in desperation I angrily accused God. "Why did You make us so different? Do You get some kind of sadistic pleasure out of making us miserable?"

It wasn't an audible voice, but I heard what I believed was the Lord's quiet response in my thoughts. "No, Sharon. I didn't design the two of you differently to frustrate you. I made you different because there is no better way for you both to experience the incredible joy that comes only through giving."

Gradually I began to realize that the greatest pleasure in life does not come from being pampered, catered to or showered with attention. Rather the most meaningful moments come when I choose to give to others. I discovered that giving changes me … for the good.

Recently I realized that I have actually acquired some of the very qualities I initially resented in John, and that some of my quirks have rubbed off on him. How like a loving heavenly Father to put two very different people together for a lifetime—not as a torturous endurance test, but so we can both be blessed, changed and enriched by the other.

What an intriguing thought: If I've become like he used to be, and he has become like I used to be, we're still different! Which means, of course, that opportunities to give continue. Now that makes being married to an opposite very attractive indeed.

Jesus, You perfectly modeled a life of giving. Please empower me to be a giver, not a taker today.

Sharon Charles assists her husband, John, director of Abundant Living, a family counseling ministry in Lititz.

NOVEMBER 18

When I Am Weak He is Strong

"My grace is sufficient for you, for my power is made perfect in weakness." 2 Corinthians 12:9

One year ago my wonderful father was dying of chronic leukemia. He was a strong robust man for being eighty-seven years old, and I watched as his body slowly faded and he became frail and weak. He spent many weeks in the hospital, and I was by his side as much as I could be to offer support to him. My body and soul grew weary as I walked through this journey with my dad.

On one of these particular days, I was driving home from the hospital and knew that I would have only a few moments at home before I would need to leave for an appointment with a congregant to do a long evening session of inner healing. These sessions are usually pretty intense and I just didn't feel like I had the emotional strength to give it my all. I knew the young lady would understand if I canceled, but something within me really didn't want to cancel. On the way to the meeting I laid my heart bare before the Lord and I prayed, "Lord, You know how emotionally and physically spent I am, but You promise us in Your word that Your power is made perfect in weakness. Tonight I am claiming Your promises over me for strength as I minister."

The Lord heard my cry and anointed and strengthened me so much that it was one of the most powerful inner healing sessions that I have ever taken someone through. God showed up in a very big way that evening and even offered an unexpected physical healing for this young woman as well. As she was being healed, I was being encouraged to keep allowing the power of the Holy Spirit to work through me—a weary and worn vessel but a conduit of the Lord's healing power.

Lord, help me to daily be reminded that no matter what state or circumstance I find myself in, Your grace is sufficient for me, and Your power is made perfect in my weakness.

Mim Hurst lives in Lititz and is a wife and a mother of three young adult sons. She serves in leadership alongside her husband, Deryl, at DOVE Westgate Church in Ephrata.

NOVEMBER 19

Rescued from Mighty Waters

"Reach down your hand from on high; deliver me and rescue me from the mighty waters." Psalm 44:7

Every Memorial Day weekend, relatives on my dad's side of the family head to the Springhouse in Mifflin County, where we go on a long canoe trip in the Juniata River.

Last year, rain had swollen the river and the adults decided it was too dangerous for our canoe trip. By the next day, the water was still high, but we didn't want to miss our canoe trip, so ten of us decided it was safe enough.

My seventeen-year-old cousin, Josh, and I paddled one canoe. We unbuckled our life jackets because they were so uncomfortable, and we considered ourselves strong swimmers. Big mistake.

We were snacking on Cheez-Its when we noticed huge rapids, the size of waves, ahead. As our canoe was swept over the rapids, it tipped. I tried to buckle my life jacket, but the force of the water kept twisting it around my arm. In the water, Josh and I grabbed hold of the canoe and tried to steer it toward calmer waters, but it was no use. The water sucked the boat, Josh and I into tree branches that grew from an island covered with flood waters. The canoe got stuck in the branches right side up, but the strong undercurrent kept pulling me beneath the boat. Several times I was sucked beneath the surface, but one time I was able to grab the top edge of the canoe. My adrenalin kicked in and amazingly I was able to pull my upper body over the side of the boat. I can't even do a chin-up in gym class. It felt as if angels lifted me from the mighty waters.

Josh helped me into the boat. I was fixing my life jacket when I saw my Uncle Pat climbing through the tree branches. He told us to abandon the canoe and showed us how to jump as far as possible from the branches and swim with the current to shore where the others in our group had gathered. Although three out of the five canoes had flipped, we were so happy and thankful that no was injured or had drowned. But I admit that when we got out of the water, my legs shook for at least a half hour.

Dear Jesus, thank You for rescuing me from mighty waters.

Seth Good, son of Todd and Marie Good, is a ninth grader at Manheim Central High School and a member of Newport DOVE.

NOVEMBER 20

Crisis Is Normal in Life

"In the world you will have tribulation; but be of good cheer, I have overcome the world." John 16:33 (New King James Version)

The one thing I know, Jesus doesn't lie. He also said to be of good cheer because He has overcome the world. And so can we overcome the world if we believe and trust in Him. "For whatever is born of God overcomes the world. And this is the victory that has overcome the world—our faith" (1 John 5:4).

My husband and I recently faced a crisis. We were sitting in church and without any warning, he lost the sight in his eye. When he reached out for my hand and told me what had happened, I was rocked with fear and panic for a moment. Then the Holy Spirit whispered into my heart and brought peace and comfort.

In the emergency room, we heard all the bad news—he would never see again, his eye was totally damaged and the cells were dead. Yet through the clamor I heard a still small voice ask, "Whose report do you believe?"

I thanked the doctor for everything he was doing to treat my husband and said how much I appreciated his care. Then I added, "We are Christians and we believe in miracles. My husband's eyesight will return."

The doctor smiled and told me it was impossible. I said, "With man it is, but all things are possible with God!"

It was a crisis in our lives. There were times I felt like giving up, but the Holy Spirit would bring a scripture to my remembrance and faith would arise and I knew that victory was ours.

Today, Bill is driving, reading and thanking God for His faithfulness.

Did we enjoy the crisis? Of course not—but I am fully persuaded that God will make a way of escape for every crisis I face in this world.

Lord, I thank You that You said You will never leave us or forsake us, and that we are not alone because You are with us.

Joyce Tilney is publisher of *The Voice of Grace and Truth*, a Christian newspaper distributed throughout the region.

NOVEMBER 21

Thanksgiving Lifestyle

"In everything give thanks, for this is the will of God in Christ Jesus concerning you." Thessalonians 5:18

During my faith journey I decided to choose the life verse of Thessalonians 5:18. God has used it many times since to bless and sometimes challenge me. He even used it before I had chosen it. As an early teen, I broke my leg. The "blessing part" was that I was excused from my usual chores on my dad's farm. Another blessing was for my sister-in-law teaching me how to crochet. I was getting bored, so she decided to teach me something creative. It has been a blessing all my life.

The Lord challenged me with this verse when He gave me the responsibility to care for my ailing husband. In the beginning of this path I chose the "got to" attitude. My husband sensed this and asked why I was sad. Soon afterward the Lord said to me, "I want you to take good care of Richard, he is My special child." When I chose to say, "Yes, Lord," my attitude changed to "get to" care for him.

It was then that my song returned. The Lord showed me it would give Him glory if I responded with "I'm blest and grateful," when asked how I'm doing.

One day a grocery clerk asked how I was doing. I replied that I'm blest and grateful. He smiled, wanted to shake hands and said, "It's good to meet another Christian." So I realized that it showed how God takes good care of His children to respond in this way.

Now I look forward to people asking how I am so I can tell them that I'm blest and grateful. Sometimes I add, "even if I don't feel like it."

Dear Father, thank You for giving us the grace to choose to glorify You, ignore our feelings and focus on You and Your love, goodness and mercy. You are precious!

Mary Ruth Lehman is blessed and grateful for eight children, fifteen grandchildren and seventeen great-grandchildren. She is a member of ACTS Covenant Fellowship.

NOVEMBER 22

Thankful in All Things

"Rejoice always, pray without ceasing, in everything give thanks; for this is the will of God in Christ Jesus for you." 1 Thessalonians 5:15-17

A day that is forever etched in the crevices of my spirit, soul and body is about gratefulness for having legs to walk. It began when a sweet-spirited, sixty-two-year-old, mostly wheelchair-bound woman came to the health center where I was working to have blood drawn. During the last few visits, I had been getting to know her better. On that special day, I asked her how much she was able to be on her feet before needing her wheelchair. She replied, "only a few steps." Immediately, her eyes welled up with tears as she quietly said she was watching how I walked as I led her through the hall to the lab.

I was silenced, humbled, and felt a Holy Spirit "oomph" in my abdomen. I couldn't move. At that moment I realized the Lord had just shown me I needed to be thankful for legs to walk, not to take them for granted, and to keep His command to be thankful in all things.

As she continued to talk, she shared how her son and daughter both had severe medical issues. She replied, "They are fighters and never quit." Immediately I replied, "You've taught them well." At first she was puzzled at the meaning of what I said, but in her "ah-ha" moment she was silenced and realized the trait was one which she instilled in her children. She beamed as she pondered. She, too, was thankful. It was a day of healing for us both as we each took a step toward wholeness.

Thank You, Lord, for teachable moments that help us become more like You. Thank You for Your great love that shows up unannounced and at Your choosing. Help us grow toward health and wholeness of spirit, soul and body each day.

Jo Farner is married to Sam and has two adult children. Her vocation includes being a registered nurse, educator and wholistic health and wellness consultant. She attends the Worship Center.

NOVEMBER 23

Sold Out

"Love the Lord your God with all your heart and with all your soul and with all your mind." Matthew 22:37

Some of you may be part of the clientele who arise early on Black Friday morning in order to be the first in line when the door opens at your favorite store or mall. It is the anticipation of being able to purchase merchandise at an all-time low price that gets you out of bed at that hour.

It would be great if people got that excited about getting to the next gathering of believers. Imagine if they would get ready an hour early in order to arrive before the doors open. How about if people showed up fifteen minutes early so that they wouldn't miss anything at small group or twenty minutes early for Sunday morning so that they could be part of everything that is happening?

There are a few people like that and I am always encouraged to meet them.

Sometimes it's only a few minutes after a store opens on Black Friday when a sign appears with the words Sold Out. The term in retail jargon means there is nothing left to sell. It is also a term used for wholehearted Christians. I think the meaning is the same, "there is nothing left to sell."

I have sold my whole being to Jesus Christ. There is nothing else of me that can be bought because He owns it all.

Everything I do should be seen through the lens and mind-set of being totally sold out for Christ. He doesn't just capture part of my heart for me to devote a portion of my life to Him. I am totally sold out to Him and His will for my life. There is nothing left for sale.

So the next time the enemy tries to buy part of your affections, just put up the sign, Sold Out. Everything has already been purchased and there is nothing else to sell.

Lord, I'm selling out to You. Take all of me. I want nothing left to sell.

Ron Myer is director of DOVE USA.

NOVEMBER 24

A Matter of Perspective

"Jesus looked at them and said, 'With man this is impossible, but with God all things are possible.'" Matthew 19:26

We were hosting two Brazilian teenagers who had never seen snow in their lives. What fun to see their reactions when our area was hit with about ten inches of snow! We bundled up our guests and sent them out to experience a white winter.

Watching them took me back to my childhood in Canada. Whenever it snowed (which was pretty often), residents shoveled their sidewalks, making giant mounds along the edges of their lawns.

How I loved those huge piles of snow! Walking to and from school each day, those mountains begged to be climbed! I imagined myself a great adventurer, scaling towering cliffs and reaching unconquered summits! At times my weight would break through a crusty top layer and I'd sink to the top of my thigh. I would arrive at school with boots packed with melting balls of ice.

As a child those snow piles looked enormous. Now that I'm an adult I see them accurately.

I recognize that life's challenges that seem massive and daunting to me actually appear miniscule to the King of the universe. When I am going through a tough situation, it seems gigantic. But when I look at it from God's perspective, it suddenly diminishes in size.

To put it simply, the difference between a mountain and a molehill is simply perspective.

So, the next snowfall will remind me once again of God's supernatural power that He lovingly offers to me. I don't know what mountain-like challenges I may be faced with today or tomorrow, but I plan to put on my spiritual boots, march up to those problems and scramble over them, knowing that one day I'll look back and see them for the tiny bumps they really were.

Lord, help me to look at today's trials from Your perspective and watch them shrink!

Sharon Charles assists her husband, John, director of Abundant Living, a family counseling ministry in Lititz. She attends Lancaster Evangelical Free Church.

NOVEMBER 25

God's Influence through an Eight-Pound Pup

"In all your ways acknowledge him and he will direct your path." Proverbs 3:6

My wife and I attended a friend's graduation at a southern university. My friend asked me to speak to the president of the university about a problem with his doctorate degree. I was greatly intimidated to ask to speak to the president of a university to challenge him on his decision because I was aware of my own lack of education. But, because I thought my dear friend's request was reasonable, I asked God to direct my path.

I went to the office and asked to speak to the president. His assistant informed me the president was a very busy man and that he would not have time for a private matter. I walked out feeling frustrated.

When I arrived at my motor home, a neighbor knocked on my door. He asked if we were the people with a little Pomeranian. I said, "Yes." The stranger said he was a professor of philosophy at the University, and his wife saw someone with a dog. She loved dogs and wanted to meet the dog. Through that contact, I found out the professor knew the president very well. I asked the professor if he would be willing to speak to the president about my friend's problem with his degree.

The professor said he was having lunch with the president that day and I was welcome to join them for lunch. He added that I would be able to ask the question myself. I thought, *Wow, Lord, it can't get better than that.*

We had lunch with the president and his wife and hit it off so well that we spent the next four hours fellowshipping and were able to resolve my friend's problem.

Lord, You respect all persons, regardless of their education or background. Your ways are not our ways, but thankfully, Your ways are unsurpassed.

Tom Zeager is a member of DOVE Westgate, president of Hershey Farm Restaurant in Strasburg and president of Justice and Mercy, a Christian judicial and prison reform group.

NOVEMBER 26

The Place above Everyday Experiences

"For she said to herself, 'If only I may touch His garment, I shall be made well.' But Jesus turned around, and when He saw her He said, 'Be of good cheer, daughter; your faith has made you well.' And the woman was made well from that hour." Matthew 9:21-22 (New King James Version)

Stepping out in faith and motivated by love to lay hands on the sick suggests a desire to be that conduit that brings the kingdom to be on earth as it is in heaven. Believing Jesus' words that "Thy Kingdom is at hand," we step out in boldness. When circumstances don't immediately line up to the authority in which we can walk in Jesus' name, we can get discouraged and lose our boldness.

Let us not look at the circumstances of our fallen world to be the barometer on what is truth. Instead, let us be like the woman with the issue of blood, as she continued to press past her circumstances until she deeply connected.

Touching His garment is symbolic of trusting in His authority. Reaching this kind of intimacy allows us to truly be effective conduits whereby His kingdom is truly on earth as it is in heaven, made possible at the very moment when His word was spoken on the cross, "It is done."

I thank You, Father, that You call me to come up higher to a place above my circumstances, thus being able to see from a different perspective. I also thank You that in my diligence to seek a closer relationship with You, I become placed in a position where I can be an effective conduit for heaven. I thank You, especially, that through us, the body, thy kingdom can truly come on the earth as it is in heaven because as You are in us and we are in You, the Kingdom truly is at hand.

Wendy S. Domkoski is restored by understanding her identity in Christ. She attends Harvest Chapel in Abbottstown.

NOVEMBER 27

Promises

"His compassions never fail. They are new every morning."
Lamentations 3:22-24

The fall air filled with the scent of crayons, glue and freshly sharpened pencils takes me back to that wonderful first day of a new school year. That was when all of my crayons were crisp and unbroken and the prospect of exciting new adventures stretched out before me. It never bothered me then to know that by October all of my crayons would be showing their wear and new adventures would give way to hard work. I just lived for the joy of the newness of that one day.

As an adult, living in the daily world filled with demands on our time, energy and patience, I long to start each of my days in that frame of mind: Focusing, like a child with new crayons, on allowing the Lord to show me the wonder in the small things He gives me each day.

Because of His faithfulness we can begin our days with excitement and anticipation rather than looking ahead and focusing on all the hardships. His promise doesn't mean that we won't encounter difficulties. But when we start with our minds settled on Christ, we can more easily remember that He is there for us when we feel overwhelmed or when our world begins to spin out of control. He has given us a promise for those times, too. It's the scripture 2 Corinthians 12:9, "My grace is enough; it's all you need. My strength is made perfect in weakness."

After all, worn-out crayons usually mean that learning has taken place. Hard work forces us to remember to lean on Him for strength. Every new day focused on the pure joy of walking with the Lord can make each of our days feel like that first day of a new school year—fresh, new and full of promise.

Heavenly Father, thank You for watching over us with mercy and strength for each day. Keep our eyes open so that we are aware of every good thing You give us. Help us rejoice in Your promises!

Karen Knight is a former actress with Sight & Sound Theaters. She is an inspirational speaker, dramatist and concert artist for Heartsongs Ministries, Inc., Lancaster.

NOVEMBER 28

Not Ashamed

"Everyone I meet—it matters little whether they're mannered or rude, smart or simple—deepens my sense of interdependence and obligation. And that's why I can't wait to get to you in Rome, preaching this wonderful good news of God. It's news I'm most proud to proclaim, this extraordinary Message of God's powerful plan to rescue everyone who trusts him, starting with Jews and then right on to everyone else! God's way of putting people right shows up in the acts of faith." Romans 1:14-17 (The Message)

As I meet people, I frequently pray, "Lord what do you want me to say?" It's exciting, it's fun and it's amazing how God answers that prayer.

Paul is proud to proclaim the Message. He's not intimidated in going to the capital of the world. Why? Because his message is extraordinary. It has power to change lives, power to transfer people from one kingdom to another. No wonder he was not ashamed of the Gospel. I believe one reason so many in the United States are not sharing the Gospel is because they have not experienced this powerful transformation. Perhaps their transformation was so gradual they forget how Jesus has changed them.

If you found a great doctor, a mechanic you could really trust or even a terrific diet, you probably would tell your friends about it. Since you've found the One who forgives sin and gives you a new life, don't you think that's something you ought to share?

Don't be discouraged if people don't respond immediately. Some studies indicate that it usually takes many contacts before a person comes to Jesus. I have worked in phone evangelism for years. I call new movers for six months and then say to them, "I don't want to waste your time or mine. I am going to take you off my phone list unless you prefer that I continue to call you." It is amazing how many people say, "Continue to call."

Lord, help me to tune into Your Holy Spirit's voice to hear how and what to share concerning the powerful plan of salvation to someone today.

Dave Eshleman served as pastor and church planter for fifty years.

NOVEMBER 29

The King and His Daughter

"It is more blessed to give than to receive." Acts 20:35

While dining in a quaint café with my friend, Beth, I spotted an unusual candelier in the adjoining antique shop. I immediately named the fixture, "The King and His Daughter," for it had a large, crown-shaped ring with hanging votives and a second identical, but smaller, ring. Of course I interpreted the large ring to represent God as the king and the smaller ring as me, His daughter. The next day this light fixture became mine.

After my brother Sam hung this prized acquisition, I stood on a chair dropping candles into each holder. But the circumference was too great for my safety, and I fell headfirst on the wooden floor. Blood flowed from my forehead and my one hand was at a ninety-degree angle, Sam drove me to the hospital. Stitches and a reset wrist were in order.

God had a lesson for me in my helplessness, and it quickly became apparent: I must learn to accept help from others, and to do so graciously.

Oh, no! I took great pride in being self-reliant. I was a single, working woman responsible for myself—from finances to yard work to everything in between.

Friends and family came to my rescue. With every meal and gift, I gritted my teeth and smiled my thanks, while inside I was screaming for independence.

Everyday care required creativity. For instance, I flossed my teeth by tying one end of the floss to a doorknob, while holding the other end and kneeling by the door. At the office, a friend helped with the final touches of my wardrobe, from fasteners to jewelry, and the company president arranged for me to have a personal typist.

Yes, it is better to give than to receive, but I struggled to be an appreciative recipient. It helped whenever I clung to the awesome fact that my heavenly Father instructs gently and provides abundantly.

Lord, thank You for Your patience and care.

Sally K. Owens lives with her husband, Don, in Lancaster, where they participate in two home fellowship groups. They share many children and oodles of amazing grandchildren.

NOVEMBER 30

Search and Rescue

"For the Son of Man has come to seek and to save that which was lost. . . ." Luke 19:10

A few years ago, God impressed my husband, Mike, and me of the need to pray for the salvation of Mike's family. Periodically, God would awaken Mike at 3 a.m. to pray for them.

During holiday gatherings, Mike's family always asked him to pray for the meals. Following Thanksgiving 2009, God again awakened Mike at 3 a.m. and increased the burden for his family. Mike sensed that God wanted him to share a message with his family at the Christmas dinner.

At the family's Christmas 2009 dinner, Mike was again asked to pray for the meal. Before he prayed, Mike told them that God had been waking him up at 3 a.m. to pray for them, and that God wanted him to share something with them. Mike shared the plan of salvation with everyone gathered together. There wasn't a dry eye in the house.

Since then, six members of Mike's family have accepted Jesus into their hearts as their Lord and Savior and attend church with us. Not only that, but they have invited friends who have accepted Jesus and these newly-saved Christians are bringing their friends to church.

Shortly after the first of Mike's family members accepted Jesus into their hearts, Mike and I started a Bible study group with his family members. We call the group Search and Rescue based on two scriptures: Luke 19:10 "For the Son of Man has come to seek and to save that which was lost. . . ." and in Ephesians 6:17-20 "Take the helmet of salvation and the sword of the Spirit, which is the word of God. And pray in the Spirit on all occasions with all kinds of prayers and requests. With this in mind, be alert and always keep on praying for all the Lord's people. Pray also for me, that whenever I speak, words may be given me so that I will fearlessly make known the mystery of the gospel, for which I am an ambassador in chains. Pray that I may declare it fearlessly, as I should."

Lord, we are expecting You to call more family members into Your kingdom and to do more miracles in the Search and Rescue group.

Pam Rittle and her husband, Mike, are small group leaders at the Fireplace Christian Fellowship, Myerstown.

Photo by Mark Van Scyoc

December

DECEMBER 1

Books

"And further, by these my son, be admonished: of making many books there is no end: and much study is a weariness of the flesh." Ecclesiastes 12:12 (King James Version)

Recently my husband and I were rummaging through an attic in Lebanon that was filled with books. The entire house of this prominent doctor was filled with more than two thousand books, which he accumulated during his lifetime.

In preparation for the estate sale, the auctioneer told us to fill a box with the books we hoped to bid on. I was like a kid in a candy store. I love books, from old tales of history to the latest Beverly Lewis novel. I'm told that if I owned a Kindle, I could choose from any book in the world to read. Imagine that!

The Apostle John wrote something fascinating in the Book of books. He tells of his experiences during three years with his best friend. He ends by saying that if all the things that Jesus did could be written, he supposed even the world itself could not contain all the books that should be written! He also recorded that Jesus told his disciples they would do even greater works than these.

If I were to record what I've accomplished in my sixty-eight years of life, it would seem like just a grain of sand. As the Apostle Paul summed up his life, he considered his works as refuse compared to knowing Christ and being found in His righteousness.

I'm eternally grateful that it's not works of righteousness that I have done, but His mercy alone that saved me. That is not a license to spend my life in my easy chair, reading books about what others have accomplished. I want to be a part of those "greater works" still to be done in the Body of Christ.

Father, thank You for giving me the Book that was inspired by You, and the Holy Spirit to bring hope, comfort and encouragement along my path.

Ruth Ann Hollinger attends Petra Christian Fellowship and absolutely loves spending an evening with old friends from my bookshelf.

DECEMBER 2

Loved to the Lord

"Therefore, accept each other just as Christ has accepted you so that God will be given glory." Romans 15:7 (New Living Translation)

As my newly wedded husband and I prepared to leave for our honeymoon, my mother-in-law sweetly mentioned her hope that we would find a nice church to attend after we moved. She was a Christian—polar opposite of my claim of being agnostic. I replied that finding a church wasn't in my plan. She smiled undaunted and hugged me good-bye.

During those tumultuous early years of our marriage, her love and acceptance remained steadfast. With retrospect, after experiencing both salvation and motherhood I am amazed at her self-control. Although I knew it was of great concern to her, "Mom" did not nag us about going to church. She was never judgmental. Quite the contrary, she encouraged me, praising my efforts as a new wife. Whenever I mentioned a problem she responded that she would pray and took the opportunity to quietly share how much the Lord loved and cared for me. I felt totally loved and accepted by her. Whenever we returned home for a visit, I noticed how she sat in her rocker faithfully praying and reading her Bible every evening before going to bed.

When faced with my own mortality following a cancer diagnosis four years later, I knew if I died, my soul was bound for hell. I willingly accepted Jesus Christ as my Lord and Savior and rested in His love and forgiveness. That was thirty-three years ago. I truly believe that Mom's prayers for my salvation and quiet acceptance of me simply "loved" me to the Lord. She exercised her faith in the Lord to draw my heart to Him. Sometimes love is spoken loudest with no words at all.

Father, thank You for everyone along our journey who prayed, accepting us with love. May all the glory be Yours forever.

Bonnie M. Evans is a member of Lancaster Christian Writer's group, traveling from Maryland to attend meetings. She enjoys sharing the Lord's love through her writing.

DECEMBER 3

Practical Ideas for Witnessing

"Forced to leave home base the Christians all became missionaries. Wherever they were scattered, they preached the Message about Jesus." Acts 8:4 (The Message)

If you have a passion to obey the Great Commission under the Holy Spirit's direction, pray for opportunities to share Jesus. My wife, Helen, suffers with three chronic medical conditions. She lives with pain but is known as an encourager. One day she walked into the physical therapy room and was greeted with, "Here comes inspiration." Prayer is the key behind her life.

Use your gift to share Jesus. Invite others to dinner. Go to a ball game or a musical drama together. Visit the park with your children. Children make great missionaries. Get to know the nonbelievers, and prayerfully seek opportunities to speak about Christ.

Community involvement should be an outreach opportunity. What are the possibilities? The parent/teacher association, the chamber of commerce, community softball leagues, a bowling or golf league, the neighborhood association, Kiwanis Club and hobby groups. In rural communities farm shows, ball teams or school events are often popular attractions where you can relate to your unchurched neighbors.

Intentionally pray for nonbelievers by name. Encourage each other by praying in groups for the unchurched. Pray for the Lord to open blinded minds, to free them from the enemy's power, to transfer them from the kingdom of darkness to the kingdom of Jesus Christ and for the Holy Spirit to make them a new creation (2 Corinthians 5:17).

Something happens to you when you pray for others. God redirects your focus, changes your thinking and moves in your heart. Start praying for nonbelievers and watch what God does as you connect with those who need to hear the Good News.

Jesus, I promise to begin praying for my unbelieving friends by name and to trust you to open doors for me to build bridges so they can hear the Good News of eternal life.

Dave Eshleman served as pastor and church planter for fifty years.

DECEMBER 4

Limit, Limiting, Limitless

"I am your servant; give me understanding." Psalm 119:125 (National Revised Standard Version)

We never know when we are going to find someone to champion us, challenge us and truly believe in us. I will not name the person I spoke to via email on Tuesday, but she will know who she is. It is thanks to her and the graciousness of her emails that I am sharing once again. Because of her I have done some soul-searching and re-evaluating within myself.

I have often prayed and asked God to help me minister to others. However, I find I limit Him by doubting myself and my own capabilities. I ask Him to use me, but I limit Him by being hesitant and afraid. I ask Him to set me on fire, but I blow out the match before the kindling is lit because I don't feel a confidence in my writing. The key word here is "my" writing.

I am limiting not only God, but myself, and the ministry that I so desperately wish to be a part of. I am limiting the light He wishes to shine through me to a dim glow. I am limiting the power of the Word reaching the person He wishes to minister to.

When will I learn that God is limitless? There is nothing he cannot do. Wasn't it Moses who felt he was not worthy to be used by God because of his disability to speak plainly? Yet he led his people out of the land of Egypt under God's limitless power. Jonah prayed from inside the belly of a fish after realizing that God's power was indeed limitless, and he could not hide to keep from going to Nineveh. These stories speak volumes to me when I feel less than capable. From now on there will be no more limiting the limitless powers of God.

Lord, thank You for clear vision into another realm that can only be seen with our spiritual eyes.

Sandy Arnold attends Rossmere Mennonite Church in Lancaster.

DECEMBER 5

Light in a Dark Night

"The people walking in darkness have seen a great light; on those living in the land of the shadow of death a light has dawned." Isaiah 9:2

"More, Mommy, more!" says my son Bennett.

He loves Christmas lights and always asks for more to be strung outside our house each year. I usually find something to add to the collection and try to get it out before the Thanksgiving turkey gets cold. My husband drags out a ladder and crate of cords to help in the task. Our son is satisfied by the warm glow that is created on our front porch for all those driving by.

As fall turns into winter we eagerly watch for lights to appear on other houses around the community. The bright strands bring such cheer to long evenings. Rides home have new excitement as we find yet another colorful display. Christmas lights are one of our family's favorite things during this special season.

My favorite piece of our Christmas lighting is the Moravian star that hangs on our porch. It is a reminder of the star that pointed the way through the night to the Christ child. I know the original Christmas did not happen in Pennsylvania during long December nights, but for me, there is rich meaning that Christmas comes during the darkest part of the year.

How about you? Does your world seem dark this year? Jesus is Lord, and He is our light in darkness wherever life finds us this Christmas.

Lord, may the hope the Christ child brought shine brightly through us. In the joyfulness of the season, may we bring that hope to others.

Sarah Sauder enjoys being a mom, works as a graphic designer and attends DOVE Westgate Church with her family.

DECEMBER 6

Sing from Your Heart

"I will praise you, Lord, with all my heart…." Psalm 138:1

Eager faces greeted us as we stepped down from the bus in front of a mission church in Peru. Smallest and poorest in town, the church was nevertheless filled to capacity with enthusiastic people of all ages who wanted to hear the visiting Americans talk about Jesus. The children especially captivated my heart as they lined up for hugs and candy. The service began and I wondered how our team, most of whom spoke no Spanish, would ever be able to adequately communicate so that people would understand the depth of the Father's love for them and the great sacrifice of Jesus.

The interpreter was quick in her translations of the Scriptures, announcements and other parts of the service, but I wondered how my music would manage to touch hearts when they couldn't understand the words. There would be no translation possible within the song.

As I prayed and asked the Lord to bless my efforts, I remembered what my grandmother had said to me when I first started singing. I could almost hear her voice saying, "Child, just sing from your heart to theirs." Her advice had always kept me mindful that music makes connection with hearts when our only intent is to praise Him and lead others in worship.

The accompanist began the introduction to my song. As I faced those beautiful people, I could feel the Lord pouring out His love to them through the notes of the music and the joy in my heart. Tears flowed freely as we each felt His power, love and grace in our own ways. We were praising with all our hearts that day in Peru and language barriers just didn't matter. It is the same today as we connect with others in our own churches. If your heart is full of praise, your song will always communicate Jesus!

Heavenly Father, we praise You for all you have done for us. Help us reach out to each other knowing that You will fill hearts that are genuinely devoted to you.

Karen Knight is a former actress with Sight & Sound Theaters. She is an inspirational speaker, dramatist and concert artist for Heartsongs Ministries, Inc., Lancaster.

DECEMBER 7

Dormant or Maturing?

"For I am planting seeds of peace and prosperity among you. The grapevines will be heavy with fruit. The earth will produce its crops, and the heavens will release the dew. Once more I will cause the remnant in Judah and Israel to inherit these blessings." Zechariah 8:12

It was a beautiful autumn day. The leaves were changing colors on the trees and the homes in our development were decorated with a harvest theme. I was walking on that beautiful day—taking a much needed break from my college studies. As I walked I reflected on the seasons that God created: seed time and harvest, a time to be set apart and a time to receive.

Later that day as I studied my biology text I read: "Near the end of a seed's maturation, the seed loses most of its water and forms a hard, resistant seed coat. The embryo, surrounded by its food supply becomes dormant; it will not develop further until the seed germinates. Seed dormancy allows time for a plant to disperse its seeds and increases the chance that a new generation of plants will begin growing and maturity is finally achieved."

Like a seed we as God's children sometimes experience times where we feel dormant, nothing seems to be happening. Yet, it is during this set apart time when we are growing into maturity. We are being prepared to produce much fruit for the Lord's harvest. If you are feeling dry and "surrounded by a hard productive seed coat" remember the promise from the Lord spoken through Zechariah. He is planting seeds of peace and prosperity and you will be heavy (or mature) with fruit. Be encouraged, He is releasing His dew upon you to inherit His blessings.

Father, thank You for Your seasons of preparation, growth and maturity in our lives. We yield to Your season and Your times knowing that You have set us apart to participate in Your great end-time harvest. Plant us and scatter us into the fertile soil of Your fields.

Patricia Denlinger is the prayer leader and administrator for Teaching the Word Ministry. She is also a teacher and founder of Forerunner Ministries.

DECEMBER 8

Grandparents' Love

"However, each one of you also must love his wife as he loves himself, and the wife must respect her husband." Ephesians 5:33

During the last couple months of my grandfather's life, I would take my grandmother to run errands and visit him in the hospital, since she didn't drive. One of the times that I took my grandmother to visit him in the hospital, the stress of her husband's failing health was starting to get to her. I remember that she started to cry. The nurse gently came and took her outside in the hall so that my grandfather would not see her upset.

In all of my years growing up, I always saw my grandfather as the strong, silent type. My grandfather was never one to cry in front of people. But right at that moment, he began to cry, too. I don't know how often he had told my grandmother he loved her, but at that instant I knew he did and how greatly he cared for her. At that moment, I saw how much they both cared for each other, even though they may not have openly expressed it.

About that same time, my grandmother said that she hoped I never had to go through what she was going through. Now that I have been married for several years, I understand. Both of my grandparents have been in heaven for several years, but I will never forget that experience. In their own way, they demonstrated to me what true love is and what it means to keep the vow to each other—until death do us part.

Dear heavenly Father, help me to openly show my family how much I love them before it's too late. May I remember to give them a hug and a kiss every day and hold them just a little bit tighter and longer with each passing year. And may my relationship with my husband resemble that of my grandparents' and grow stronger with each passing year. More importantly may our relationship with each other be an example of Your relationship with the church.

Jennifer Paules Kanode is an English-as-a-second-language instructor and part-time disc jockey on FM 90. 3 WJTL. But more importantly she is a full-time wife and mother.

DECEMBER 9

Brushes with Eternity

"Blessed are those whose strength is in you, who have set their hearts on pilgrimage." Psalm 84:5

Twelve years ago I went to the hospital for what I thought would be a routine test. I never dreamed I would be undergoing quadruple heart by-pass surgery the next day. The surgeon explained that I had blockage in what is referred to as "the widow-maker's artery," because it usually goes undetected until the victim falls over dead from a heart attack. Fortunately mine was found and fixed before that happened.

A couple of years ago, I had another close call. I thought I had a bad case of the flu that was making me feel weak. Turns out I was bleeding internally. By the time Sharon rushed me to the emergency room, I was a very sick guy. Once again a skilled doctor patched me up and I was soon feeling like a million dollars.

Crises, particularly those that are life-threatening to myself or a loved one, strike me anew with the fragility of life. Such brushes with eternity are impactful to say the least. They remind me that since I became a follower of Jesus, I have a different perspective on life and death. I am a pilgrim, not a settler. A pilgrim is on a journey, his heart set on the destination awaiting him. A settler plunks himself down right where he's at and focuses on getting the most enjoyment out of the here and now.

So I thank the Lord for these unexpected events that have caused me to examine my heart and keep my eye on eternity. But, I must admit I'm hopeful I won't need another crisis reminder for quite awhile.

Father, help me today to keep my eye on You and my heavenly destiny. May I not be sidetracked by the temporary pleasures this world offer, but live with the joyful heart of a pilgrim.

John Charles is director of Abundant Living, a family counseling ministry in Lititz. He attends Lancaster Evangelical Free Church.

DECEMBER 10

Our Strong Tower

"The name of the Lord is a fortified tower; the righteous run to it and are safe." Proverbs 18:10

Children know when the phone rings, it is time. The ringing of the phone reminds their little brains of every nagging necessity they had forgotten they were desperate without up to that point in the day. Such things as a snack, a new TV show, or the knowledge of why God created bees are needed at that immediate moment.

Children know where to find you even when you hide.

How are you supposed to concentrate on making that doctor's appointment with the office receptionist when you are on the other side of the laundry room door, pulling it closed while one child is pulling on the other end of the knob, and another child is pounding on that door for your attention? To complicate matters, there is no calendar in the laundry room.

These are the moments when I want to be wanted a little less around my house. I want to run somewhere safe. Not that my children are dangerous, just draining at times. Not just when I am with the children or on the phone, but when the trivialities of this world consume my attention. And in these times, I need a refill. I want to be where nothing else matters but my love for my Savior. I can picture the safe tower that the Lord proclaims He is. Unlike the laundry room door, I do not have to hold this one shut. He closes Himself around me.

And I am saved.

Lord, I run to You, into Your towering love for me. I want to be surrounded by You and shut out the world. Save me from a life of this world and bring me to Your presence.

Tracy Slonaker, director of Christian education at Harvest Fellowship of Colebrookedale, loves her husband and three children but longs for the presence of God even more.

DECEMBER 11

Tip of the Tongue

"… a great and strong wind rent the mountains and broke in pieces the rocks … but the Lord was not in the wind; and after the wind an earthquake, but the Lord was not in the earthquake; And after the earthquake a fire, but the Lord was not in the fire; and after the fire a still, small voice." 1 Kings 19:11, 12

Exhausted, we came home with our newborn. We'd intentionally planned our return so I could talk with my stepmother, who was watching our older three children while I was away. I wasn't thinking as I put the infant car seat with our sleeping bundle in the center of the living room floor.

As my stepmother was taking coats and briefing us on the events of the last forty-eight hours, I unconsciously heard the familiar click of Beau's trot coming down the hallway. Beau was a Labrador mix, all eighty pounds of him. He was great with kids, but occasionally we had sent him to his bed for baring his teeth at them.

There wasn't any time to yell or dive at him before he got to the carrier. He was already sniffing Tabitha from the top down. We drew in fearful breaths as he got to her feet and immediately went for her face.

His gentle snout touched her forehead and the tiniest bit of the tip of his tongue came out. It wasn't even a lick—more like a light dab. Then he turned and walked back to where he had been napping.

That incident reminds me that the awesomeness of God truly is something we can't fathom. He is pure power, creating the universe with one word and even now creates in that space miraculous celestial bodies we barely know about. In the same portion, He is also utter gentleness. He is truly the best King and Friend we could ever have.

Father, I cast my cares on You today, knowing you have all strength, might and compassion to deal with whatever I face.

Carolyn Schlicher is the mother of five children and is still learning how to hear God's still, small voice.

DECEMBER 12

God, the Perfect Planner

"I know that you can do all things; no plan of yours can be thwarted." Job 42:2

When we moved into our home, we found a small cottage at the corner of our woods that was occupied by an elderly couple. As the years passed the elderly man passed away leaving the lady living alone. God placed an idea in our minds, so we started to talk about the possibility of the cottage someday being a place for missionaries to live while on home assignment.

We prayed and asked God to give us the chance to own the cottage someday and use it for missions. In those days, I never read the obituary page; however, one day while waiting at the dentist's office, I scanned the obituary page and recognized the elderly lady's name in print.

After waiting an appropriate amount of time, I contacted a sibling listed in the obituary to inquire about the cottage property. I was directed to the executor of the estate who informed me that the property would be sold by sealed bid. How could we ever decide on the price of a small cottage in a bad state of repair? In the following days, we asked God to give us a number for a bid. The day before the sealed bid closing date, God gave us a number. The next day the estate executor called and informed us that we were the highest bidder.

That winter, we refurbished the cottage inside and out and put the word out that it was now available for use by missionaries. Today we have lost track of how many missionaries have used the cottage. What a joy to experience God's perfect plan to supply a cottage for missions.

Thank You, God, for placing ideas of Your will into our minds, allowing us to recognize Your will and nudging us into carrying out those plans to bless others.

Joe Nolt and his wife, Dawn, serve at Elizabethtown DOVE Christian Fellowship.

DECEMBER 13

Confirmation

"… for your Father knows what you need before you ask him." Matthew 6:8

While my wife and I flew to Australia, flight attendants handed out snacks to the passengers. I haphazardly glanced at the ingredient label on the snack package. The words "sunflower seed oil" sparked a message that I sensed God wanted me to deliver to the church we would be visiting and that I should use sunflower oil to anoint people who wanted to break free from strongholds.

I said to my wife, "We need to buy some sunflower seed oil before we attend the church services."

Our host family picked us up at the airport and after a time of visiting, we needed to leave for the church service. I asked our host if we could stop at a supermarket to pick up sunflower seed oil. A shocked look spread across his wife's face. "Sunflower seed oil?" she asked. She went into her kitchen and came back with a large unopened jar. Then the story poured out. She had been grocery shopping the day before and needed cooking oil. She had reached for the olive oil that she generally used, but sensed the Lord saying she was not to purchase it. She reached for a different brand, but again sensed the Lord saying no. Somewhat confused, she noticed a bottle of sunflower seed oil and reached for it. She had peace that was the one to purchase.

Her story confirmed that God wanted me to incorporate using the sunflower seed oil to anoint people at the evening service. I shared the message God had given me and told the audience that sunflowers constantly turn their faces toward the sun. I encouraged anyone in the audience who wanted prayer for freedom from strongholds to come and be anointed. While I anointed people with oil, some people standing on the street outside the church came inside and to the altar for prayer. One of those responding was a heroin addict, who remarked the following day that she hadn't felt so free before.

Thank You, Holy Spirit, for going before us and ministering encouragement and confirmation as we walk by faith and walk out our destiny in You.

Carl Zeiset and his wife, Sarah, attend Ephrata Community Church and lead a small group in their home.

DECEMBER 14

Changing Negative Thought Patterns

"Take every thought captive, making it obedient to Christ." 2 Corinthians 10:5

While texting with a client recently, we talked about how our thoughts affect our actions. She had been struggling with negative thoughts about herself: believing that she was stupid, ugly and without hope. She had acted on those false beliefs, which led her down unhealthy paths and negatively impacted her most important relationships.

Philippians 4:8 speaks to what we should think on. "Finally, brothers, whatever is true, whatever is noble, whatever is right, whatever is pure, whatever is lovely, whatever is admirable—if anything is excellent or praiseworthy—think about such things."

I wonder how much our lives would change if we actually put those commands into practice. How would it affect our relationships if instead of thinking false things, we thought true things? How would our talk be changed if we thought on noble things instead of crass things? How would we treat others if we thought of right things instead of wrong things? Pure things instead of impure things? Lovely things instead of ugly things? Admirable things instead of dishonorable things? Excellent and praiseworthy things instead of poor and unworthy things?

Changing our negative thoughts to "God-thoughts" is a huge first step to changing bad habits and unhealthy relationship patterns. What will you decide to think on today?

Lord, empower us to change our negative thought patterns into God thoughts.

Shannon Shertzer is a professional counselor at New Hope Community Life Ministry in Quarryville. She and her husband, Jere, live in Lititz and are members of Ephrata Community Church.

DECEMBER 15

Who Do You Relate To?

"By this time a lot of men and women of doubtful reputation were hanging around Jesus, listening intently. The Pharisees and religion scholars were not pleased, not at all pleased. They growled, 'He takes in sinners and eats meals with them, treating them like old friends.'" Luke 15:1 (The Message)

Jesus saw Levi at his tax collection booth and invited him to follow. "That night Levi invited Jesus and his disciples to be his dinner guests, along with his fellow tax collectors and many other notorious sinners. (There were many people of this kind among the crowds that followed Jesus.) But when some of the teachers of religious law who were Pharisees saw him eating with people like that, they said to his disciples, 'Why does he eat with such scum?' When Jesus heard this, he told them, 'Healthy people don't need a doctor—sick people do. I have come to call sinners not those who think they are already good enough'" (Mark 2:15-27).

What was it about Jesus that sinners liked to be with Him and listen to him? Was it because they knew he understood them, accepted them rather than condemned them? Was it because he condemned religious hypocrisy? Was it because they saw the miracles?

Jesus was comfortable with sinners. He came: to seek and save the lost. He came not to call the righteous but sinners. That was His life's purpose and it must be ours. We accept unbelievers because Jesus accepted them.

Did he condone their sin? No, but he accepted them as persons, persons who were valuable, people worth understanding. He related to them by entering into their life, talking and eating with them. (See Matthew 19:5.)

We will not win people for Jesus in our Christian ghettos. We must take Christ to the workplace. For salt to do its work, it has to get out of the salt shaker. Jesus instructs us to let our light shine for people to see our good works.

Lord Jesus, help me to love sinners—to understand them, to build bridges to them.

Dave Eshleman served as pastor and church planter for fifty years.

DECEMBER 16

Paid in Full

"For the law of the spirit of life in Christ Jesus has made me free from the law of sin and death." Romans 8:2 (New King James Version)

Understanding that grace breaks the chains of bondage, we boldly walk in righteousness. In the middle of the night, when I was just coming to terms with this concept, I remember telling God: "I believe Your Son went to the cross and paid the price for sin." But I still identified with my own weight of sin and felt like everyone else could be clean, but somehow, not me!

In the stillness, I heard Him say, "How dare you think that what I did on the cross was so small that it was not enough to take care of what you did? Don't you understand, Daughter, that going to the cross was not about all the bad you had done. It was about the fact that I miss you and desire to be in relationship with you! That could not happen with sin between us."

I began to understand that His righteousness is mine to receive. I felt like I climbed up into His lap. When I am in His righteousness, I am free to go boldly into His throne room to love Him and receive His love. Whatever weakness that still plagues and grieves me may cause a sad separation between us but it doesn't, however, cause me to dismay. Instead, I look to the cross, knowing that He still sees me as righteous!

I boldly keep going back to Him. I find that each time I'm in His presence, I get closer. Our interaction gets sweeter and thus the voice of those distractions, serving to pull me away, gets weaker. In continually going back to Him, sooner or later, those distractions will fall away to where it is just Him and me!

Dear Lord, help me not to reject my identity of righteousness in You, for fear that it gives license to sin.

Wendy S. Domkoski attends Harvest Chapel, Abbottstown.

DECEMBER 17

Closed Doors

"When they came to the border of Mysia, they tried to enter Bithynia, but the Spirit of Jesus would not allow them to." Acts 16:7

Apostle Paul handled closed doors much better than I do. During his second missionary journey, the Holy Spirit would not allow him and his traveling companion to enter a country in order to spread the gospel of Jesus Christ. Paul didn't blame the closed door on the devil or the political climate, antagonistic people or lack of funds. Paul and the early Christians were accustomed to seeing God open doors in supernatural ways, not close them. They experienced prison doors flung open, the mouths of lions closed. I'd think a closed door would cause him to push forward in faith. Instead, he explains the situation almost nonchalantly as we tried … but the Spirit of Jesus would not allow us to enter.

At times, I, too, have experienced closed doors. Although I didn't always attribute them to God's closing, later, I could definitely see He was in charge. One door that slammed in my face happened after I had diligently sought God, and thought I heard His direction to attend college to attain a journalism degree. I applied, paid the tuition and attended the first class. But the door slammed in my face. No explanation from God—just a crushing feeling of despair on my part.

But, like Paul and his companions, God guided me in a different direction. Within a few months of the closed door, I was offered a journalism job that I hadn't even known about, let alone applied for it. I was given on-the-job training and received the knowledge I would have needed to pursue for a four-year-degree. I didn't need to pay tuition. Instead, I received a salary for a job I loved, and many more open doors to use that knowledge.

I'm grateful to serve a God who closes and opens doors.

Lord, thank You for being more powerful than any other person or incident in my life. I'm grateful that closed doors are a part of Your direction in keeping me on the path You planned for me.

Lou Ann Good and her husband, Parke, are members of DOVE Westgate Church.

DECEMBER 18

Fine Living

"You prepare a table before me…" Psalm 23: 5

A Place Apart

Resolutely, I walked up the hill.
I needed a place serene, quiet, still.
It was from force of will, of which
Every bone, muscle and fiber agreed.

High time for readjustments, realignment,
Centering, from the core of me outward,
Spinning and twirling into proper positions
To make transformation in my disposition.

A location of no hurry, no rush;
Environment to hush distractions
And listen to the Spirit's whispers,
Teaching me a song within my soul.

No nobler goal or better decisions—
To make such excursions,
Where I can feast on Heaven's bread
And drink of kingly wine.

No dining more sumptuous;
No food more delicious, to end all strife
In the brevity of this earthly life;
No living more fine than this.

Lord Jesus, take us to that place apart with You where we can feast at your banqueting table. Thank You that you feed us with the bread of Your presence and fill us with Your holy wine.

Arnolda Brenneman is a member of the Lord's House of Prayer in Lancaster. She is multi-gifted as an artist in worship dance, poetry, prose, song and the visual arts. She and her husband, Jan, make and use worship flags and function as pastors to artists through In His Shadow Ministries.

DECEMBER 19

The Answer

"Mercy, peace and love be yours in abundance." Jude 2

My husband and I listened to my son, Bennett's, bedtime prayers one summer evening.

"How is God going to answer this one?" I thought to myself, as he prayed for a good day tomorrow. Our plans included a trip to Dutch Wonderland amusement park and there was rain in the day's forecast. It was our last chance to go before summer ended and we could not reschedule.

We got up the next day and experienced an early downpour. It drizzled when we got to the park at 10 o'clock. We picked rides that had roofs on them. We did not have to wait in lines because the showers kept others away. Then the rain stopped. We took a log boat ride through the lagoon and watched a beautiful egret pruning its feathers. The sun came out late in the afternoon.

We really did have a good day, just like Bennett had prayed for. Several unexpected blessings also happened. A friend with us commented about how relaxing it was not struggling to keep track of the boys because the weather forecast had kept away the crowds. In a café, because we were the only customers, we got to chat with an old friend who was working there. It rained, but only lightly. It wasn't cold, so things dried quickly. Yes, God answered Bennett's prayer, and in a better way than I was hoping for! While there are much bigger concerns than one day at an amusement park, I am humbled that He answered our prayers.

Thank You, Father, for caring for us and caring for our children. We are grateful for the big and the small blessings You have given us.

Sarah Sauder enjoys being a mom, works as a graphic designer and attends DOVE Westgate Church with her family.

DECEMBER 20

Raven Food

"You will drink from the brook, and I have ordered the ravens to feed you there." I Kings 17:4

Pretty much the whole world has been in a recession. I see it as I travel from state to state and country to country. So many families are suffering loss. In this scripture, we see how Elijah was fed by God ordering ravens to bring him food right by his water supply. I love this picture. For several years there was neither dew nor rain—which means a drought—which means a loss of crops—which means a loss of income. Recession was upon the land.

God's kingdom, however, is recession proof. Elijah was provided for by God Himself. A bread and meat delivery came in the morning and again in the evening. Did you ever wonder where this came from? I mean, who slaughtered and cooked the meat? Who kneaded and baked the bread? And, ravens as delivery boys? Ravens are known for finding things and returning them to their nests, not making deliveries.

Many years ago my wife and I were missionaries. Mary loved Christmas and desired a Christmas tree, although we were financially unable to purchase one. One morning a Christmas tree delivery truck drove by our home, and a beautiful fir tree fell off the truck rolling into our front yard. I called the tree farm and verified they had a truck traveling in that direction that very morning, and they would retrieve their tree from us. My wife went from ecstatic about "the miracle" to tears saying, "We can't even afford a lousy Christmas tree."

But like the meat delivery for Elijah, God cared about the desires of my wife's heart. A few days later I received a phone call that went something like this, "Steve, do you guys have a tree? Well, we won't be getting down your way anytime soon, just keep it … no charge."

Thank You, Father, for caring for me as Your child because You and Your kingdom are recession proof.

Steve Prokopchak is married to Mary for thirty-five years and a member of the Dove International Apostolic Council, giving oversight to DOVE churches in various regions of the world.

DECEMBER 21

God Takes Rain Checks

"For my thoughts are not your thoughts, neither are your ways my ways declares the Lord." Isaiah 55:8

At the end of the sermon, the head of our prayer ministry said she had a sense that God was calling people with knee problems to come forward for prayer.

I had been having problems with arthritis in my right knee, which was twice the size of the other knee. The doctor had sent me for physical therapy, which helped a little. But recently, I had to cut back my time of exercising from four days a week to two because of the pain and swelling.

I was excited to hear that God was particularly interested in knees; however, it was my turn to work in the church resource center. I was extremely busy and did not have time to respond to the altar call for healing.

The following week my knee was at its worst. Not only was I limping, but my knee buckled a few times.

The next Sunday I went to the altar and told the prayer minister that I hoped that God accepted rain checks and would carry over His wishes to heal knees from the Sunday before since I had been unable to come forward when I should have. She prayed for me and even got down on her knees to touch my knee in prayer.

As Sunday progressed, it was cold and rainy, but my knee remained pain free. When I was getting ready for bed, I compared my knees and the swelling had reduced considerably. I am thrilled to know that God understands the concept of rain checks and has met my need.

Thank You, Lord, that Your ways are not our ways and that Your timing is on eternal timing and not necessarily on our timing.

Connie Martin goes to Petra Christian Fellowship and offers prayer ministry counseling for women in her home.

DECEMBER 22

Saved to the Uttermost

"Whosoever will call on the name of the Lord shall be saved." Acts 2:21

Our family had moved to Tulsa, Oklahoma, three months before Christmas. During the holidays we were invited to a Christmas party hosted by some church acquaintances. Toward the end of the evening, we gathered in a group in the living room. We took turns sharing how God had blessed us in many different ways.

One couple told a story about a tornado experience. When a tornado was about to hit their neighborhood one night, the fear caused them to remember that some friends had previously told them "they needed to ask Jesus to save them." As the tornado started to "touch down" in the neighborhood, the couple screamed in unison, "Jesus save us."

A few minutes after the tornado passed, the couple went outside to see the damage. The entire neighborhood had been completely flattened. Their house was the only one untouched by the storm.

Jesus had saved them from their sins that night and also saved them from the tornado damage. From that time on the couple's lives were different.

Father, help us all to appreciate the completeness of our salvation.

Betty Cowley is a member of Ephrata Community Church, a member of HarvestNet and vice president of Papa's New Generals Corporation (an outreach to Papua New Guinea).

DECEMBER 23

Greater Plans

"He will give you the desires of your heart." Psalm 37:4

My husband, Shannon, and I have always had an intense love for our two beautiful daughters. Despite that, I had a longing for a son to complete our family. When I needed a hysterectomy at the age of thirty-four and my husband seemed closed to the idea of adoption, I thought this desire would never be fulfilled.

Hoping to distract myself with other things, I began working with children and adolescents in a mental health facility. These tough and troubled children and teens showed me the need for loving adoptive and foster parents. When I brought up the idea of becoming a foster/adoptive parent to Shannon, he was receptive to learning more and we soon were officially approved as foster-to-adopt parents. The next six months were filled with frustrating experiences of hearing about children who needed homes but unavailable, often because of paperwork.

In December 2010 our Christmas tree was up. The presents were wrapped. The ornament with the blue bow that we had so hopefully purchased the year before was hanging on the tree. I cried and poured out my heart to God that I wanted so desperately for our son to be home with us for Christmas.Three days later, our caseworker said that an emergency placement was needed for an eleven-year-old boy. His profile revealed a life that had been filled with loneliness and poverty with abusive parents dealing with addictions. He had been placed in ten different foster homes within three years.

Would he fit into our family or was it a mistake to take an older child than our daughters? Despite the questions, we felt absolute peace. Our son came home for Christmas. We were a family.

We recently completed our son's adoption and his journey in foster care ended. Our journey of faith continues. It has not always been easy. There are still hurdles to overcome, but through it all, I have been awed and amazed by God's leading.

Lord, I am awed and privileged to see just a glimpse of Your greater plan in my life. I trust You with the desires of my heart and know that You never give anything less than Your absolute best.

Heather Weaver lives with her husband, Shannon, and three children in Lititz.

DECEMBER 24

Celebrate the Day

"The Word became flesh and made his dwelling among us. We have seen his glory, the glory of the One and Only, who came from the Father, full of grace and truth." John 1:14

Imagine with me, if you will, what it was like on that day, two-thousand or so years ago. A young couple, having traveled many miles for many days, finally reaches their destination only to find reminders of the shame of her pregnancy.

With the order from the Roman government that sent all Jews back to the hometown of their forefathers to be counted and taxed, Bethlehem was crowded.

Joseph and Mary could not sleep in the same room with relatives because of the cultural shame of her pregnancy. But they could stay in an alternate location, a small stable attached to the house.

In that humble, unfriendly locale, the Savior of the World is born. John's Gospel states that even though the Word made the world, the world didn't recognize Him.

Yet, for those who believe in the Word, He will transform their lives. That Babe in the manger came so that humanity could have an intimate relationship with their Creator for all of eternity. God was offering the world the greatest gift ever. We pause today, on the day set aside to designate His birth, to worship the One who came from the Father full of grace and truth. He came to change the world that He created. Today, thank Him for the way that He changed your life. If you have never allowed Jesus to change your life, today would be a great day to do so.

Lord Jesus, thank You for coming to this world so that we can know the Father and have eternal life through a relationship with You. Bless us as we pause to celebrate Your birth and encourage us to tell others about You in the coming year.

Pastor Kevin Kirkpatrick is the pastor of Terre Hill Bible Fellowship Church and former missionary with the Pocket Testament League.

DECEMBER 25

Return to Simplicity

"After coming into the house they saw the Child with Mary His mother; and they fell to the ground and worshiped Him. Then, opening their treasures, they presented to Him gifts of gold, frankincense, and myrrh." Matthew 2:11 (New American Standard Bible)

To the natural eye he was simply a baby, but these great kings of the earth fell to the ground and worshipped Him. They saw the King of the Universe and bowed low.

Each year we celebrate Christmas we are reminded how the Creator of all chose to enter the world as the Savior of all mankind. The inconspicuous manger scene urges us to recall our own humble beginnings and bids us to kneel before the Babe of Bethlehem.

From there it is easier to accept the truth that the kingdom of heaven is for the lowly and the simple. Our hearts are quieted and comforted that Jesus looks upon us as His very own and His desire is that we live in simple and pure devotion to Him.

Our response is much like the magi from the east. With our hearts bowed before the Christ child king we open our treasures and present them to Him. We offer our gifts: gold (our money), frankincense (our adoration and worship) and myrrh (our willingness to lay down our lives to live for Him instead).

In being reminded of Jesus' humble birth, we are invited to let go of the complexities of our lives that are drowning out His still, small voice. We remember that "only one thing is necessary," and like Mary of Bethany, we choose the good part, which shall not be taken away from us.

Lord, thank You for giving us such a profound reminder that we are called to simplicity and that we are created to worship You and You alone. May our lives be poured out for You and Your glory. Amen.

Kathi Wilson and her husband, Mark, are co-authors of *Tired of Playing Church*, co-founders of Body Life Ministries and serve as church planters for the Lancaster Mennonite Conference in Lancaster.

DECEMBER 26

Little by Little, Layer by Layer

"Therefore, since we have so great a cloud of witnesses surrounding us, let us also lay aside every encumbrance and the sin which so easily entangles us, and let us run with endurance the race that is set before us, fixing our eyes on Jesus, the Author and Perfecter of our faith …" Hebrews 12:1, 2 (New American Standard Version)

When I look back at my life, I'm amazed that God didn't give up on me when I carried so much excess baggage of sin and emotional wounds, which had built up over the years. Instead, He lovingly and patiently worked with me. Little by little, year after year, He convicted and cleansed me and then healed me of each sin and emotional wound—one at a time.

The layers He is continuing to lay bare in recent years are wrong inner attitudes toward others and life situations that encompassed attitudes of a critical spirit and judgmental sin. He also continues healing—layer by layer—several longtime wounds of embarrassment and humiliation from being singled out and criticized in front of others.

God has been helping me understand why I react negatively when attention is turned my way; while at the same time, I inwardly long for positive affirmation.

My deep, heartfelt prayer for many years can be expressed in this hymn: "And can it be that I should gain an interest in the Savior's blood? Died He for me, who caused such pain? For me, who Him to death pursued, amazing love! How can it be? That Thou, my God, shouldest die for me."

Thank You, Lord, for not giving up on me and for continuing to set me free of so many burdens. Your amazing love continually leaves me in awe!

Sandra Kirkpatrick is a special needs tutor and a member of DOVE Westgate.

DECEMBER 27

Semester Break Surprise

"If you shall ask anything in My name I will do it." John 14:14 (King JamesVersion)

It was Christmas break from college for our son and his next tuition payment was due when he returned. We had been earnestly praying for the one thousand dollars that was needed. We did not have the money because my husband was out of work. It seemed like an impossible situation, but we continued to pray for the money.

One day our son Scott was helping us to install some insulation at the top of the outside walls of the basement level between the joists, above the dropped ceiling. He was on a ladder doing the work, when suddenly he came down the ladder with a stack of twenty-dollar bills in his hands. We were in shock. We counted the money and it was one thousand dollars—enough to send him back to school.

Praise God! The money had a dry feel to it, as though it had been in the ceiling for a long time, long before we owned the house. We never found out who had been living in the house before we had taken possession. We did not know where the money came from or to whom it may have belonged to years before. So we accepted it as God's answer to our prayers and need.

Does God answer prayer? Yes, He does! Keep on praying—He will do it.

Father God, help us not to put limits on how You choose to answer our prayers.

Betty Cowley is a member of Ephrata Community Church, a member of HarvestNet and vice president of Papa's New Generals Corporation (an outreach to Papua New Guinea).

DECEMBER 28

Willing and Obedient

"If you are willing and obedient...." Isaiah 1:19

Last year, God really spoke to a group of us about reading through the Bible in one year. Little did we know how much our lives would be challenged and changed. When we began reading Isaiah, God really showed us about revival and our nation. Dr. Larry Crabb puts it this way: "Prepare to be slapped, then hugged."

In Isaiah 1, beginning in verse 4, a sinful nation wasn't like we might think. The nation Isaiah was talking to was Israel, the church if you will. Us. Let's reread those verses in Isaiah 1: "Alas sinful church, laden with iniquity, evildoers." Ouch.

We pray many times for our nation and officials to "get revival" or to be healed and we should, but how much of this really should be directed inward to us? The church?

Again Isaiah declares that God is sick of mindless worship, heartless religious rituals, to wash yourselves and make yourself clean. He wasn't telling the government, he was telling the church. It is easy to point the finger at the "lost," and see their sin, but never look inward to ourselves and see our lies, dishonesty, gossip, slander and other sins.

It becomes easy to say "they"' need saved and revived, and to pray for them. Revival is about us, the church, returning, weeping, mourning, fasting, praying. Verse 19: "if we are willing and obedient." Verse 16: "cease to do evil, learn to do good, seek justice, rebuke the oppressor, defend the fatherless, plead for the widow."

Wow! Just by typing these words, I am moved to get on my face and beg for forgiveness.

What would happen if every believer, in every fellowship, prayed the same prayer: "Lord we return to you."

For corporate revival to begin, personal revival must happen—"if we are willing and obedient."

God, we are willing and we will be obedient.

Kim and Brian Zimmerman are the founders and directors of City Gate Lancaster and the City Gate Prayer room.

DECEMBER 29

Awaiting Our Healing

"As waters break out, the Lord has broken out against my enemies before me. So that place was called Baal Perazim (lord who breaks out)." 2 Samuel 5:20

It was the second night of the ladies' conference conducted at the Lord's Sanctuary in Kenya. God's Spirit was moving in healing. Many were coming for deliverance and healing of tumors, growths and back pain.

While praying for one lady with a growth in her abdomen, I realized that she was touched by God's love for her. She left that night praising God for His touch and believing for evidence of a physical healing. I trust God will reveal the depth of the healing to His glory.

Another lady came who had lost her hearing in one ear. After praying what I sensed the Holy Spirit was speaking, the lady was very quiet. As she went back to her seat, I wondered if she could hear at all or had felt God touch her in any way.

Later that night Pastor Lucy, who translated while I prayed, came over to me with the lady who could not hear. I was told she wanted me to know that God had healed her and she could hear. She said, first she felt something like a swish of water breaking through her head and then she heard a car horn beep outside. She was rejoicing because she could hear.

Father, it was Your presence that quieted her and she could not respond other than to be still until her healing came. Oh God, You are mighty to save. You take great delight in us, You quiet us with Your love, You rejoice over us with singing.

Debbie Davenport, married to Bill, is executive director of Cornerstone Pregnancy Care Services. Her passions are intercession and mentoring young leaders for kingdom purposes.

DECEMBER 30

Mr. Magoo Anointing

"Surely he will save you from the fowler's snare and from the deadly pestilence." Psalm 91:3

Margie Flaurant was a special speaker at church one Sunday. At one point she stood directly in front of my husband, Steve, and said, "You are coming out of your comfort and going into the place God has always had for you." She also quoted Jeremiah 29:11 " 'For I know the plans I have for you,' declares the Lord, 'plans to prosper you and not to harm you.' " It was powerful!

As we drove home from the service, Steve told me he needed to take a nap before he took our son to Baltimore Airport. "I'll nap on the hammock, so try not to wake me," he said. We decided to both rest on the two hammocks we had set up because it was very warm that day. Steve went into the house to put shorts on, and I climbed into my hammock to rest waiting for him to come back—but he did not come back. I stepped out to see where he was when suddenly a ten-foot tree limb came crashing down on his hammock. Had he been there, or I hadn't gone to look for him, we both would have been seriously injured, if not killed.

I ran into the house to tell him what had just happened. He told me he was just about to come out but wanted to check on the Eagles' score. We walked outside and picked up the limb, which had split in half on impact. We held each other tight recalling the words of protection that had been spoken over us that very morning. Steve said, "I would like to think that I am led by God." He certain was!

We thanked the Lord together for His protection and love for us. Every morning Steve and I pray, "Father, keep us one step ahead of the enemy at all times, just like You kept David ahead of Saul. I call this the "Mr. Magoo Anointing"—Mr. Magoo was a cartoon character who always evaded mishaps.

God is so faithful.

Heavenly Father, You are our protector, and we trust in You for our spiritual and physical care. Thank You so very much.

Valerie Morris and her husband, Steve, direct Palabra Viviente Ministries (Living Word Ministries) in Honduras. They attend Gateway International Church in York.

DECEMBER 31

Love One Another

"A new commandment I give to you, that you love one another: just as I have loved you, you also are to love one another. By this all people will know that you are my disciples, if you have love for one another." John 13:34-35 (English Standard Version)

In my naivete, one year I chose this verse as my New Year's Resolution. By the end of the year, I expected to have its message and accomplishment under my belt. So I sent out Christmas cards bearing this and other related scripture. Surely God would bless this worthy endeavor and help me achieve its goal. But I was humbled to learn that such success is a lifetime process.

Why is it so difficult to follow Jesus' command? Shouldn't we want to love the brethren? Yes, we want to do so, but are hampered by our sinful natures. The Apostle Paul describes this struggle as follows: For what I do is not the good I want to do; no, the evil I do not want to do—this I keep on doing" (Romans 7:19).

During a short-term mission trip, I experienced this battle in living color. A missionary couple came through the town in which we were working and joined our accommodations. These missionaries asked me to bring tea to their room.

What, my brain screamed! We are as busy as you are; you can get it yourself. Fortunately, the Lord rendered me mute and I fulfilled the request.

How do we love the brethren with a smile on our faces, as well as in our hearts? It is a work of God's grace. Paul shares his secret of success in Philippians 4:13, "I can do all things through Christ who strengthens me." And we have that same power in us to obey. How wonderful it will be to have others see that we are Christ's disciples.

Lord, may we submit to You and to each other.

Sally K. Owens lives with her husband, Don, in Lancaster, where they participate in two home fellowship groups. They share many children and oodles of amazing grandchildren.

Index

A Celebration of Partnership

The following regional networks within South Central Pennsylvania partnered in publishing this devotional. We invite you to contact them to learn more about how God is at work to bring transformation in your local region.

The Regional Church of Lancaster County

Box 311, Leola, PA 17540
Phone: (717) 625-3034 www.theregionalchurch.com

We are a network of Christian congregational, marketplace and
ministry leaders dedicated to the growth of God's kingdom in Lancaster County through relational partnership.

To attain spiritual and social transformation of Lancaster County, we actively cultivate partnerships to:

PRAY: fill the region with continual united prayer and worship
WITNESS: communicate the gospel of Jesus Christ to every person in each local community and culture group
LOVE: mobilize initiatives to transform our communities with the love of God
PROTECT: promote biblical unity, reconcile relationships and provide spiritual discernment for the well-being of the Church.

Many partnerships; one mission: Lancaster County transformed by the gospel of Jesus Christ.

Reading Regional Transformation Network

Craig Nanna, Director
P.O. Box 8188, Reading, PA 19603
Phone: (610) 371-8386 Email: craignanna@readingdove.org

Reading House of Prayer

Chad Eberly, Director
Phone: (610) 373-9900 Email: ChadE@rhop.net www.rhop.net

Uniting leaders together in strategic kingdom relationships for the purpose of transformation in the Reading region. Our priorities include advancing the kingdom of God in the Reading region through relationship, the unity of the body of Christ, the house of prayer and strategic initiatives that will produce transformation.

Transforming Ministries: Coatesville Regional

Bill Shaw, Executive Director
643 East Lincoln Highway, P.O. Box 29, Coatesville, PA 19320
Phone: (610) 384-5393 Email: www.QuietRevolution.org

A catalyst in the movement for church unity and community transformation. Generated out of humility and united prayer, the mission of LTM is to feature the Lordship of Jesus by being a conduit for the development of trusting cross-cultural relationships and an incubator of collaborative ministry initiatives.

Lebanon Valley Prayer Network

Stephen J. Sabol, Executive Director
825 North Seventh Street, Lebanon, PA 17046
Phone: (717) 273-9258

This network exists to lay a foundation of worship and intercessory prayer for the purpose of birthing transformation in the Lebanon Valley.

Lebanon 222

Jay McCumber, Director
515 Cumberland Street, Lebanon, PA 17042
Phone: (717) 279-5683

The Lebanon 222 Team exists to discern and implement God's heart for the Lebanon Valley.

Capital Region Pastors' Network

Dave Hess, Coordinator
Christ Community Church, Camp Hill, PA 17001
Phone: (717) 761-2933

We are a network of pastors in the Capital Region of Pennsylvania committed to Christ and to developing relationships among pastors, rooted in prayer, which lead to partnerships in ministry bearing the fruit of revival.

For more copies of this book or other editions of God Stories

Visit www.theregionalchurch.com.